THE PICTORIAL WORKBOOK OF THE CODE
By Tom Henry and Tim Henry

Based on the 2008 NEC®

Copyright © 2008 by Tom Henry. All rights reserved. No part of this publication may be reproduced in any form or by any means: electronic, mechanical, photocopying, audio/video recording or otherwise, without prior written permission of the copyright holder.

While every precaution has been taken in the preparation of this book, the author and publisher assumes no responsibility for errors or omissions. Neither is any liability assumed from the use of the information contained herein.

National Electrical Code® and NEC® are Registered Trademarks of the National Fire Protection Association, Inc., Quincy, MA.

ISBN 978-0-945495-80-2

ENRY PUBLICATIONS SINCE 1985

Preface

I have found over the years the English language can be confusing to someone born in the USA let alone someone from another country and language. Did I hear you say right? Or did you say wright or rite?

Most likely you've heard the expression, "A picture is worth a thousand words." I've always maintained that a smile means the same in any language. A picture is like a poem without words. In my writing of books I take text and massage it and put it into a picture where possible.

I have written 5 volumes "The Pictorial Workbook of the Code" which covers the first five chapters of the Code in pictures. The first four chapters I have always referred to as "the meat of the Code."

The 5 volumes *"The Pictorial Workbook of the Code"* are excellent study guides for the apprentices, electricians, inspectors, technical schools and even for the electrical engineer that had zero hours of Code study at the University.

The 5 volumes total **1721 Code questions**, 165 quizzes or exams, 9 final exams all with answers and Code references.

These volumes are the answer for an instructor teaching the Code.

There's a tremendous amount of work that must be done in electrical training. The one area I feel we are lacking in is "learning" the Code. You can't just read the Code book, it must be taught to you.

Today, electricians must be better than they have ever been. With the tremendous growth in technology, new products, new wiring methods, etc. the industry has moved forward while many of us have stood still. Many electrical jobs are in jeopardy because individuals have stood still.

With the increasing threat of legal liability, it is time the electrician understands the **minimum** requirements of the Code.

The quality of American life depends upon the safety and effectiveness of electrical application.

CONTENTS

	PAGE
Article 280 - Surge Arrestors, Over 1kv	1
Article 285 - Surge Protective Devices, 1kv or less	6
Article 280 - Quiz	9
Article 300 - Wiring Methods	10
Article 300 - Quiz #1	29
Article 310 - Conductors For General Wiring	36
Article 310 - Quiz #1	60
Article 312 - Cabinets, Cutout Boxes & Meter Enclosures	68
Article 312 - Quiz	73
Article 314 - Boxes and Conduit Bodies	75
Article 314 - Quiz #1	101
Article 320 - Armored Cable	111
Article 322 - Flat Cable Assemblies	117
Article 324 - Flat Conductor Cable	120

CONTENTS

	PAGE
Article 326 - Integrated Gas Spacer Cable	125
Article 328 - Medium Voltage Cable	128
Article 330 - Metal-Clad Cable	130
Articles 320-330 - Quiz #1	135
Article 332 - Mineral-Insulated Cable	139
Article 334 - Nonmetallic-Sheathed Cable	143
Article 336 - Power and Control Tray Cable	152
Article 338 - Service-Entrance Cable	157
Article 340 - Underground Feeder & Branch Circuit Cable	160
Articles 332-340 - Quiz #1	164
Article 342 - Intermediate Metal Conduit	170
Article 344 - Rigid Metal Conduit	175
Article 348 - Flexible Metal Conduit	180
Article 350 - Liquidtight Flexible Metal Conduit	185

CONTENTS

PAGE

Article 352 - Rigid Polyvinyl Chloride Conduit 187

Article 353 - High Density Polyethylene Conduit 193

Article 354 - Nonmetallic Underground Conduit 197

Article 355 - Reinforced Thermosetting Resin Conduit ... 199

Article 356 - Liquidtight Flexible Nonmetallic Conduit __ 201

Article 358 - Electrical Metallic Tubing 203

Article 360 - Flexible Metallic Tubing 208

Article 362 - Electrical Nonmetallic Tubing 210

Articles 342-362 - Quiz #1 213

Article 366 - Auxiliary Gutters 219

Article 368 - Busways 223

Article 370 - Cablebus 227

Article 372 - Cellular Concrete Floor Raceways 229

Article 374 - Cellular Metal Floor Raceways 231

Article 376 - Metal Wireways 233

CONTENTS

	PAGE
Article 378 - Nonmetallic Wireways	234
Article 380 - Multioutlet Assembly	235
Article 382 - Nonmetallic Extensions	235
Articles 366-382 - Quiz #1	236
Article 384 - Strut-Type Channel Raceway	242
Article 386 - Surface Metal Raceways	244
Article 388 - Surface Nonmetallic Raceways	245
Article 390 - Underfloor Raceways	246
Article 392 - Cable Trays	249
Article 394 - Concealed Knob-and-Tube Wiring	254
Article 396 - Messenger Supported Wiring	254
Article 398 - Open Wiring on Insulators	254
Articles 384-398 - Quiz #1	255
Final Exam	263
Answers	271

DEFINITION of ELECTRICIAN

ELECTRICIAN
A specialist in electricity
One who installs, maintains, operates or repairs electrical equipment

SPECIALIST
One who devotes himself to a special occupation or branch of learning

DEVOTE
To give to a cause, enterprise or activity
Devote means to set apart for a special and often higher end

SPECIAL
Distinguished by some unusual quality
Being in some way superior
Held in particular esteem
Readily distinguishable from others of the same category
Being other than usual

LEARNING
Knowledge or skill acquired by instruction or study

ARTICLE 280
SURGE ARRESTORS, Over 1 kV

I. General

Article 100 *Definitions*: A surge arrester is a protective device for limiting surge voltages by discharging or bypassing surge current.

280.3. Where used, a surge arrester shall be connected to each ungrounded (hot) conductor.

280.4. Surge arresters installed on a circuit of more than 1000 volts shall comply with all of the following:

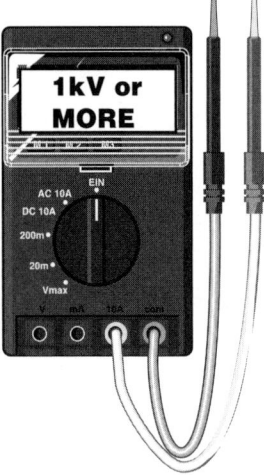

(A) The rating of the surge arrester shall be equal to or greater than the maximum continuous operating voltage available at the point of application.
(1) On solidly grounded systems, the maximum continuous operating voltage shall be the phase to ground voltage of the system.
(2) Impedance or Ungrounded systems the maximum continuous operating voltage shall be the phase to phase voltage of the system.

280.4(B)

1000 VOLTS and OVER

280.4(B). The rating of a silicon carbide-type surge arrester of circuits 1000 volts and over shall not be less than 125% of the rating specified in 280.4(A).

FPN2. The selection of a properly rated metal oxide arrester is based on considerations of maximum continuous operating voltage and the magnitude and duration of over-voltages at the arrester location as affected by phase-to-ground faults, system grounding techniques, switching surges, and other causes. Manufacturer's application data on rating and other characteristics and the minimum duty-cycle voltage rating of an arrester for a particular method of system grounding must be observed carefully.

280.5. The surge arrestor device **shall be** listed.

II. Installation

280.11. Surge arresters shall be made inaccessible to unqualified persons, unless listed for installations in accessible locations. They are permitted to be located indoors or outdoors.

Article 100 DEFINITIONS - **Qualified Person.** One who has the skills to the construction and operation of the electrical equipment and installations and has received safety training to recognize and avoid the hazards involved.

280.12. Conductors to surge arresters shall not be any longer than necessary and shall avoid any unnecessary bends. This is important because bends in the conductors increase the impedance to lightning discharges which tends to eliminate the effectiveness of a grounding conductor.

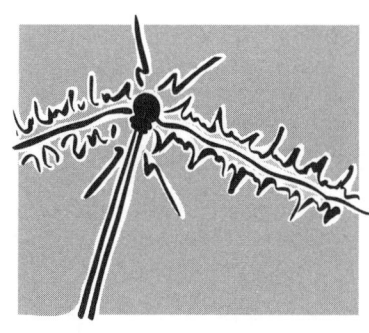 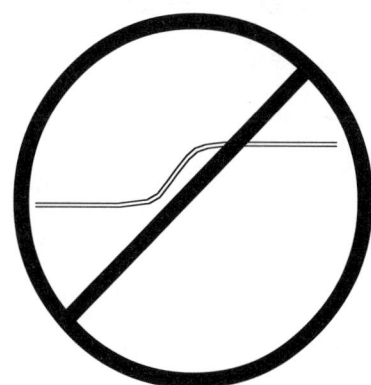

III. Connecting Surge Arresters

280.21. Services of more than 1000 volts: The arrestor grounding conductor shall be connected to one of the following:

MORE THAN 1000 VOLTS

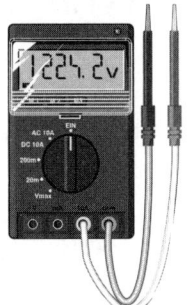

(1) Grounded service conductor

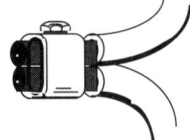

(2) Grounding electrode conductor

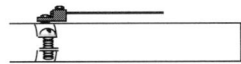

(3) Grounding electrode for the service

(4) Equipment grounding terminal in the service equipment

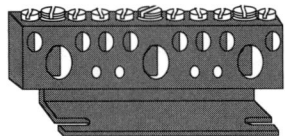

280.23. The conductor between the surge arrester and the line and the surge arrester and the grounding connection of circuits of over 1000 volts shall not be smaller than #6 copper or aluminum.

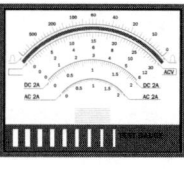

280.24. Interconnections of circuits over 1000 volts are aimed at ensuring more effective lightning protection of transformers. Lightning protection of a transformer cannot be provided by a primary arrester that is connected only to a separate electrode. Common grounding of gaps or other devices must be used to limit voltage stresses between windings and from windings to case.

280.25. Surge arrester grounding connections shall be made as specified in Article 250 (Grounding) except as indicated in Article 280 (Surge Arresters). Grounding conductors shall not be run in metal enclosures unless bonded to both ends of the enclosure. The reason is when conducting lightning currents, the impedance of a lightning arrester grounding conductor is materially increased if run through a metallic enclosure, especially if of a magnetic material. The voltage drop in this impedance may be sufficient to cause arcing to the enclosure, and in any event it reduces the effectiveness of the lightning arrester. Bonding of the conductor to both ends of the enclosure is necessary to eliminate this detrimental effect where metallic enclosures are used.

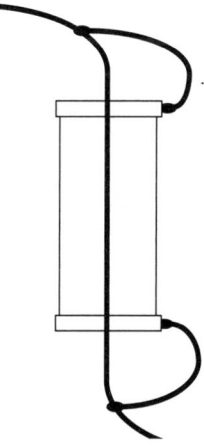

ARTICLE 285
Surge Protective Devices: SPDs
1 kv or less

I. General

285.1. This covers the rules for hardwired installation of surge suppressors (arresters) on systems of 1kV or less that are commonly used today to prevent voltage spikes that result from a lightning strike or system switching that damage sensitive electronic equipment, such as computers.

285.3. An SPD (surge arrester) or TVSS device shall NOT be installed in the following:

(1) Circuits exceeding 1000 volts.
(2) On ungrounded systems, impedance grounded systems, or corner grounded delta systems unless listed specifically for use on these systems.
(3) Where the rating of the SPD (surge arrester) or TVSS is less than the maximum continuous phase-to-ground power frequency voltage available at the point of application.

285.4. The SPD (surge arrester) or TVSS shall be connected to each ungrounded conductor where used at a point on a circuit.

285.5. A SPD (surge arrester) or TVSS shall be listed.

285.6. The SPD (surge arrester) or TVSS shall be marked with a short circuit current rating and shall not be installed at a point on the system where the available fault current is in excess of that rating. The marking does not apply to receptacles.

II. Installation

285.11. Surge arresters or TVSSs shall be made inaccessible to unqualified persons, unless listed for installations in accessible locations. They are permitted to be located indoors or outdoors.

285.12. Conductors used to connect the surge arrester or TVSS to the line or bus to ground shall not be any longer than necessary and shall avoid any unnecessary bends.

III. Connecting SPDs.

285.23. Type 1 SPDs - Single phase or 3 phase grounded or ungrounded services are permitted to have a Type 1 SPD installed on the line side of the service disconnecting means. When installed at the service the Type 1 SPD grounded conductor shall be connected to one of the following:
(1) Grounded service conductor
(2) Grounding electrode conductor
(3) Grounding electrode for the service
(4) Equipment grounding terminal in the service equipment

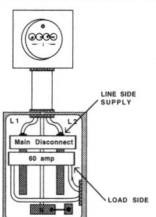

285.24. Type 2 SPDs must be installed on the load side of the service disconnect overcurrent protection. On a separately derived system the SPD shall be connected on the load side of the first overcurrent device.

285.25. Type 3 SPDs shall be permitted to be installed anywhere on the load side of branch circuit overcurrent protection up to the equipment served, provided the connection is a minimum 30 feet of conductor distance from the service or separately derived system disconnect.

285.26. Line and ground connecting conductors shall not be smaller than #14 copper or #12 aluminum.

285.27. A SPD (surge arrester) or TVSS shall be permitted to be connected between any two conductors - ungrounded conductor(s), grounded conductor, grounding conductor. The grounded conductor and the grounding conductor shall be interconnected only by normal operation of the SPD or TVSS during a surge.

285.28. Grounding conductors shall not be run in metal enclosures unless bonded to both ends of the enclosure.

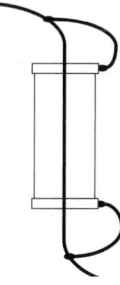

Article 280-285 Quiz #1 - Open Book

QUIZ #1

1. Ground connecting conductors for surge arresters of less than 1,000 volts shall not be smaller than ____ copper.

(a) #14   (b) #12   (c) #10   (d) #8

2. When installing a Type 1 surge arrester at the service of less than 1000 volts, the grounding conductor shall be connected to ____.

I. the grounded service conductor
II. the grounding electrode conductor
III. the grounding electrode for the service
IV. the equipment grounding terminal in the service equipment

(a) I and II only   (b) I and III only   (c) III and IV only   (d) I, II, III, or IV

3. Surge arresters shall be permitted to be located ____ and shall be made inaccessible to unqualified persons unless listed for installation in accessible location.

I. outdoors   II. indoors

(a) I only   (b) II only   (c) either I or II   (d) neither I nor II

4. The rating of the surge arrester shall be ____ the maximum continuous phase-to-ground power frequency voltage.

I. equal to   II. less than   III. greater than

(a) I only   (b) I or II   (c) I or III   (d) II only

5. The conductor between a lightning arrester and the line for installations operating at more than 1000 volts must be at least ____.

(a) #14 copper   (b) #6 copper   (c) #8 copper   (d) none of these

6. SPD (TVSS) surge arrester ratings are based on the magnitude and duration of overvoltage at the arrester location as affected by ____.

I. switching surges   II. system grounding techniques   III. phase-to-ground faults

(a) I only   (b) II only   (c) III only   (d) I, II and III

CHAPTER 3

ARTICLE 300

WIRING METHODS

300.1(A). This article covers wiring methods for all wiring installations unless modified by other articles.

300.1(B). Article 300 is not intended to apply to the conductors that form an integral part of equipment, such as motors, controllers, motor control centers, or factory assembled control equipment, or listed utilization equipment.

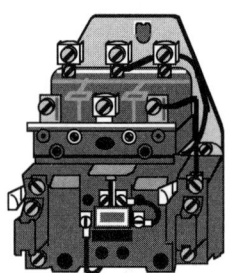

300.1(C). Metric designators and conduit sizes, etc. shall be as designated in Table 300.1(C).

Table 300.1(C)

Metric Designator	Trade Size
12	3/8"
16	1/2"
21	3/4"
27	1"
35	1 1/4"
41	1 1/2"
53	2"
63	2 1/2"
78	3"
91	3 1/2"
103	4"
129	5"
153	6"

Note. The metric designators and trade sizes are for identification purposes only and are not actual dimensions.

300.2 Limitations.

(A) Wiring methods specified in Chapter 3 shall be used for 600 volts, or less where not specifically limited in Chapter 3.

600 volts or less

300.2(B). Temperature limitation of conductors shall be in accordance with 310.10. Section 310.10 states that no conductor shall be used in such a manner that its operating temperature will exceed that designated for the type of insulated conductor involved.

300.3(A). This article requires that single conductors shall be installed using an recognized wiring method in Chapter 3.

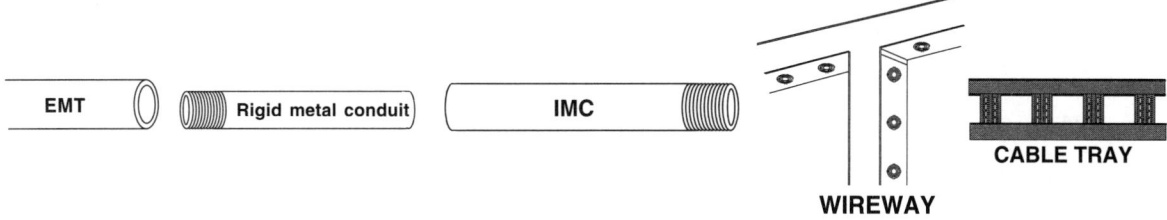

300.3 (B). All conductors including the neutral if used and the grounding conductor must be installed in the same raceway, cable, cable tray or trench.

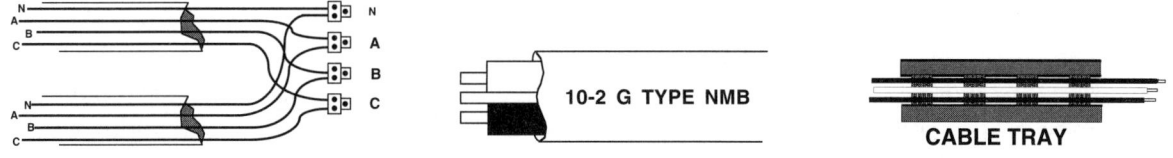

300.3(B3). Warns against the need for preventing induced currents where nonmetallic or nonmagnetic sheathed conductors are run through metallic walls or ceilings as in 300.20(B).

300.3(C1). With the exception of solar photovoltaic systems (690.4(B), the conductors of different systems such as direct current and alternating current 600 volts or less may be installed in the same raceway, cable, or wiring enclosure if all of the conductors have an insulation rating at least equal to the highest voltage of any conductor.

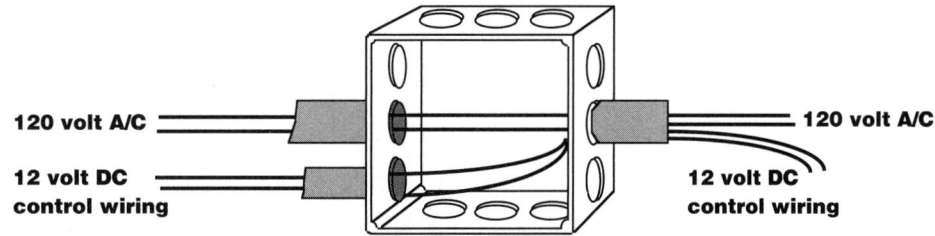

300.3(C2)

300.3(C2). This section prevents circuits rated over 600 volts from being installed in the same raceway, cable, or wiring enclosure with circuits rated 600 volts or less.

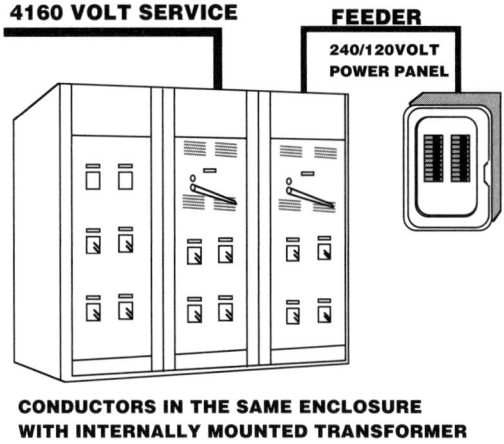

CONDUCTORS IN THE SAME ENCLOSURE WITH INTERNALLY MOUNTED TRANSFORMER

300.4. Protection from physical damage is required for conductors.

300.4(A1). This section requires that the outer edge of bored holes for cables or conduit be no more than 1 1/4 inches from the outer edge in wooden joists, rafters, studs or other wood members. In a standard 2" x 4" stud this is in most cases is not possible, so a provision is made for protection to prevent nails or screws from damaging the conductors to be installed if the hole is less than 1 1/4 inches from the outer edge. This protection can be a steel plate at least 1/16 inch thick, a bushing must be used in steel studs, and the protection must be of the appropriate length and width to cover the area of the wiring.

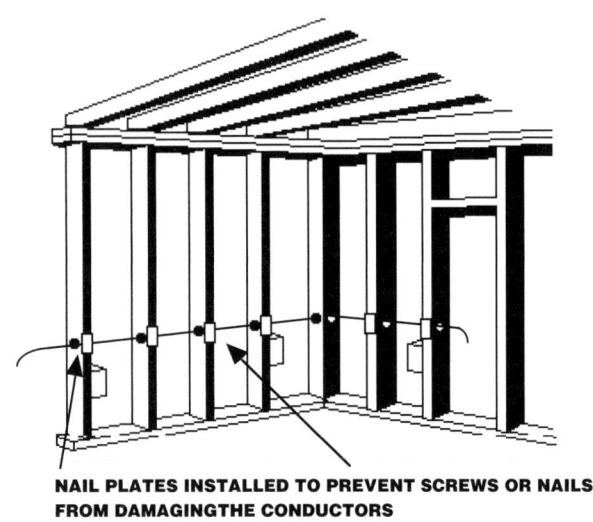

NAIL PLATES INSTALLED TO PREVENT SCREWS OR NAILS FROM DAMAGING THE CONDUCTORS

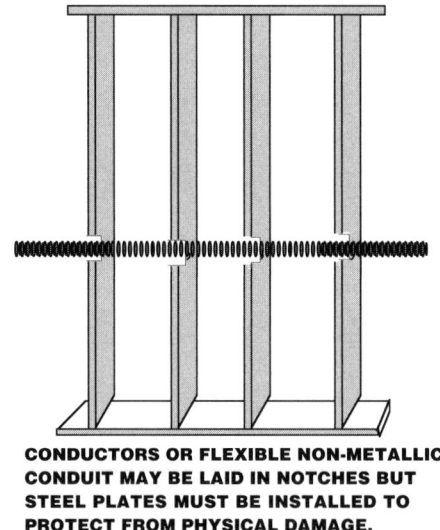

CONDUCTORS OR FLEXIBLE NON-METALLIC CONDUIT MAY BE LAID IN NOTCHES BUT STEEL PLATES MUST BE INSTALLED TO PROTECT FROM PHYSICAL DAMAGE.

300.4(A2) Conduit or cable is permitted to be laid in notches in wood studs, joists and rafters if protected by steel nail plates at least 1/16 inch thick and the notches do not cause any weakening.

300.4(B1)

300.4(B1) When steel framing members are used, nonmetallic sheathed cable is allowed to be installed through either factory or field punched holes. A bushing or grommet must be installed in the hole to protect the cable from damage that may be caused by the sharp edges.

RUBBER GROMMET OR BUSHING MUST BE INSTALLED TO PREVENT DAMAGE TO CABLE

300.4(D). When cables or raceways are installed parallel to joists, rafters, or studs the cable or raceway must be installed so that it is not less than 1 1/4 inches from the nearest edge where nails or screws may de driven. If this 1 1/4 inch distance cannot be maintained, then steel plates or metal sleeves must be used.

300.4(E). Cables and raceways installed below a metal corrugated sheet roof decking installation require at least a 1 1/2 inch of separation from any of the roof decking surface. This requirement does not apply to Rigid metal or Intermediate metal conduit.

300.4(F). Raceways containing ungrounded conductors #4 or larger that enter a cabinet, box, or raceway, the conductors shall be protected by a substantial fitting providing a smooth rounded insulated surface, unless the conductors are separated by insulation securely fastened.

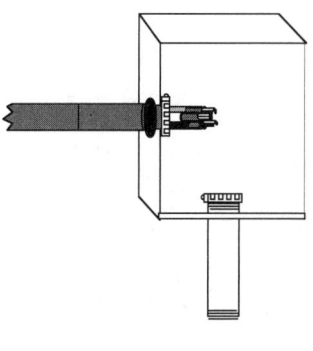

TH

300.5. Underground Installations.

When conduit or cable listed for direct burial are installed underground, they must be buried to a depth so that it is unlikely to be damaged by someone digging in the area at a later date. The depth requirements vary according to the type of raceway or cable. Rigid non-metallic conduit will not be damaged by someone trenching with a shovel but UF cable might be, so UF cable must be buried deeper than PVC conduit.

300.5(A). The minimum cover requirements of Table 300.5 must be met for underground wiring installations. Table 300.5 lists five different wiring methods and the minimum cover requirements for each one in several different locations. The general rule for direct burial cables or conductors is 24 inches and for rigid metal or intermediate metal conduit is 6 inches. This table also lists some special problems that may be encountered such as in solid rock, if rigid metal conduit is installed with a minimum of 2 inches of concrete, the minimum cover requirement is reduced from 6 inches to 2 inches.

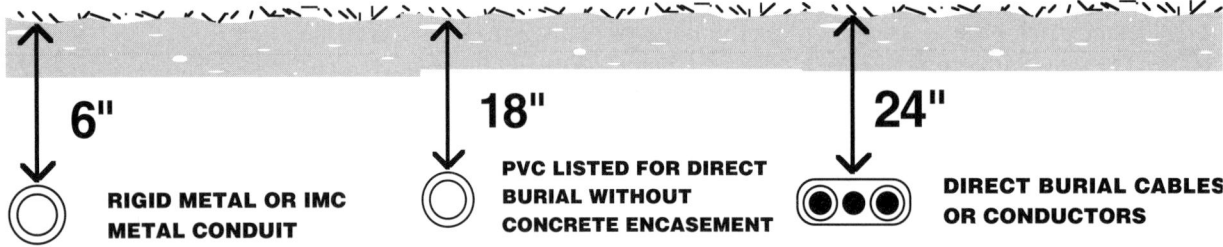

300.5(B). The inside of **all** raceways and enclosures installed underground are considered a wet location. All insulated conductors within those underground raceways and enclosures shall be listed for use in wet locations and comply with 310.8(C).

300.5(C). When underground cables are installed under a building they shall be installed in a raceway. The required raceway must extend beyond the outside walls of the building.

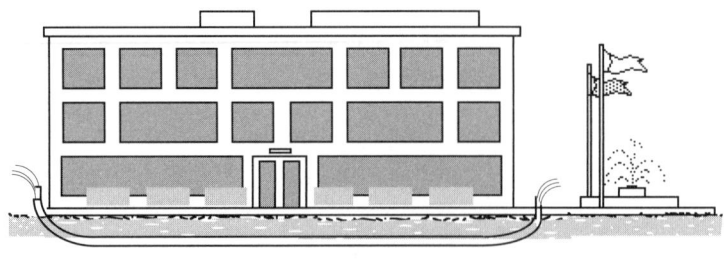

A CABLE INSTALLED UNDER A BUILDING MUST BE IN A RACEWAY

300.5(D1) Where direct buried conductors emerge from the ground and are specified in columns 1 and 4 of Table 300.5 they shall be protected by enclosures or raceways from the burial depth to at least 8 feet above the ground. This protection shall not be required to be more than 18 inches below grade level.

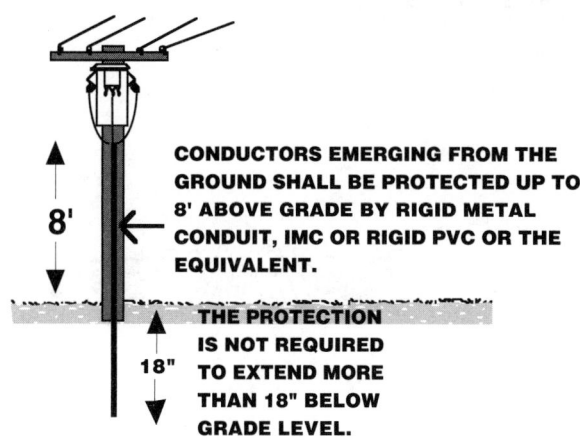

300.5(D2). Conductors entering a building shall be protected to the point of entrance.

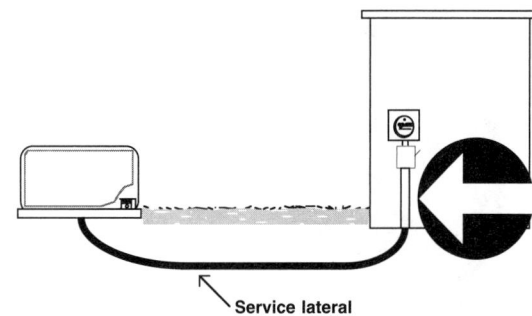

300.5(D3). A warning ribbon is required to be placed 12" above underground service conductors that are not buried 18" or more or encased in concrete.

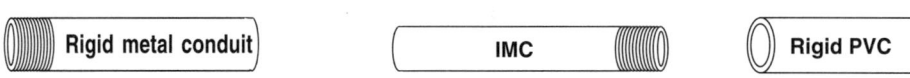

300.5(D4). Where the enclosure or raceway is subject to physical damage, the conductors shall be installed in rigid metal conduit, intermediate metal conduit, Schedule 80 PVC, or equivalent.

300.5(E). Underground conductors or cables shall be permitted to be spliced or tapped without the use of splice boxes.

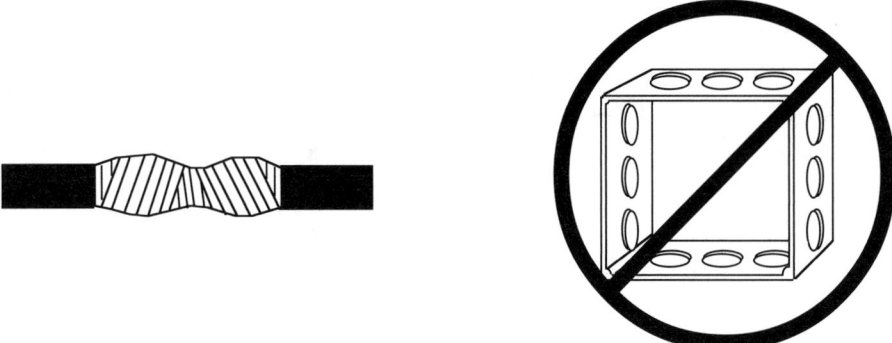

300.5(F). Backfill must contain sand or suitable running boards or other protection where backfill consists of heavy stones or sharp objects that could damage the conductors.

300.5(G). If moisture can contact live parts the underground raceway must be sealed or plugged at either or both ends.

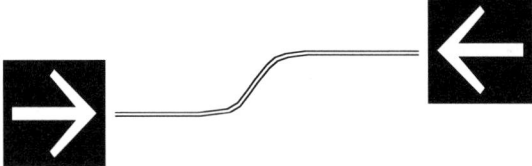

300.5(H)

300.5(H). Where a conduit system is changed to direct burial cable, a bushing must be installed where the conductors emerge as a direct wiring method.

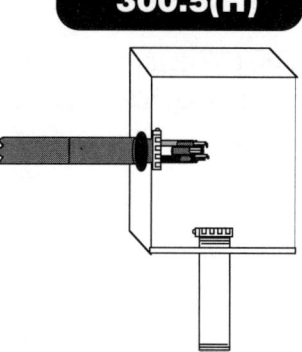

300.5(I). All conductors of the same circuit and, where used, the grounded conductor and all equipment grounding conductors shall be installed in the same raceway or cable or shall be installed in close proximity in the same trench.

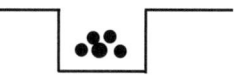

300.5(J). Direct buried conductors, raceways or cables that are subject to movement by settlement or frost shall be arranged so as to prevent damage to the enclosed conductors or to the equipment connected to the raceways.

FPN: This section recognizes "S" loops in underground direct burial to raceway transitions, expansion fittings in raceway risers to fixed equipment, and, generally, the provision of flexible connections to equipment subject to settlement or frost heaves.

300.5(K). Cables or raceways installed using directional boring equipment shall be approved for the purpose.

300.6. Metal raceways, cable armor, cable sheath and fittings must be suitable for the conditions in which they are installed. The material must be resistant to moisture and corrosion. It must be strong enough to withstand the continued loading. Metal raceways buried in the soil can corrode, and should be coated before the installation to prevent the corrosion. Cable sheath may develop a fungus or rot easily in the dampness of the soil, so the sheath must be resistant to fungus and rot.

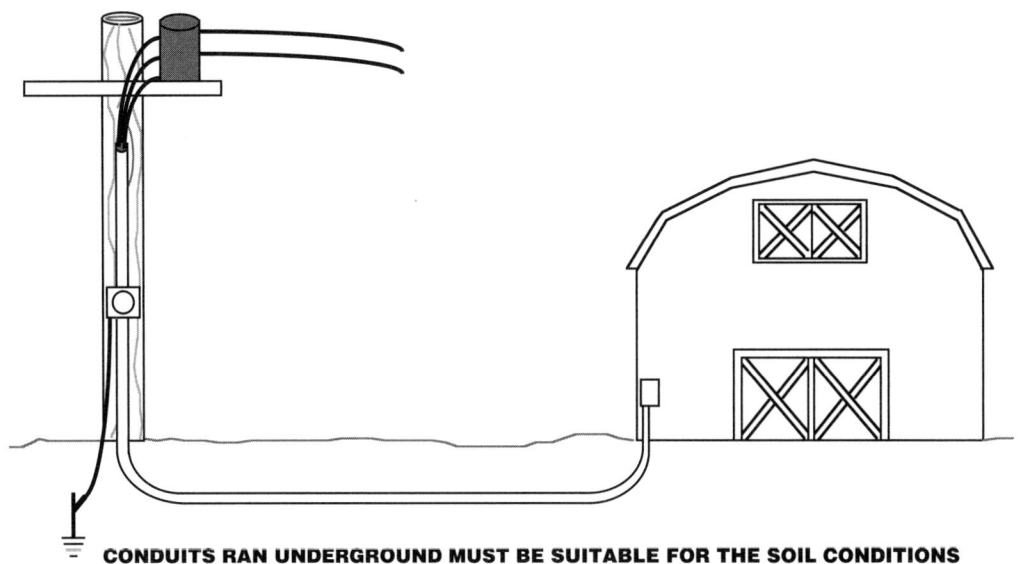

CONDUITS RAN UNDERGROUND MUST BE SUITABLE FOR THE SOIL CONDITIONS

300.6(A). Ferrous metal equipment shall be suitably protected against corrosion inside and outside (except threads at joints) by a coating of listed corrosion-resistant material.
Defintion of ferrous: Containing iron.

Exception. Stainless steel shall not be required to have protective coatings.

300.6(A1). Ferrous metal equipment protected from corrosion solely by enamel shall not be used outdoors or in wet locations.

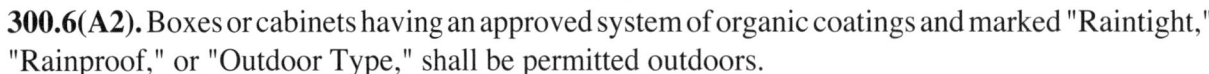

300.6(A2). Boxes or cabinets having an approved system of organic coatings and marked "Raintight," "Rainproof," or "Outdoor Type," shall be permitted outdoors.

300.6(A3). Ferrous metal equipment shall be permitted to be installed in concrete or in direct contact with earth where made of material approved for the condition. or where provided with corrosion protection approved for the condition.

TH

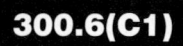

300.6(C1). Nonmetallic equipment where exposed to sunlight, the materials, shall be listed as sunlight resistant or shall be identified as sunlight resistant.

300.6(D). Indoor wet locations where walls are washed frequently all electrical equipment shall be mounted so that there is at least 1/4" airspace between the equipment and the wall.

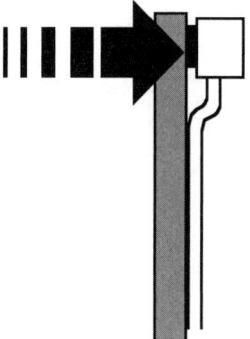

Exception: Nonmetallic equipment shall be permitted without the airspace on a concrete, masonry, tile, or similar surface.

300.7(A). This section requires protection against moisture accumulation. If air is allowed to circulate from warmer to the colder section of the raceway, moisture in the warm air will condense in the cold section of the raceway. Most often this can be prevented by sealing just outside the cold rooms.

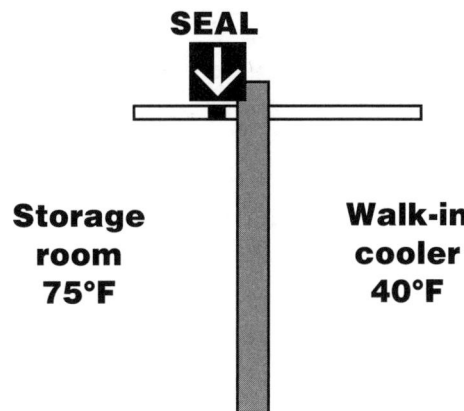

300.7(B). Raceway shall be provided with expansion fittings where necessary to compensate for thermal expansion and contraction.

FPN: Data regarding the use of expansion fittings for PVC, IMC, EMT, and rigid steel conduit.

300.8

300.8. Any raceway or cable tray that contains electric conductors shall not contain any pipe, tube, or equal for steam, water, air, gas, drainage or any service other than electrical.

300.9. Raceways and enclosures that are installed in wet locations abovegrade, shall contain insulated conductors and cables listed for use in wet locations.

300.10. This section requires a permanent and continuous bonding together of all non-current-carrying metal parts of electrical equipment to the system grounding electrode to provide a low impedance path for fault-current flow along the equipment to ensure the opening of overcurrent devices due to a fault.

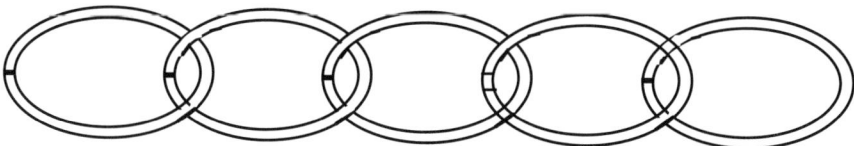

If you have a loose connection you have a high-resistance connection which causes heat. The chain is as strong as the weakest link.

Exception 1: Short sections of metal enclosures or raceways used to protect or support cable assemblies are not required to be grounded. Metal elbows installed in underground nonmetallic conduit where 18" of earth covers any part of the elbow, no grounding of the metal elbow is required.

Exception 2: An insulating spacer may be used to interrupt the electrical continuity of a metal conduit at the point of connection to the metal enclosure to reduce electromagnetic noise or interference.

300.11(A). The rule calls for fastening, not just support. The equipment must be fastened in place using as recognized method. Unfastened cables and raceways are prohibited.

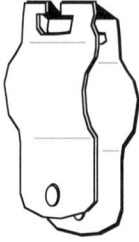 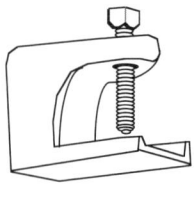

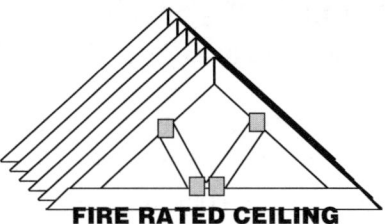

300.11(A1). This section requires an independent means of support for wiring within **fire-rated ceilings**. Where additional ceiling support wires are used as the support for wiring within a hung ceiling, such wires must be identified by marking, tagging, painting, or any method that will permit the ceiling support wires to be readily distinguished from the electrical system support wires.

300.11(A2). This rule does NOT permit the use of additional support wires for use with the wiring methods run within the ceiling cavity in a **NON-fire-rated** ceiling. Some other means must be provided and shall be permitted to be attached to the assembly to support raceways and cables.

Exception: Manufacturers are now producing ceilings that have been investigated and tested to support fixtures and other equipment. Where the hung ceiling is listed for use as a support of equipment and conductors no additional means of support is required.

300.11(B). In general, raceways are NOT to be used as a means of support for cables or nonelectrical equipment. Telephone or other communication, signal, or control cables must NOT be fastened to raceways by plastic straps or any other means.

(1) Raceways can be used for support when identified for the purpose.

(2) Raceways can be used for support when they contain power supply conductors for control equipment and is used to support Class 2 circuit conductors or cables.

(3) Raceways can be used for support in accordance with 314.23 or 410.36(E).

300.11(C). Cable wiring shall NOT be used to support other cables, raceways, or nonelectrical equipment.

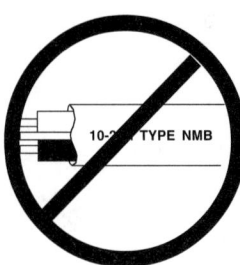

300.12. All raceways shall be continuous between boxes, cabinets, fittings, etc.

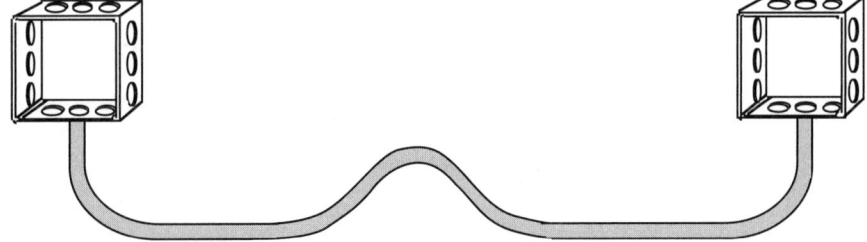

Exception: Short sections of raceways used to protect or support cable assemblies are not required to be mechanically continuous..

300.13(A)

300.13(A). The general rule is when conductors are spliced a box is needed. The second sentence then allows certain cases to be permitted.

300.13(B). In multiwire circuits the continuity of a grounded conductor shall **not** be dependent upon device connections, such as lampholders, receptacles, etc., where the removal of such devices would interrupt the continuity. A pigtail is required to connect the neutral to the receptacle.

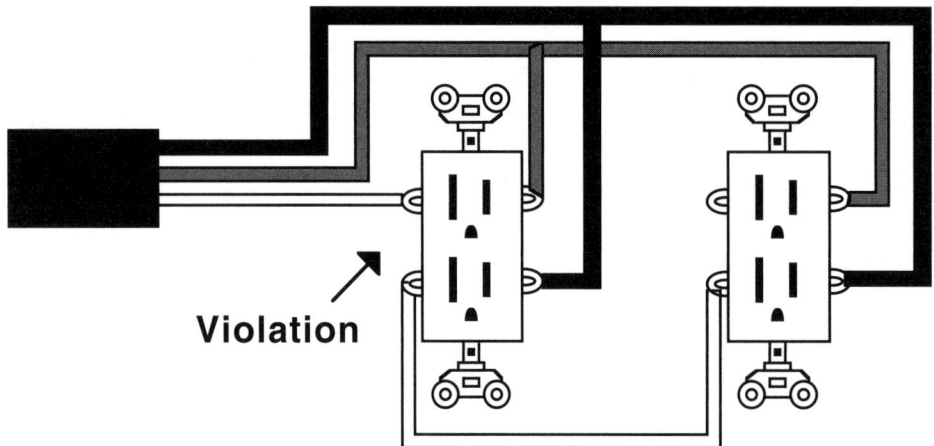

If the duplex receptacle on the left was removed, the grounded conductor would be disconnected and would not feed the receptacle on the right. Because of this "open" neutral condition, it can cause higher than normal voltages on one part of the multiwire circuit and damage the equipment.

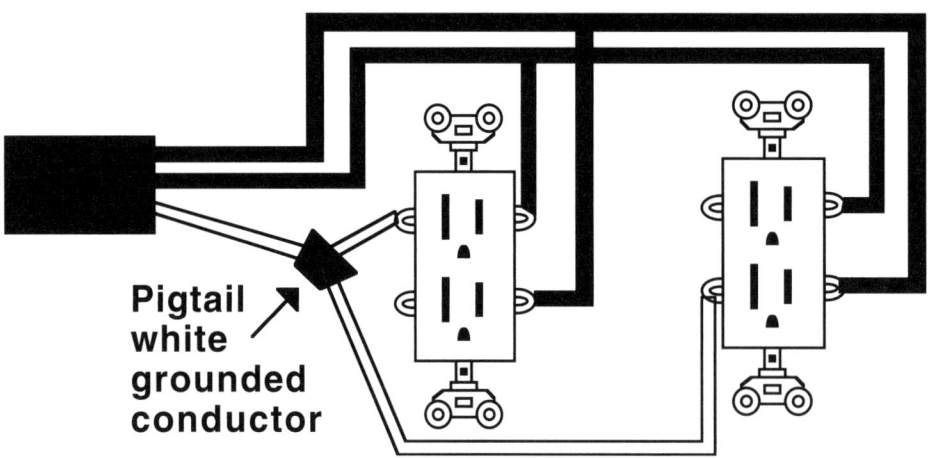

300.14. At least 6" of free conductor measured from its raceway or cable sheath shall be left at each box for the connection of fixtures or devices. Where the opening to a box is less than 8" in any dimension, each conductor shall extend beyond the outside of the opening by at least 3".

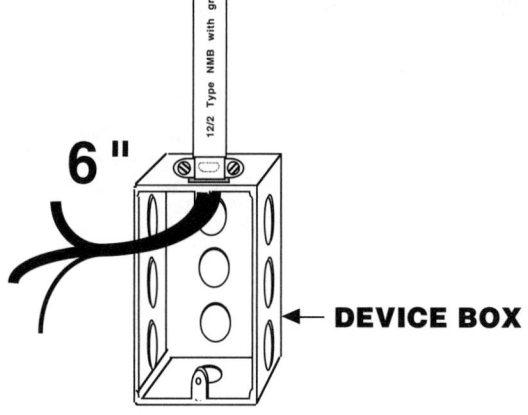

300.15. A box or conduit body is to be used at splice points or connection points in raceway systems.

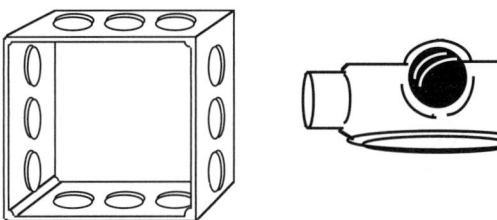

300.15(A). A box or conduit body is not required at outlet points with removable covers, such as wireways, multioutlet assemblies, gutters, and surface raceways.

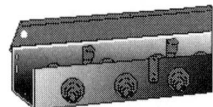

300.15(B). An integral junction box or wiring compartment as part of approved equipment shall be permitted in lieu of a box.

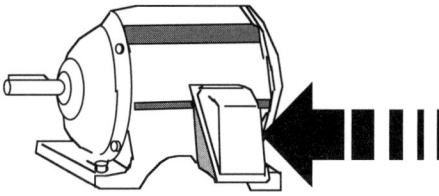

300.15(C). A box or conduit body is not required where cables enter or exit from conduit used to support or protect the cable. A fitting is required on each end of the conduit to protect the cable from abrasion.

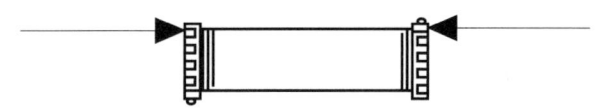

300.15(D). A box or conduit body is not required where accessible fittings are used for straight through splices in MI cable.

300.15(J). A box or conduit body is not required where light fixtures are listed as a raceway.

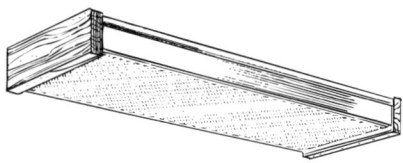

300.16(A). A box, conduit body, or fitting having a separately bushed hole for each conductor shall be used wherever a change is made from conduit to cable.

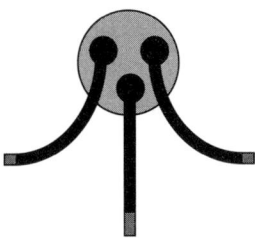

300.17. The number and size of conductors in any raceway shall not be more than will permit dissipation of heat and ready installation or withdrawal of conductors without damage.

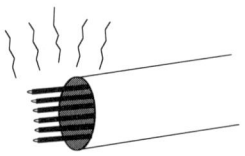

300.18(A). A general rule that requires all raceways to be installed completely before pulling any wires.

300.18(B). Metal raceways shall not be supported by welding.

300.19(A). Long vertical runs of conductors should NOT be supported by the terminal to which they are connected. Table 300.19(A) lists the spacing for conductor supports.

300.19(B). Support methods and spacing for fire rated cables and conductors shall comply with the listing of the electrical circuit protective system used and in no case exceed the values in Table 300.19(A).

300.20(A). When all alternating current conductors are kept close together in a raceway, box, etc. the magnetic fields around the conductors tend to oppose or cancel each other minimizing the inductive reactance of the circuit. The neutral must be run with the phase conductors. The equipment grounding conductor must also be run close to the circuit conductors to minimize the impedance of the fault-current return path.

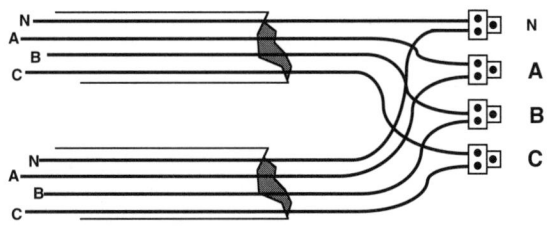

300.20(B)

300.20(B). Where a single conductor carrying alternating current passes through metal with magnetic properties, the inductive effect shall be minimized by:

(1) cutting slots in the metal between individual holes through which the individual conductors pass or
(2) passing all the conductors in the circuit through an insulating wall sufficiently large for all of the conductors of the circuit.

FPN: Because aluminum is not a magnetic metal, there will be no heating due to hysteresis; however, induced currents will be present.

300.21. Electrical installations in hollow spaces, vertical shafts, and ventilation or air handling ducts shall be made so that the possible spread of fire or products of combustion will not be substantially increased.

FPN: A minimum 24" horizontal separation usually applies between boxes installed on opposite sides of the wall per Building Codes.

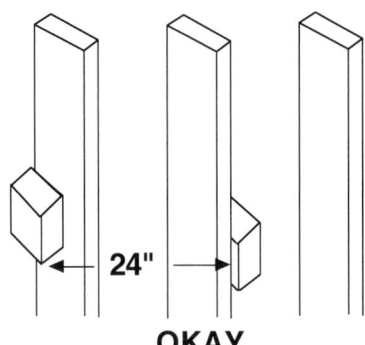

The Building Code requires outlet boxes on opposite sides of the fire resistant wall or the shaft enclosure shall be separated by a horizontal distance of not less than 24".

The exception is openings for electrical outlet boxes of any material are permitted provided such boxes are listed for use in fire resistant assemblies and are installed in accordance with their listings.

Back to back boxes or boxes in the same stud chase to opposite rooms are not permitted in fire rated walls. A good example would be a hotel room where a fire in one room could spread to an adjoining room through the boxes even though the wall is fire rated. Some codes permit boxes if in a different stud chase.

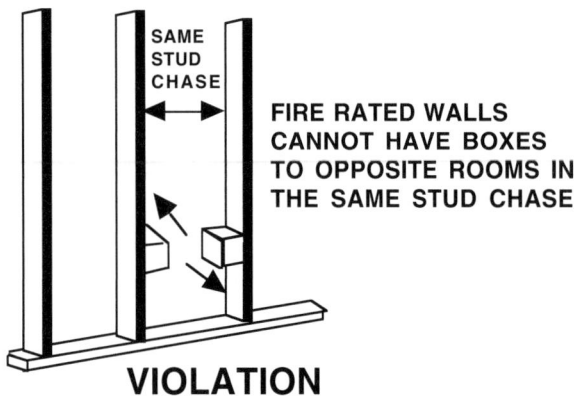

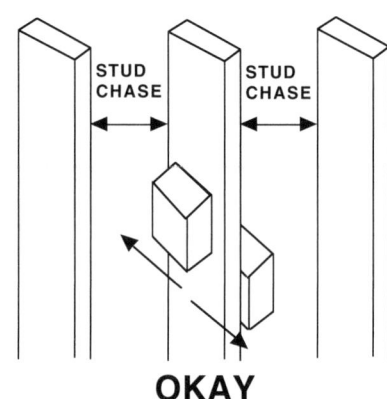

300.22(A). No wiring system shall be installed in ducts used to transport dust, loose stock, or flammable vapors or ducts used for the removal or for ventilation of commercial-type cooking equipment.

300.22(B). Only MI cable, MC cable, EMT, flexible metal tubing, Flexible metal conduit not over 4', IMC, or rigid metal conduit without nonmetallic covering shall be installed in ducts or plenums specifically fabricated to transport environmental air.

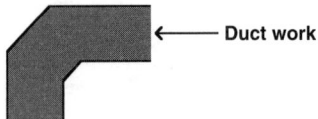

Definition of duct system: A continuous passageway for the transmission of air which, in addition to ducts, may include duct fittings, dampers, plenums, fans, and accessory air handling equipment.

Definition of a plenum: An air compartment or chamber to which one or more ducts are connected and which forms part of an air distribution system.

• Generally speaking it has been made clear that the Code panel oppose nonmetallic wiring methods in ducts and plenums, except for nonmetallic cable assemblies that are specially listed for such use. Using PVC would not propagate a fire, it would contribute to the smoke and provide additional flammable material in the air duct.

II. Requirements for Over 600 Volts

300.31. Covers are required on all boxes, fittings, etc. to prevent accidental contact with energized parts.

300.34. The conductor shall not be bent to a radius less than 8 times the overall diameter for nonshielded conductors or 12 times the overall diameter for shielded or lead-covered conductors during or after installation.

Article 300   Quiz #1   -   Open Book

QUIZ #1

1. Electric equipment with a metal enclosure or with a nonmetallic enclosure listed for the use and having adequate ____ producing characteristics, and associated wiring material suitable for the ambient temperature shall be permitted to be installed in other space used for environmental air unless prohibited in this Code.

I. fire-resistant   II. low-smoke

(a) I or II   (b) I and II   (c) I only   (d) II only

2. ___ of the following is a true statement.

I. Wiring above a nonfire rated ceiling shall not be supported by the ceiling support wires.
II. Wiring above a fire rated ceiling shall not be supported by the ceiling support wires.
III. Cables and raceways shall not be permitted to be supported by ceiling grids.
IV. The ceiling support wires shall be permitted to support branch circuit wiring if in accordance with the ceiling manufacturer's instructions.

(a) I & II only   (b) II & III only   (c) IV only   (d) I, II, III & IV

3. In areas where walls are frequently washed, conduit should be mounted with ____ inches of air space between the wall and the conduit.

(a) 1/8"   (b) 1/4"   (c) 3/8"   (d) 1/2"

4. Because aluminum is not a magnetic metal, there will be ____ present when aluminum conductors are grouped in a wireway.

(a) no heat due to voltage   (b) no heating due to hysteresis
(c) no induced currents   (d) none of these

5. Underground service conductors carried up a pole must be protected from mechanical injury to a height of at least ____ feet.

(a) 10   (b) 8   (c) 12   (d) 15

6. Bored holes in wood members for cable or raceway-type wiring shall be bored so that the edge of the hole is not less than ____ inches from the nearest edge.

(a) 1 1/4"   (b) 1 1/8"   (c) 1 1/2"   (d) 1 1/16"

Article 300 Quiz #1 - Open Book

QUIZ #1

7. Insulating bushings are required on conduit entering boxes, gutters, etc. if it contains conductors as large as ____.

(a) #2   (b) #4   (c) #0   (d) #6

8. The minimum length of free conductor left at each outlet and switch point in a dwelling shall not be less than ____ inches.

(a) 4   (b) 6   (c) 8   (d) 10

9. Electrical installations in hollow spaces, vertical shafts, and ventilation or air-handling ducts shall be so made that the possible spread of fire or products of combustion will not be ____.

(a) substantially increased   (b) allowed   (c) exposed   (d) underrated

10. Underground service conductors that are encased in concrete and that are buried ____ inches or more below grade shall have their location identified by a warning ribbon.

(a) 12   (b) 14   (c) 16   (d) 18

11. When connections are made in the white wire in a multi-wire circuit at receptacles, they are required to be made ____.

(a) connected to the silver terminals on the duplex
(b) to the brass colored terminal
(c) with a pigtail to the silver terminal
(d) none of these

12. Conductors of light and power systems of all voltages may occupy the same enclosure or raceway ____.

(a) if less than 600 volts and if insulated for maximum voltage of any conductor within the enclosure or raceway
(b) if power system is over 600 volts and light system under 600 volts
(c) if power system is over 600 volts and individual circuits are AC
(d) in most instances without qualification

TH

Article 300 Quiz #2 - Open Book

1. All but which of the following shall be continuous between cabinets, boxes, fittings or other enclosures or outlets?

(a) short sections of raceways used to provide support or protection of cable assemblies
(b) metallic or non-metallic raceways
(c) cable armors
(d) cable sheaths

2. Only wiring methods consisting of _____ shall be installed in ducts or plenums used for environmental air.

I. EMT   II. type NMC   III. type MI   IV. flexible metallic tubing

(a) I and II only   (b) I, II and III only   (c) I, III and IV only   (d) I, II, III and IV

3. All of the following may be used on services of 2300/4600v except _____.

(a) MI cable   (b) MV cable   (c) cable bus   (d) busway

4. The bending radius for nonshielded cables operating at 4160v shall be less than _____ times the diameter.

(a) 6   (b) 8   (c) 10   (d) 12

5. Which of the following methods is **not** approved for conductor supports?

(a) deflecting of cables in junction boxes   (b) insertion of boxes
(c) clamping devices   (d) loop connectors

6. A box or conduit body shall not be required for each splice, junction, switch, pull, termination, or outlet points in wiring methods with removable covers such as _____.

I. surface raceways   II. wireways   III. cable trays

(a) I only   (b) II only   (c) I and II only   (d) I, II and III

Article 300   Quiz #2   -   Open Book

QUIZ #2

7. Where a single AC conductor carrying current passes through metal with magnetic properties, the inductive effect shall be minimized by _____.

I. cutting slots in the metal between the individual holes through which individual conductors pass
II. passing all the conductors in the circuit through an insulating wall sufficiently large for all the conductors of the circuit

(a) I only   (b) II only   (c) both I and II   (d) neither I nor II

8. The Code requires all conductors carrying AC current installed in metal raceways to be grouped together because _____.

(a) it's cheaper   (b) it's easier to test   (c) it's easier to maintain   (d) of inductive current

9. Open runs of braid-covered insulated conductors used for over 600 volts shall have a flame retardant saturant applied to the braid covering after installation unless this protectant is factory installed. This treated braid covering shall be stripped back a safe distance at conductor terminals, a distance of not less than ___ for each kilovolt of the conductor to ground voltage of the circuit.

(a) 1"   (b) 2"   (c) 3"   (d) 6"

10. Where the ends of a conduit terminate in areas of widely differing temperatures, _____.

(a) conduit ends should be filled with an approved material
(b) rigid metallic conduit should be used
(c) electrical metallic conduit should be used
(d) flexible metallic conduit should be used

11. Type JM or SM cable may be run through an environmental return air duct when enclosed in _____.

(a) metal raceways   (b) PVC   (c) ENT   (d) flexible nonmetallic tubing

12. Non-shielded high-voltage cables shall be installed in _____ conduit encased in not less than 3" of concrete.

I. rigid PVC   II. IMC   III. rigid metal

(a) I only   (b) II only   (c) III only   (d) I, II or III

Article 300 Quiz #3 - Open Book

1. Which of the following wiring methods is permitted through an air conditioning duct?

(a) electrical metallic tubing
(b) PVC
(c) no wiring method is permitted in an A/C duct
(d) romex

2. The Code requires all conductors that attach to a cablebus to be in the same raceway because ____.

(a) of less voltage drop   (b) the cost is less   (c) it is easier to service   (d) of inductive current

3. Cable or raceway that is installed through bored holes in wood members, holes shall be bored so that the edge of the hole is not less than 1 1/4" from the nearest edge of the wood member. Where this distance cannot be maintained the cable or raceway shall be protected from penetration by nails and screws by a steel plate or bushing, at least ____ inch thick, and of appropriate length and width installed to cover the area of the wiring.

(a) 1/16   (b) 1/8   (c) 3/16   (d) 1/4

4. Conductors of AC or DC circuits rated 600 volt or less, shall be permitted to occupy the same conduit if ____.

(a) all conductors shall have an insulation voltage rating equal to the maximum circuit voltage rating of any conductor in the conduit
(b) all conductors shall have a 600 volt insulation rating
(c) conductors must have a dividing barrier in the raceway
(d) AC and DC are not permitted in the same raceway

5. Because aluminum is not a magnetic metal, there will be no heating due to ____.

(a) electrolysis   (b) hysteresis   (c) hermetic   (d) galvanic action

6. Which of the following is a false statement?

(a) direct buried conductors are required to be spliced in a splice box.
(b) direct buried conductors are permitted to be soldered.
(c) where wire connectors are used for splicing direct buried conductors, the connectors must be listed for such use.
(d) where necessary to prevent physical damage, direct buried conductors shall be protected by raceways, boards sleeves, or other approved means.

QUIZ #3

Article 300   Quiz #3   -   Open Book

7. Suitable covers shall be installed on all boxes, fittings, and similar enclosures to prevent accidental contact with ____ parts or physical damage to parts or insulation. Over 600v nominal.

(a) energized   (b) mechanical   (c) electrical   (d) none of these

8. Underground cable installed under a building shall be in a ____ ?

(a) sleeve   (b) duct bank   (c) gutter   (d) raceway

9. Where raceways are exposed to widely different temperatures they shall be ____.

(a) sealed   (b) bonded   (c) grounded   (d) isolated

10. Which of the following wiring methods may be used inside the duct used for vapor removal and ventilation of commercial type cooking equipment?

(a) nonmetallic sheathed cable   (b) EMT   (c) rigid steel conduit   (d) none of these

11. If laid in notches in wood studs, joists, rafters, or other wood members ___ shall be protected against nails or screws by a steel plate at least 1/16" thick.

(a) EMT   (b) rigid nonmetallic conduit   (c) intermediate steel conduit   (d) flexible conduit

12. A vertical run of 4" rigid conduit is installed to a height of 250 feet. The conduit contains four #500 kcmil THHN copper conductors. How many conductor supports are required?

(a) none   (b) 3   (c) 4   (d) 5

13. A 2400 volt lead cable can be bent up to ___ times its diameter.

(a) 6   (b) 8   (c) 10   (d) 12

14. Ferrous raceways, boxes, fittings, etc., shall not be used outdoors or in wet locations if protected solely by ____.

(a) zinc
(b) PVC
(c) cadmium
(d) enamel

Article 300   Quiz #3   -   Open Book

QUIZ #3

15. Which of the following wiring methods may be installed in notches cut into wood framing members without being protected by a steel plate 1/16" thick?

(a) Rigid nonmetallic conduit   (b) Armored cable
(c) Nonmetallic sheathed cable   (d) Metal clad cable

16. Conductors of light and power systems of 600 volts or less may occupy the same enclosure, without regard to whether the individual circuits are AC or DC, only where all conductors are ____.

(a) insulated for the maximum of 300 volts
(b) insulated for the maximum temperature within the enclosure
(c) insulated for the maximum voltage of any conductor within the enclosure
(d) none of the above

ARTICLE 310

CONDUCTORS FOR GENERAL WIRING

310.1. The rules are general requirements for conductors and their insulations, markings, type designations, mechanical strengths, ampacity ratings, and uses. These requirements do NOT apply to conductors that form an integral part of equipment, such as motors, motor controllers, and similar conductors.

FPN: For flexible cords and cables, see Article 400. For fixture wires, see Article 402.

310.2(A). Conductors are generally required by this section to be insulated, but bare conductors are permitted for equipment grounding conductors, for bonding jumpers, for grounding electrode conductors, and for grounded neutral conductors.

A conductor can be round, solid, stranded, rectangular, copper, aluminum, etc.

SOLID   **STRANDED**   **RECTANGULAR**

Note the larger gage numbers actually are the smaller size wires. Example: A #14 (larger number) is a smaller size wire than a #6 (smaller number). A #0 wire is much larger than a #12.

Solid wires are used in the smaller sizes generally in *cable*, such as the nonmetallic sheathed cable used in house wiring, often called *romex* by the electrician.

SOLID WIRES

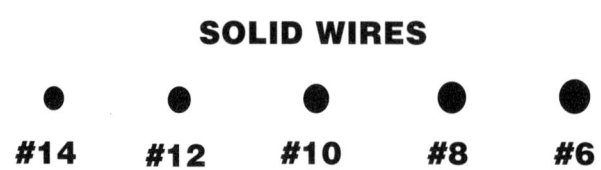

310.2(B)

STRANDED WIRES

The units used in measuring wires are mils and circular mils. A mil is one thousandth (.001) of an inch. Circular is round. So a circular mil is about the size of a hair.

Wires can be measured with a wire gage or a micrometer.

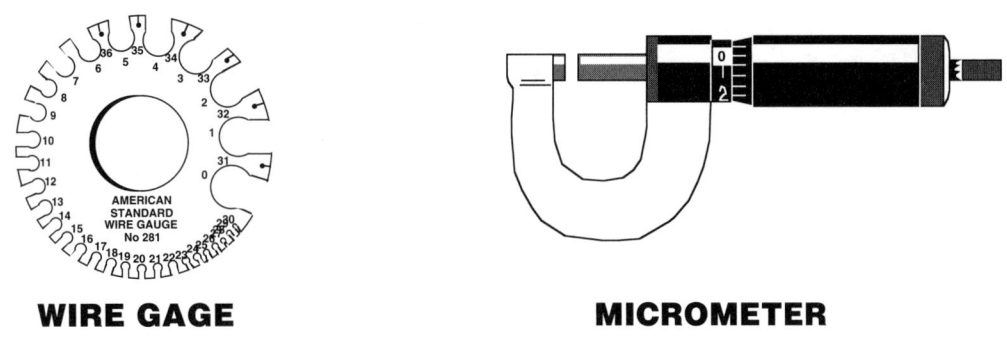

WIRE GAGE   **MICROMETER**

#0, #00, #000, and #0000 are called one-naught, two-naught, three-naught and four-naught. On the insulation they will be marked #1/0, #2/0, #3/0 or #4/0.

Example: A #2/0 (#00) is called a two-naught. When you hear an electrician pronounce it, sometimes it sounds like he's saying two-OUGHT.

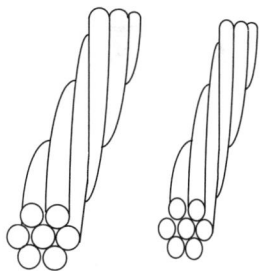

Wire size is like water pipe size; the larger the water pipe the more water it will carry. The larger the wire the more amperes it will carry.

310.2(B). Conductors in Article 310 shall be aluminum, copper-clad aluminum. or copper unless otherwise specified.

Section 110.5: *Conductors normally used to carry current shall be of COPPER unless otherwise provided in the Code. Where the conductor material is not specified, the material and sizes given in the Code shall apply to COPPER conductors.*

•Note. Copper-clad aluminum is the newest conductor material in the Code. A copper-clad aluminum conductor has the copper bonded metallurgically to an aluminum core. The copper forms a minimum 10% of the cross-sectional area of the solid conductor or of that of each strand of a stranded conductor.

The ampacity of copper-clad aluminum conductors is the same as that of aluminum conductors. Copper-clad aluminum conductors are suitable for intermixing with copper and aluminum conductors in terminals for splicing connections only when the wire connectors are specifically recognized for such use. These connections are limited to dry locations.

310.3. Stranded wire is used in the larger size wire as it is easier to install than a solid wire because of its bending and flexing. The Code does not allow #8 and larger *solid* wires to be installed in a conduit (pipe) for that reason. The smaller wire has fewer strands than the larger size wire.

310.4. Conductors size #1/0 amd larger, comprising each phase, shall be connected in parallel (electrically joined at both ends). There are four exceptions to the rule.

The parallel conductors in each phase, polarity, neutral, grounded circuit conductor, or equipment grounding conductor shall comply with all of the following:

(1) Be the same length
(2) Have the same conductor material
(3) Be the same size in circular mil area
(4) Have the same insulation type
(5) Be terminated in the same manner

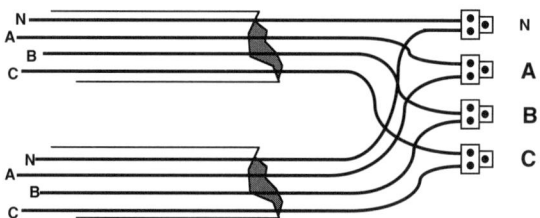

•Note. All the conductors of any PHASE or the neutral must satisfy the five rules, but **A** phase does not have to be the same as **B** phase or **C** phase. Each PHASE must be the SAME. It is important to follow the five rules for all the phases as is most commonly done to prevent voltage drop from causing an unbalance with the other phases.

FPN: Differences in inductive reactance and unequal division of current can be minimized by choice of materials, methods of construction, and orientation of conductors.

310.4

Proper design is to parallel smaller conductors rather than installing one large conductor.

The reason for paralleling conductors is to get the most ampacity per circular mil area.

#12 CONDUCTOR
6530 cm

#6 CONDUCTOR
26240 cm

A #6 conductor has a cross sectional area approximately four times larger than a #12 (6530cm x 4 = 26120cm).

But, the ampacity of a #6 conductor is *not* four times larger than a #12 conductor. A #12 TW has an ampacity of 25 and a #6 TW has an ampacity of 55. About twice as large.

A #6 conductor has only twice the surface area (circumference) of a #12 and not four times. The heat produced in the wire can only be dissipated through the surface area.

Using smaller conductors to obtain the required current carrying ampacity reduces the total cross section of the conductor which produces a higher resistance and a greater voltage drop.

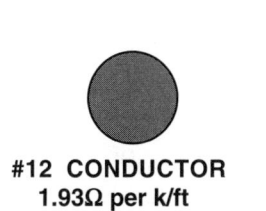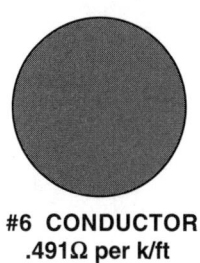

#12 CONDUCTOR
1.93Ω per k/ft

#6 CONDUCTOR
.491Ω per k/ft

The circumference of a #6 is only twice as large as a #12 even though the cross sectional area is four times greater.

A #1/0 conductor at 105600 cm is ten times larger in cross sectional area than a #10 conductor at 10380 cm. The #1/0 does not have ten times the ampacity of a #10.

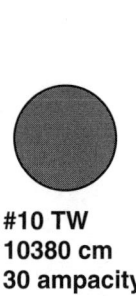

#10 TW
10380 cm
30 ampacity

#1/0 TW
105600 cm
125 ampacity

A #700 THW kcmil conductor has an ampacity of 460 amps. Two #4/0 THW conductors paralleled have an ampacity of 460 amps.

A #700 kcmil has 700,000 cm whereas two #4/0 have a combined circular mil area of 423,200 (2 x 211,600); 40% less conductor with the same ampacity. This is why the paralleling of conductors is to be considered in electrical designing.

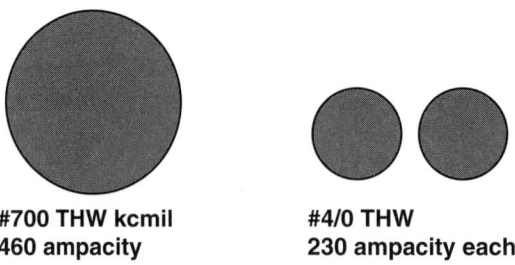

It is seldom economical to use conductors of larger sizes. It's more economical to parallel smaller conductors as you can see why.

310.5. In general, the minimum size of conductors is shown in Table 310.5, unless permitted elsewhere in the Code.

310.6. Shielding of high-voltage cables protects the conductor assembly against surface discharge or burning from corona, which can damage the insulation.

310.7. This section also requires direct burial high-voltage cables to be "identified for such use".

310.8(C2). Any conductor installed in a wet location must designated with the letter "W".

310.8(D). Conductors or cables exposed to direct rays of the sun shall comply with one of the following:

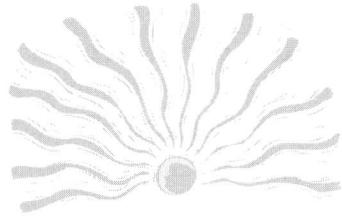

(1) Conductors and cables shall be listed, or listed and marked, as being sunlight resistant
(2) Conductors and cables shall be covered with insulating material, such as tape or sleeving, that is listed, or listed and marked, as being sunlight resistant

310.9. Conductors exposed to oils, greases, vapors, gases, fumes, liquids, or other substances having a deleterious effect on the conductor or insulation shall be of a type suitable for the application.

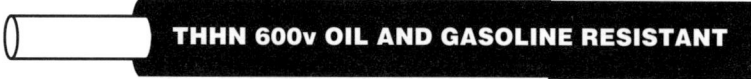

310.10. This section is very important and is the basis of safe operation of insulated conductors.

FPN1: The principal determinants of operating temperature are:

(1) Ambient temperature may vary along the conductor length as well as from time to time.
(2) Heat generated internally in the conductor as the result of load current flow, including fundamental and harmonic currents.
(3) The rate at which generated heat dissipates into the ambient medium. Thermal insulation that covers or surrounds conductors affects the rate of heat dissipation.
(4) Adjacent load-carrying conductors have the dual effect of raising the ambient temperature and impeding heat dissipation.

310.11(A). All conductors and cables shall be marked to indicate:

(1) The maximum rated voltage
(2) The proper type letter or letters for the type of wire or cable
(3) The manufacturer's name, trademark
(4) The AWG size or circular mil area (found in Table 8 Chapter 9)
(5) Cable assemblies where the neutral conductor is smaller than the ungrounded conductor it shall be so marked

310.11(B). The following conductors and cables shall be durably marked on the surface. The AWG size or circular mil area shall be repeated at intervals not exceeding 24". All other markings shall be repeated at intervals not exceeding 40".

(1) Single-conductor and multiconductor rubber and thermoplastic-insulated wire and cable
(2) Nonmetallic-sheathed cable
(3) Service-entrance cable
(4) Underground feeder and branch-circuit cable
(5) Tray cable
(6) Irrigation cable
(7) Power-limited tray cable
(8) Instrumentation tray cable

310.12(A). Insulated or covered grounded conductors shall be white or gray in color.

310.12(B). Equipment grounding conductors shall be green or bare.

310.12(C). The hot (ungrounded) conductor shall be clearly distinguished from the grounded or grounding conductor.

310.15. Ampacities for Conductors Rated 0 - 2000 Volts.

310.15(A2). Where more than one calculation of ampacity could apply for a given circuit length, the LOWEST value shall be used.

Definition of ampacity: The current, in amperes, that a conductor can carry continuously under conditions of use without exceeding its temperature rating.

310.15(B). Ampacities of conductors may be determined by either of two methods. The first method is the old, tested, and familar method based on Tables 310.16 through 310.21. The second method is mentioned in 310.15(C) which is a defective method not used today.

310.15(B2). Adjustment Factors.

When there are more than three current-carrying conductors in a raceway or cable, the ampacity of each conductor must be reduced as indicated in Table 310.15(B2a) to compensate for heating effects and reduced heat dissipation due to reduced ventilation of individual conductors. Each current-carrying conductor of a paralleled set of conductors shall be counted as a current carrying conductor.

Table 310.15(B2a). Adjustment Factors.
(a) More than Three Conductors in a Raceway or Cable. Where the number of conductors in a raceway or cable exceeds three, the ampacities shall be reduced as shown in the following table:

Number of Conductors	Percent of Values in Tables as Adjusted for Ambient Temperature if Necessary
4 through 6	80
7 through 9	70
10 through 20	50
21 through 30	45
31 through 40	40
41 and above	35

*Some conductors are **not** counted when applying 310.15(B2a):*

310.15(B2) ex. 1	Conductors of different systems
310.15(B2) ex. 2	Cable trays
310.15(B2) ex. 3	Nipples
310.15(B2) ex. 4	Outdoor trench
310.15(B4a)	The neutral conductor in a normally balanced circuit is **not** counted

Definition of a nipple: A nipple is 24" or less.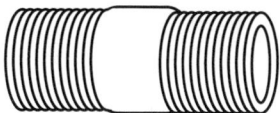

310.15(B3). Where bare or covered conductors are installed with insulated conductors, the temperature rating of the bare or covered conductor shall be equal to the lowest temperature rating of the insulated conductor for the purpose of determining ampacity.

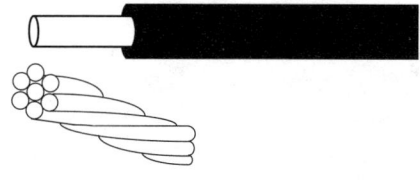

TH

310.15(B4a)

310.15(B4a). The neutral conductor in a normally balanced circuit is **not** counted.

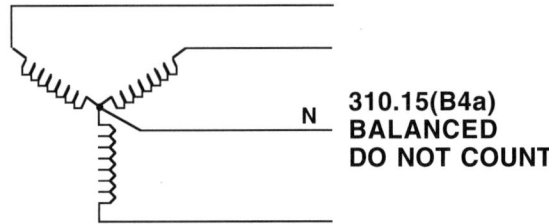

310.15(B4b). The neutral conductor is **counted** in a 3-wire circuit consisting of 2-phase wires of a 3-phase wye system.

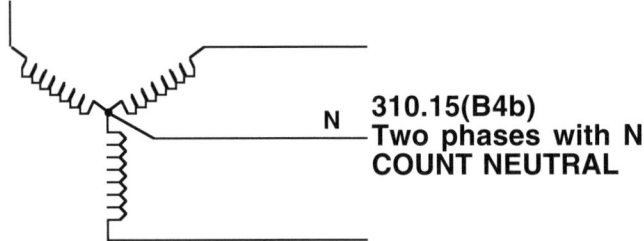

310.15(B4c). The neutral is considered a **current carrying** conductor in nonlinear loads. Circuits such as discharge lighting (fluorescent, mercury, sodium) data processing, or similar equipment. The Harmonic currents in the nonlinear loads can cause the neutral currents to rise a little higher than the line current.

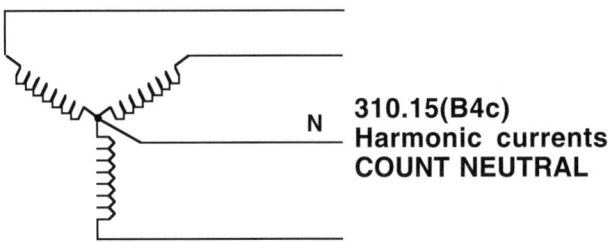

310.15(B5). A grounding or bonding conductor shall **not** be counted when applying the provisions of Table 310.15(B2a). The grounding conductor (green or bare wire) only carries fault current to trip the overcurrent device. This is **not** a heat factor.

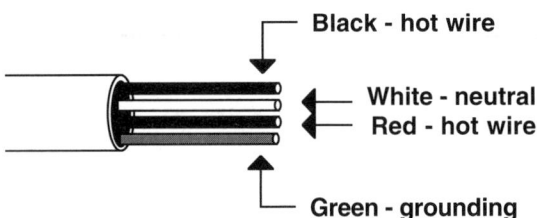

310.15(B6). Services and feeders 120/240v, 3-wire, single-phase for individual dwelling units of one family, two-family, and multifamily dwellings, conductors listed in Table 310.15(B6), shall be permitted as service-entrance, service lateral and feeder conductors. The grounded (neutral) conductor shall be permitted to be smaller than the ungrounded (hot) conductors.

Table 310.15(B6). Conductor types for 120/240v, 3-wire, 1ø dwelling services and feeders. Conductor types RHH, RHW, RHW-2, THHN, THHW, THW, THW-2, THWN, THWN-2, XHHW, XHHW-2, SE, USE, and USE-2.

Conductor (AWG or kcmil)		
Copper	Aluminum or Copper-Clad Aluminum	Service or Feeder Rating (Amperes)
4	2	100
3	1	110
2	1/0	125
1	2/0	150
1/0	3/0	175
2/0	4/0	200
3/0	250	225
4/0	300	250
250	350	300
350	500	350
400	600	400

310.15(c). This method of calculating ampacity is complex, confusing, incomplete, and a defective procedure that was presented in the 1987 Code as the basic method, based on an elaborate formula.

$$I = \sqrt{\frac{TC - (TA + \Delta TD)}{RDC(1 + YC)RCA}}$$

Table 310.16.

Even if the electrician does not use the Code often, at one time or another you have referred to the table of ampacity to determine how many amps a certain size wire can carry. Table 310.16 lists these ampacities for conductors.

This is probably the most misused table in the Code book as the ampacities listed in Table 310.16 are generally **never** correct. This is a very important table that you must learn to use correctly.

Table 310.16. Allowable Ampacities of Insulated Conductors
Rated 0-2000 Volts, 60° to 90°C (140° to 194°F)
Not More Than Three Conductors in Raceway or Cable or Earth
(Directly Buried), Based on Ambient Temperature of 30°C (86°F).

Size	Temperature Rating of Conductor. See Table 310.13.						Size
	60°C (140°F)	75°C (167°F)	90°C (194°F)	60°C (140°F)	75°C (167°F)	90°C (194°F)	
AWG kcmil	TYPES TW, UF	TYPES RHW, THHW, THW, THWN, XHHW, USE, ZW	TYPES TBS, SA, SIS, FEP, FEPB, MI, RHH, RHW-2, THHN, THHW, THW-2, THWN-2, USE-2, XHH XHHW, XHHW-2 ZW-2	TYPES TW, UF	TYPES RHW, THHW, THW, THWN, XHHW, USE	TYPES TBS, SA, SIS, THHN, THHW, THW-2, THWN-2, RHH, RHW-2, USE-2, XHH, XHHW, XHHW-2, ZW-2	AWG kcmil
	COPPER			ALUMINUM OR COPPER-CLAD ALUMINUM			
18	....	....	14	....	....	....	....
16	....	....	18	....	....	....	....
14*	20	20	25	....	....	....	....
12*	25	25	30	20	20	25	12*
10*	30	35	40	25	30	35	10*
8	40	50	55	30	40	45	8
6	55	65	75	40	50	60	6
4	70	85	95	55	65	75	4
3	85	100	110	65	75	85	3
2	95	115	130	75	90	100	2
1	110	130	150	85	100	115	1
1/0	125	150	170	100	120	135	1/0
2/0	145	175	195	115	135	150	2/0
3/0	165	200	225	130	155	175	3/0
4/0	195	230	260	150	180	205	4/0
250	215	255	290	170	205	230	250
300	240	285	320	190	230	255	300
350	260	310	350	210	250	280	350
400	280	335	380	225	270	305	400
500	320	380	430	260	310	350	500
600	355	420	475	285	340	385	600
700	385	460	520	310	375	420	700
750	400	475	535	320	385	435	750
800	410	490	555	330	395	450	800
900	435	520	585	355	425	480	900
1000	455	545	615	375	445	500	1000
1250	495	590	665	405	485	545	1250
1500	520	625	705	435	520	585	1500
1750	545	650	735	455	545	615	1750
2000	560	665	750	470	560	630	2000

CORRECTION FACTORS

Ambient Temp. °C	For ambient temperatures other than 30°C (86°F), multiply the ampacities shown above by the appropriate factor shown below.						Ambient Temp. °F
21-25	1.08	1.05	1.04	1.08	1.05	1.04	70-77
26-30	1.00	1.00	1.00	1.00	1.00	1.00	78-86
31-35	.91	.94	.96	.91	.94	.96	87-95
36-40	.82	.88	.91	.82	.88	.91	96-104
41-45	.71	.82	.87	.71	.82	.87	105-113
46-50	.58	.75	.82	.58	.75	.82	114-122
51-55	.41	.67	.76	.41	.67	.76	123-131
56-60	....	.58	.71	....	.58	.71	132-140
61-70	....	.33	.58	....	.33	.58	141-158
71-80	....	....	.41	....	....	.41	159-176

* See Section 240.4(D)

The reason for the misuse of the table comes from not reading the heading which states the ampacities shown for the various conductors are correct if you don't: (1) install over three current carrying conductors in a raceway or cable (2) exceed 30°C or 86°F in ambient temperature.

Table 310.16. Ampacities of Insulated Conductors Rated 0-2000 Volts, 60° to 90°C (140° to 194°F) **Not more Than Three Conductors in Raceway or Cable or Earth** (Directly Buried), **Based on Ambient Air Temperature of 30°C (86°F).**

Common sense would remind you that normally you are installing more than three conductors in a conduit and also the surrounding temperature of these conductors would be above 86°F. The **normal** ampacities listed in the table must be corrected if either condition (1) or (2) is present.

The conductor ampacity is the current carried **continuously** without increasing the temperature of its insulation beyond the danger point. The conductor ampacity varies with the type of insulation and the method of installation.

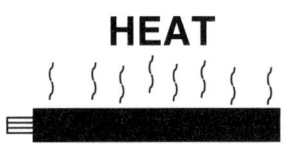

Except for mechanical abuse, the greatest hazard that conductors must endure is **heat**. Conductor insulation can be damaged by excessive heat in various ways, depending on the type of insulation and the degree of overheating. Continued exposure to excessive heat causes insulation to become soft, perhaps to melt, and in extreme cases to burn.

This heat comes from two sources: From the ambient air surrounding the conductors or from the current the conductors must carry. There is a point where an increase in current causes excessive heat even though conducting materials such as copper or aluminum have a low resistivity.

For many years natural rubber was used to insulate conductors, but age along with heat caused such rubber insulation to dry out, to crack, and to become brittle. Today we have better quality rubber and thermoplastic materials that not only permit thinner insulation on conductors but also withstand temperature better resulting in higher ampacities of conductors.

The maximum temperature permitted for conductor insulation is called the **temperature rating** of the conductor. **Table 310.13** shows the **maximum** temperature that the insulation type is permitted to reach. That maximum temperature will be reached when a conductor is loaded to its full ampacity in an ambient temperature of 30 degrees C or 86 degrees F.

The type letter on the insulation indicates its insulation, maximum operating temperature, and application provisions.

RHW insulation, the "R" indicates rubber insulation. The "H" indicates 75°C - 167°F maximum operating temperature (insulation rating). The "W" indicates moisture resistant.

THHN insulation, the "T" indicates thermoplastic insulation. The "HH" indicates 90°C - 194°F maximum operating temperature (insulation rating). The "N" indicates nylon covering.

Remember in the proper sizing of conductors you must consider the **worst** heat condition the conductor would ever encounter. I recently read an article in the newspaper where all 50 states in the U.S.A. have reached a temperature over 100 degrees F at some time. The ampacity Table 310.16 is based on an ambient temperature of 86 degrees F. If the conductor is subject to a temperature higher than 86 degrees F, the **correction factor** must be applied.

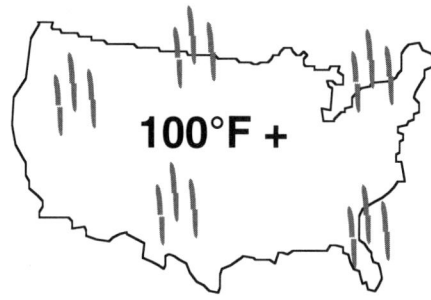

Table 310.16. Ampacities of Insulated Conductors Rated 0 -2000 Volts,
60° to 90°C (140° to 194°F) Not more Than Three Conductors in Raceway or Cable or Earth (Directly Buried),
Based on Ambient Air Temperature of 30°C (86°F).

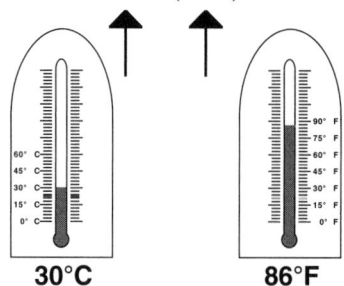

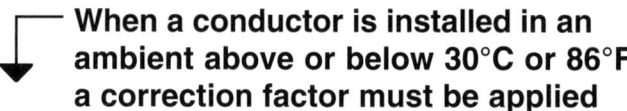

When a conductor is installed in an ambient above or below 30°C or 86°F a correction factor must be applied

	CORRECTION FACTORS						
Ambient Temp. °C	For ambient temperatures other than 30°C (86°F), multiply the ampacities shown above by the appropritate factor shown below.						Ambient Temp. °F
21-25	1.08	1.05	1.04	1.08	1.05	1.04	70-77
26-30	1.00	1.00	1.00	1.00	1.00	1.00	78-86
31-35	.91	.94	.96	.91	.94	.96	87-95
36-40	.82	.88	.91	.82	.88	.91	96-104
41-45	.71	.82	.87	.71	.82	.87	105-113
46-50	.58	.75	.82	.58	.75	.82	114-122
51-55	.41	.67	.76	.41	.67	.76	123-131
56-60	....	.58	.71	....	.58	.71	132-140
61-70	....	.33	.58	....	.33	.58	141-158
71-80	....	....	.41	....	....	.41	159-176

For ambient temperatures above 30 degrees C or 86 degrees F **multiply** the **ampacities** shown above by the appropriate correction factor shown below. Remember, correction factors change with different temperatures and different **types of insulations**.

A #10 TW copper conductor in an ambient temperature of 106 degrees F has a correction factor of .71, whereas a #10 **THW** copper conductor in the same ambient temperature has a correction factor of .82. A #10 **THHN** copper conductor in the same ambient temperature has a correction factor of .87.

T. 310.16

A #10 TW copper conductor has an ampacity of 30. In an ambient temperature of 106 degrees F the ampacity shall be reduced: 30 ampacity x .71 correction factor = 21.3 amps. This is the reduced ampacity and the maximum load that can be applied to this conductor at 106 degrees F without exceeding the temperature rating of 140 degrees F for TW insulation.

An error I have seen made by students trying to select the correct multiplier from the correction factor table is called a **line of sight** error. As you can see when selecting the 106 degrees F from the far right column, that you now have to go back to the second column from the left (TW insulation copper) to select the correction factor of .71. I suggest when using tables from the Code to use a **straight edge** such as a **ruler** so that you can follow the same line across the table and avoid selecting wrong numbers. Columns, numbers and lines have a tendency to "jump around". Your eyes can become weary after several exam hours of working calculations. **Use a straight edge**.

The left half of Table 310.16 is for **copper** and the right half of this table is for **aluminum or copper-clad aluminum** conductors. A #10 TW **aluminum** conductor has an ampacity of 25. In an ambient temperature of 106 degrees F, the correction factor is .71. The ampacity shall be reduced 25 ampacity x .71 correction factor = 17.75 amps. This is the reduced ampacity and maximum load on this conductor at 106 degrees F.

A #10 **THHN** copper conductor has an ampacity of 40. In an ambient temperature of 106 degrees F the correction factor **changes** to .87. 40 ampacity x .87 = 34.8 reduced ampacity, **but** the **maximum load** is limited to 30 amps by **overcurrent protection** device per the **asterisk (*)** at the bottom of Table 310.16:

" * 240.4(D) Unless otherwise specifically permitted in (e) through (g), the **overcurrent protection** shall not exceed 15 amperes for #14 AWG, 20 amperes for #12 AWG, and 30 amperes for #10 AWG **copper**; or 15 amperes for #12 AWG and 25 amperes for #10 AWG **aluminum and copper-clad aluminum** after any **correction factors for ambient temperature and number of conductors have been applied**."

Example: A #14 TW copper conductor has an ampacity of 20. The **overcurrent protection** (fuse or circuit breaker) shall not exceed 15 amps.

When answering exam calculations, watch the **wording**. Ask yourself: "Is the question asking for **conductor ampacity** or asking for **overcurrent protection**?"

I've had students ask, "What good is it to have a conductor with an ampacity of 20, if you can only fuse it at 15 amps?"

TH

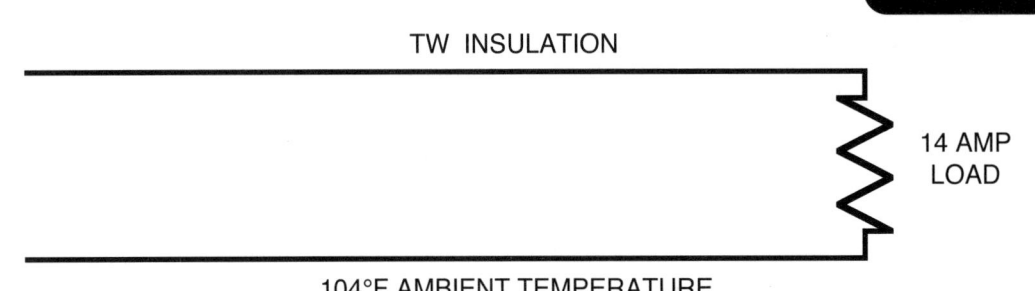

Even though a #14 conductor can only be **fused** at a maximum of 15 amps, the conductor is **derated** from the **20 ampacity** rather than 15.

In an ambient temperature of 104°F #14 TW copper has an ampacity of 20 x .82 correction factor = 16.4 reduced ampacity. A #14 TW copper conductor will carry a 14 amp load in an ambient temperature of 104°F.

In the 1978 Code a #14 TW copper conductor had an ampacity of **15**. From the 1978 Code 15 ampacity x .82 correction factor = 12.3 ampacity. A #14 TW copper conductor would not be permitted under the 1978 Code. A #12 TW copper conductor would have been the minimum size permitted. In the 1981 Code the ampacities were increased for some conductors due to better products of thermoplastics, etc.

A #14 TW copper conductor can carry 20 amperes continuously @ 86°F, but the devices you connect the conductor to are not rated for these higher currents. The asterisk (*) limit of 15 amps on the overcurrent protection is because the protective device will not protect the conductor from short-circuit currents, it will protect the conductor from overcurrent but not short circuit.

Conductors and devices must be used as listed in Section 110.3(B). An example of a daily **misuse** of Table 310.16 would be using the ampacities of a 90°C conductor such as the popular **THHN** insulation. Table 310.16 shows a #6 THHN copper conductor with an ampacity of 75, **but** this ampacity applies when the 90°C conductor is connected to devices with a rating of 90°C.

From the UL Electrical Construction Materials Directory and Code section 110.14(C): "The termination provisions on equipment are based on the use of 60°C conductors in circuits rated 100 amperes or less and the use of 75°C conductors in higher rated circuits.

If the termination provisions on the equipment are based on the use of other conductors, the equipment is either marked with both the size and temperature rating of the conductors to be used. If the equipment is marked only with the temperature rating of the conductors to be used, that temperature rating is required for the ambient temperature in the equipment and the 60°C ampacity (100 ampere or less circuits) or 75°C ampacity (over 100 ampere circuits) should be used to determine the size of conductors.

Higher temperature rated conductors may be used, though not required, if the size of the conductors is determined on the basis of the 60°C ampacity (100 ampere or less circuits) or 75°C ampacity (over 100 ampere circuits)."

T. 310.16

Example: A #6 TW has a normal ampacity of 55 amps. Which means when the conductor is loaded to 55 amps in an ambient of 86°F or 30°C it will reach an **operating temperature** of 140°F or 60°C.

When the conductor insulation is exposed to a temperature **above** 86°F or 30°C it is subject to insulation damage when loaded to its ampacity value. This is why a **correction factor** is applied when the ambient temperature exceeds 86°F or 30°C.

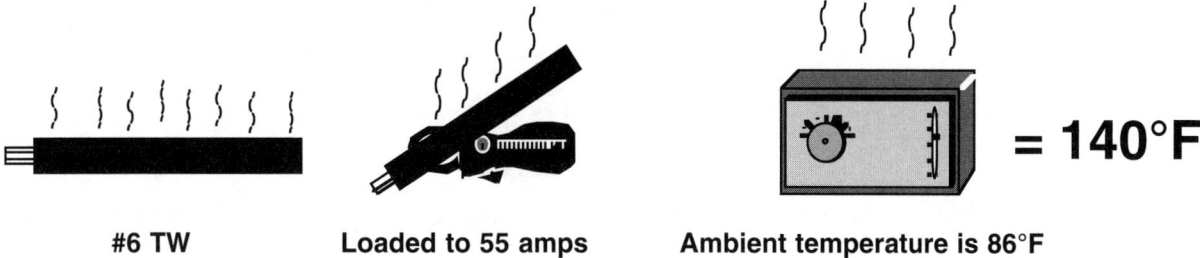

#6 TW   Loaded to 55 amps   Ambient temperature is 86°F

If you lay your ruler on 140°F and read the column for TW insulation (60°C-140°F) you'll see there is **no** correction factor. This simply means you are not permitted to use this insulation in this high of an ambient temperature.

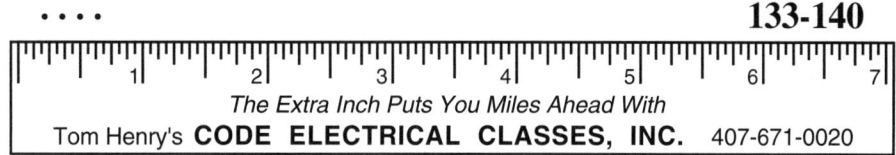

When the ambient temperature is **below** 86°F or 30°C the ampacity can be adjusted to a **higher** value than shown.

Example: The #6 TW has a normal ampacity of 55 amps. If the ambient temperature is 70°F the correction factor is now **1.08**. 55 ampacity x 1.08 = **59.4 ampacity**.

Cooler ambient allows a higher ampacity

SUMMARY OF 310.15(B) and Table 310.16

It is very important to get started off on the right foot by completely understanding the function of a conductor, the insulation and how temperature effects the conductor.

A conductor is a component of the electrical circuit and is used to carry the current to and from the load in the circuit. The current flowing through the conductor produces heat.

The capacity of current the conductor can carry is referred to as the *ampacity* (amp-capacity).

Ampacity is defined as the current in amperes that a conductor can carry *continuously* under the conditions of use without exceeding its temperature rating.

Conductor ampacities are listed starting at Table 310.16 through 310.86. **Table 310.16** is the ampacity table used for wiring buildings.

The current a conductor can safely carry is determined by several factors. The size of the conductor, the alloy (copper or aluminum), the type of insulation, the environment, etc.

Table 310.16 lists different types of insulations, different ampacities and different temperature ratings for the same size conductor.

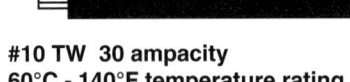 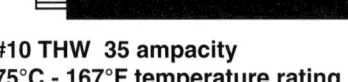 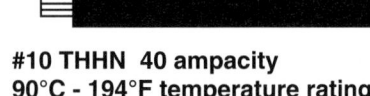

#10 TW 30 ampacity
60°C - 140°F temperature rating

#10 THW 35 ampacity
75°C - 167°F temperature rating

#10 THHN 40 ampacity
90°C - 194°F temperature rating

A #10 wire is the same size with a circular mil area of 10,380, but as you can see, it has three different ampacities and different temperature ratings.

Insulation around a conductor is like a pipe carrying water. With the water pressure (voltage) and the flow (amperes) of water, the pipe (insulation) is used to contain the water. If the pipe were to "spring a leak" you would lose some of the water pressure.

"Good" insulation means a high resistance to current to keep it from "leaking".

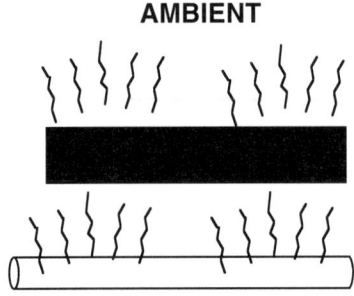

AMBIENT

As current is passed through the conductor, the heat that is produced (I^2R) must be dissipated through the insulation to the ambient. Ambient is that which encompasses on all sides.

Ambient temperature is the temperature surrounding the conductor into which the heat of the conductor is dissipated. If the ambient temperature is higher it slows down the dissipation of the heat.

TH

T. 310.16

A conductor in free air, as shown below, can carry more amperage than one that is installed in a conduit, as the conduit will entrap the heat. The conductors installed in attics, around a furnace, or a boiler encounters higher ambient temperatures that requires lowering the current flow on the conductor to prevent insulation damage. Table 310.17 is for conductors in free air.

DIFFERENT AMBIENT CONDITIONS

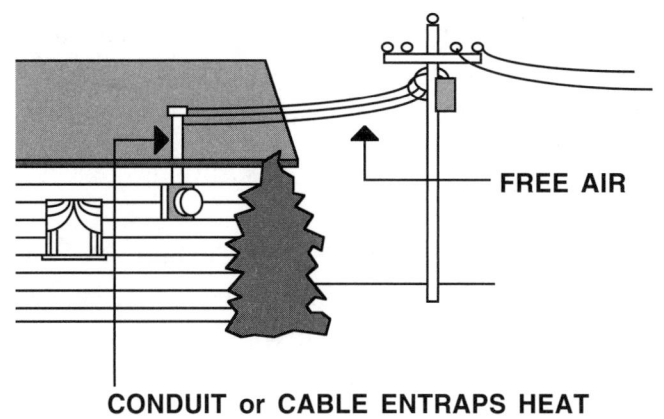

FREE AIR

CONDUIT or CABLE ENTRAPS HEAT

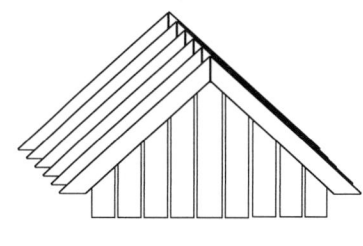

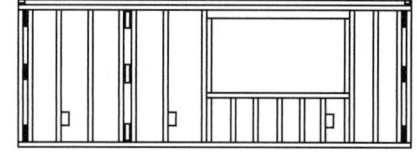

It is important to understand how a conductor dissipates heat.

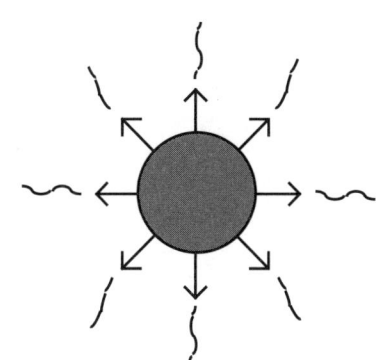

The heat produced from the current flowing through the conductor is dissipated through the skin in all directions.

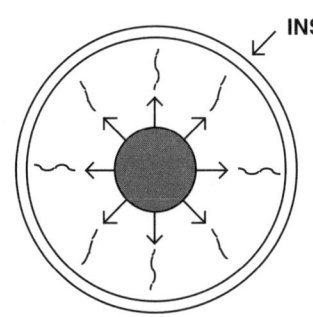

INSULATION

The heat dissipates through the insulation into the surrounding ambient.

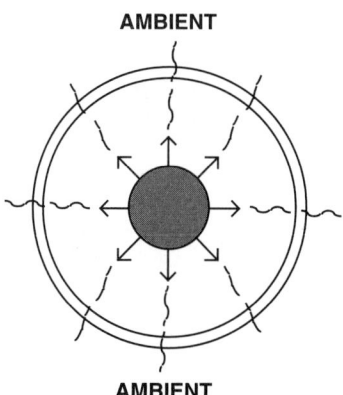

AMBIENT

AMBIENT

TH
54

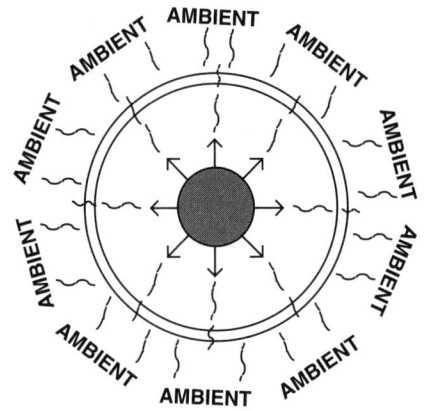

If the surrounding ambient temperature is higher it opposes the dissipation of the heat through the insulation. The ampacity of the conductor must be reduced for the higher ambient temperature. If the ampacity is not reduced the heat is contained longer in the conductor and the insulation, thus causing insulation damage. Even though the ambient is cooler when a conductor is buried, it is slower in dissipating heat the deeper it is buried.

Example: A conduit contains six #8 TW current-carrying conductors. The normal ampacity is 40 amps. But, an adjustment factor of 80% from Table 310.15(B2a) must be applied for the six current-carrying conductors. 40 amps x 80% = 32 amps is the maximum current that can be passed through a #8 TW conductor without subjecting it to insulation damage.

The type letter on the insulation indicates its insulation, maximum operating temperature, and application provisions.

#10 RHW

The #10 RHW, the "R" indicates rubber insulation. The "H" indicates 75°C - 167°F maximum operating temperature (insulation rating). The "W" indicates moisture resistant.

#10 THHN

The #10 THHN, the "T" indicates thermoplastic insulation. The "HH" indicates 90°C - 194°F maximum operating temperature (insulation rating). The "N" indicates nylon covering.

T. 310.16

The #10 THW has a maximum operating temperature of 75°C which is 167°F.

The #10 THHN has a maximum operating temperature of 90°C which is 194°F. A "HH" rated insulation will allow more heat to be dissipated faster than an "H" rated insulation thus raising the ampacity (the current the conductor can carry safely without damage).

The maximum operating temperature is the insulation rating of the conductor and must not be exceeded. Proper designing is a very important factor.

You must first understand what words mean; such as ampacity, ambient temperature, insulation rating, etc.

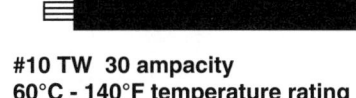

#10 TW 30 ampacity
60°C - 140°F temperature rating

A #10 TW conductor has an ampacity of 30 amperes. The insulation rating is 60°C or 140°F.
This does *not* mean that a TW insulation can be installed where the ambient temperature reaches 140°F.

What this means is: If a #10 TW conductor is loaded to the allowable ampacity, 30 amperes in an ambient that has a temperature of 30°C or 86°F, the temperature of the *insulation* will reach 60°C or 140°F.

Table 310.16 the table of ampacity is aimed at designating a level of current that will permit the conductor to reach its thermal limit, but not exceed it.

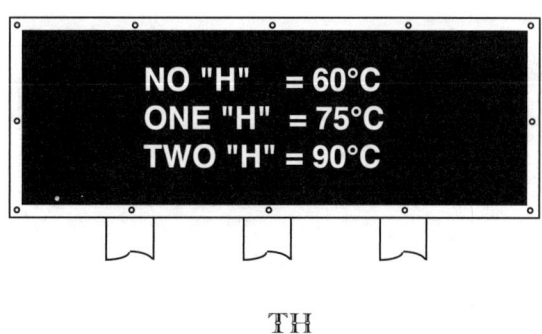

TH

T. 310.16

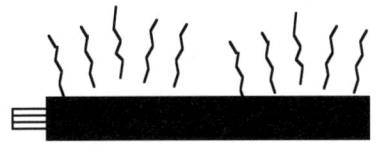

#10 TW 30 amps of current flowing

The 30 amps of current flowing produces heat in the conductor which must dissipate through the insulation to the ambient.

With the ambient temperature at 86°F and with 30 amperes of current flowing through the conductor, a thermometer placed on the *insulation* would read 140°F which is maximum operating temperature for this type insulation (TW).

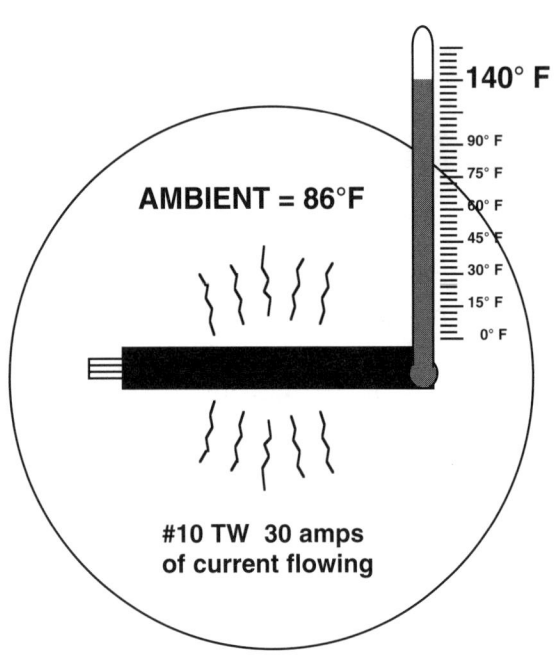

For a #10 TW conductor, any current above 30 amps or any ambient temperature above 86°F will cause insulation damage, as you will exceed the maximum operating temperature of the conductor; 140°F.

Maximum operating temperature = Full ampacity at 86°F.

140°F - 86°F = 54°F for the 30 amperes of current flow in the #10 TW conductor.

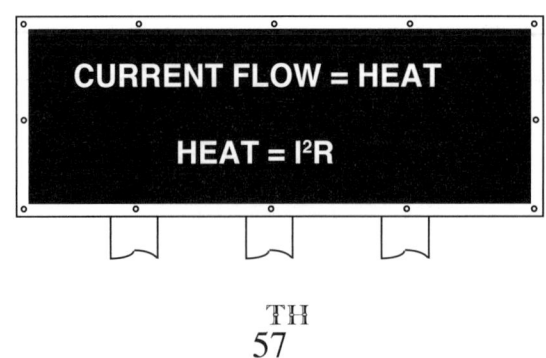

CURRENT FLOW = HEAT

HEAT = I^2R

T. 310.16

Shown below are the three different insulations; TW, THW and THHN. A #10 TW will allow 30 amperes of current flow through this insulation with an ambient temperature of 86°F without insulation damage. A #10 THW will allow 35 amperes of current flow at 86°F. A #10 THHN will allow 40 amperes at 86°F.

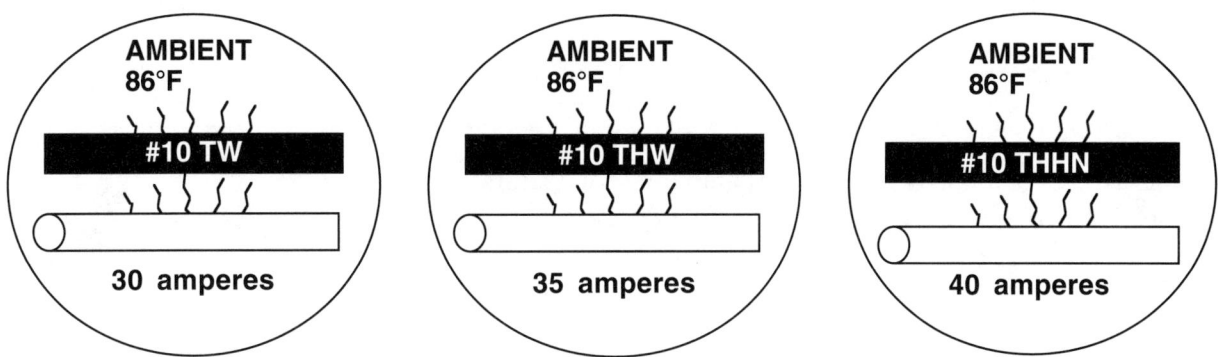

As you can see different insulation types have different ampacities. The better grade of insulation will allow the dissipation of the heat faster so the current carrying capacity (ampacity) is higher.

But, ampacities are based on 30°C which the equivalent is 86°F. If the ambient where the conductor is being placed is higher than 30°C or 86°F, the normal ampacity shall be *lowered*.

With a higher ambient it slows down the dissipation of the heat, so the heat produced by the current flow must be reduced to prevent damage.

AMPACITY IS BASED ON AN AMBIENT OF 86°F

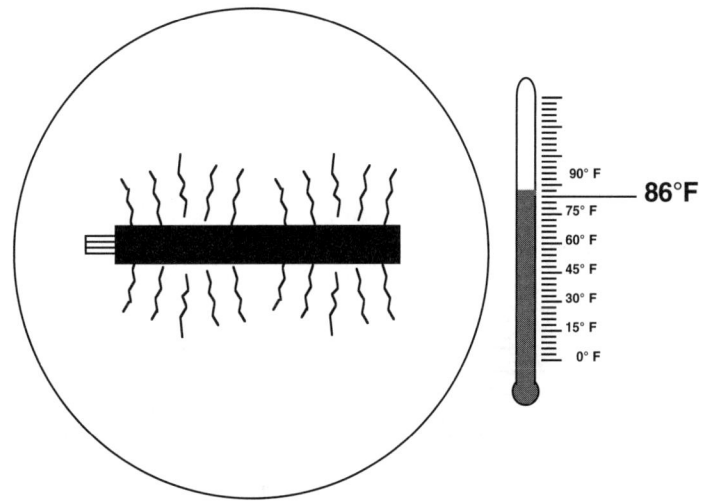

TH

T. 310.16

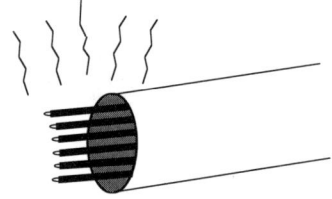
When there are more than three current-carrying conductors in a raceway or cable, the ampacity of each conductor must be reduced as indicated in Table 310.15(B2a) to compensate for heating effects and reduced heat dissipation due to reduced ventilation of individual conductors.

Table 310.15(B2a) also applies when paralleling conductors per section 310.4.

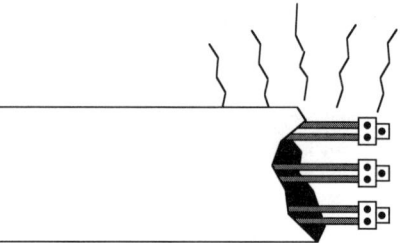

It is wrong to think since you connected two conductors in parallel on one lug that you now only have one conductor. Heat is measured by $W = I^2R$. In parallel you have *two* conductors carrying current producing heat.

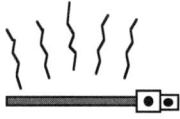 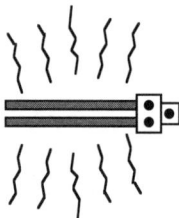

It is wrong to think that by using a larger size conduit than required would satisfy the Table 310.15(B2a) reduction of ampacity. The larger conduit would have more volume area, but it's like heating a rock; it may take a little longer but it will still reach the same temperature.

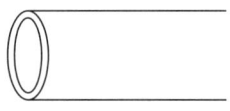 

To avoid applying Table 310.15(B2a) ampacity adjustment deration you can install two separate conduits as shown below. Now you only have 3 current carrying conductors in each conduit.

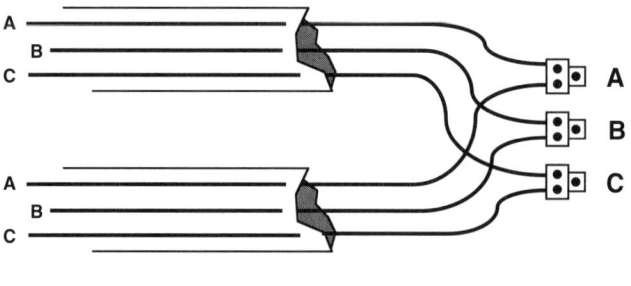

QUIZ #1

Article 310   Quiz #1   -   Open Book

1. Conductors ____ and larger shall be stranded when installed in raceways.

(a) #12   (b) #10   (c) #8   (d) none of these

2. Solid dielectric insulated conductors operated above 2000 volts in permanent installations shall have ____ insulation and shall be shielded.

(a) ozone-resistant   (b) asbestos   (c) hi-temperature   (d) perfluoro-alkoxy

3. What is the ampacity of four #6 THW copper current-carrying conductors enclosed in schedule 80 PVC conduit, 8 feet in length entering a trench?

(a) 65 amps   (b) 52 amps   (c) 44 amps   (d) 40 amps

4. A raceway contains 45 current-carrying conductors. The ampacity of each conductor shall be reduced ____ percent.

(a) 80   (b) 70   (c) 60   (d) 35

5. The following letter suffixes shall indicate the following:

____ for two insulated conductors laid parallel within an outer nonmetallic covering.

(a) D   (b) M   (c) R   (d) N

6. When bare grounded conductors are used with insulated conductors, their ampacities are limited to ____.

(a) 60 degrees C
(b) 75 degrees C
(c) 90 degrees C
(d) the lowest temperature rating of the insulated conductors

7. Insulated wires shall be marked or tagged with which of the following?

(a) maximum rated voltage
(b) proper type letters
(c) manufacturer indentification
(d) all of these

Article 310 Quiz #1 - Open Book

8. All of the following about paralleling conductors are true except ____.

(a) must terminate in the same manner (b) must be same material
(c) must be same length (d) must be enclosed in the same raceway

9. Surface marking of conductors and cables shall be durably marked on the surface at intervals not exceeding ____ inches.

(a) 6 (b) 12 (c) 18 (d) 24

10. Electrical ducts shall include any of the electrical conduits recognized in Chapter 3 as suitable for use ____.

(a) over 600v (b) as bus bars (c) underground (d) exposed

11. Spacing between conduits, tubing, or raceways shall be ____.

(a) 1/4" (b) insulated (c) 1" (d) maintained

12. Insulated conductors used in wet locations shall be ____.

(a) MTW (b) asbestos (c) THHN (d) varnished cambric

13. A nipple contains six #8 THW copper current-carrying conductors. The ampacity of each conductor would be ____ amperes.

(a) 24 (b) 50 (c) 35 (d) 40

14. Branch circuit conductors within 3" of a ballast, within the ballast compartment shall be recognized for use at temperatures not lower than 90 degrees C, such as insulation types ____.

I. THHN II. THW III. TW IV. FEP

(a) I only (b) I and IV only (c) I, II and IV (d) I, II, III and IV

Article 310 Quiz #2 - Open Book

QUIZ #2

1. Solid dielectric insulated conductors operated above 2000 volts in permanent installations shall have ozone-resistant insulation and shall be ____.

(a) covered   (b) protected   (c) shielded   (d) surface mounted

2. Type USE-2 is rated at ____.

(a) 60°C   (b) 75°C   (c) 90°C   (d) 86°F

3. When the letters THHN are stamped on the insulation of a conductor, the HH indicates that the conductor insulation has a temperature rating of ___ degrees C.

(a) 60   (b) 75   (c) 90   (d) 110

4. If a nipple 18" long contains 24 conductors, the ampacity for each conductor must be reduced to ____ of Table 310.16 and Table 310.18.

(a) 80%   (b) 70%   (c) 60%   (d) 0%

5. A raceway containing 30 current carrying conductors, the ampacity of each conductor shall be reduced ____ percent.

(a) 80   (b) 70   (c) 45   (d) 50

6. The principal determinants of operating temperature are ____.

I.   heat generated internally in the conductor as the result of load current flow
II. the rate at which generated heat dissipates into the ambient medium
III. adjacent load-carrying conductors
IV. ambient temperature

(a) II and IV only   (b) I and IV only   (c) I, II and IV   (d) I, II, III and IV

7. The temperature rating of a conductor is the maximum temperature, at any location along its length, that the conductor can withstand over a prolonged time period without ____.

(a) tripping the breaker   (b) serious degradation
(c) short circuiting   (d) a ground fault

Article 310 Quiz #2 - Open Book

QUIZ #2

8. When more than one calculated or tabulated ampacity could apply for a given circuit length, the ____ value shall be used.

(a) lowest   (b) average   (c) highest   (d) none of these

9. A nipple contains four #6 THW copper current-carrying conductors. The ampacity of each conductor would be ____ amperes.

(a) 65   (b) 52   (c) 39   (d) 55

10. All conductors the size below can be connected in parallel except ____.

(a) #250 kcmil   (b) #2/0   (c) #1   (d) #1/0

11. The ampacity for conductors is derated when the ambient temperature exceeds:

(a) 30 degrees F   (b) 72 degrees F   (c) 86 degrees F   (d) 104 degrees F

12. Where single conductors or multiconductor cables are stacked or bundled longer than ____ without maintaining spacing for a continuous length and are not installed in raceways, the ampacity of each conductor shall be reduced.

(a) 12"   (b) 18"   (c) 20"   (d) 2'

13. A three-wire, 240/120v single-phase 200 amp service for a dwelling requires what size THW copper conductors?

(a) #4/0   (b) #3/0   (c) #2/0   (d) #1/0

14. Conductors shall **not** be installed in locations where the operating temperature will exceed that specified for the type of ____ used.

(a) connectors   (b) protection   (c) insulation   (d) wiring

TH

Article 310 Quiz #3 - Open Book

1. The parallel conductors in each phase or neutral shall ____.

I.   have the same insulation type and conductor material
II. be the same size in cma
III. be the same length and be terminated in the same manner

(a) I only   (b) II only   (c) III only   (d) I, II and III

2. The ampacities provided by this section are based on temperature alone and do not take ____ into consideration.

(a) insulation   (b) AWG   (c) CMA   (d) voltage drop

3. Adjacent load-carrying conductors have the dual effect of raising the ____ and impeding heat dissipation.

(a) insulation rating   (b) heat above 86°F   (c) ambient temperature   (d) skin effect

4. Where the number of current-carrying conductors in a raceway is seven, the individual ampacity of each conductor shall be reduced ____.

(a) to 70% due to the number of conductors
(b) to 80% if they are continuous loads
(c) to both (a) and (b) if both conditions exist
(d) neither apply if the ambient temperature is below 30° C or 86° F

5. A conduit exposed to sunlight on a rooftop is 1" above the rooftop surface. What is the temperature adder for this installation ____°F.

(a) 25   (b) 30   (c) 40   (d) 60

6. Type THW insulation has a ____ degree C rating for use in wiring through fixtures.

(a) 60   (b) 75   (c) 85   (d) 90

Article 310 Quiz #3 - Open Book

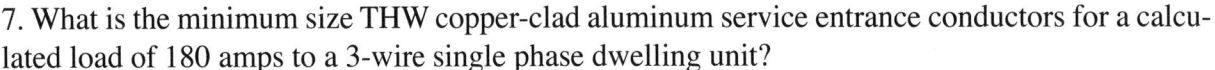

7. What is the minimum size THW copper-clad aluminum service entrance conductors for a calculated load of 180 amps to a 3-wire single phase dwelling unit?

(a) #3/0   (b) #1/0   (c) #4/0   (d) #250 kcmil

8. Of the types of conductors listed below, ____ is not permitted for use in wet locations.

(a) RHH   (b) XHHW   (c) THWN   (d) MI cable

9. What is the **MAXIMUM** allowable AWG size for a solid conductor installed in a raceway?

(a) #14   (b) #12   (c) #10   (d) #8

10. What is the allowable ampacity of a #4 THW in free air in an ambient temperature of 104°F?

(a) 74.8 amps   (b) 69.7 amps   (c) 110 amps   (d) 125 amps

11. How many conductors would be counted in a branch circuit raceway for the purpose of derating conductor ampacity given the following:
   3 bare conductors - 3 black insulated conductors - 3 white insulated conductors - 3 red insulated conductors

   The service is single-phase, the load is balanced on each circuit and there are no harmonic currents on the neutrals.

(a) 3   (b) 6   (c) 9   (d) 12

12. Where two different ampacities apply to adjacent portions of a circuit, the higher ampacity shall be permitted to be used beyond the point of transition, a distance equal to 10 feet or ____ percent of the circuit length figured at the higher ampacity, whichever is less.

(a) 10%   (b) 15%   (c) 20%   (d) 25%

QUIZ #4

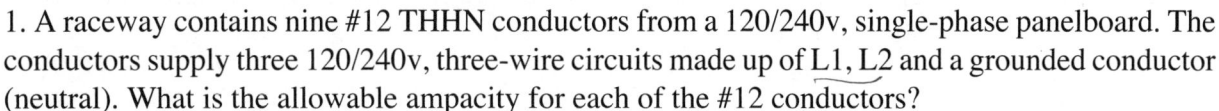

1. A raceway contains nine #12 THHN conductors from a 120/240v, single-phase panelboard. The conductors supply three 120/240v, three-wire circuits made up of L1, L2 and a grounded conductor (neutral). What is the allowable ampacity for each of the #12 conductors?

(a) 20   (b) 21   (c) 24   (d) 25

2. The ampacity of a #14 THW conductor, when there are six conductors in a conduit and the temperature is 30°C, would be _____ amps.

(a) 25   (b) 22   (c) 20   (d) 16

3. What is the maximum current allowed on a #10 THW when in a conduit with 5 other current-carrying #10 THW's and two bare #10 grounding conductors? (all are copper conductors) (this is a total of 8 conductors in the conduit).

(a) 30 amps   (b) 21 amps   (c) 28 amps   (d) 20 amps

4. A single-phase 240/120 volt service has six #3/0 THW copper conductors in parallel installed in a single raceway. What is the ampacity of each conductor?

(a) 200 amps   (b) 400 amps   (c) 160 amps   (d) 140 amps

5. 24 - #12 THW current-carrying conductors are installed in a conduit 18" in length. What is the total derating percent of value?

(a) 70%   (b) 80%   (c) 60%   (d) no derating required

6. What is the ampacity of 4 #6 THW copper current-carrying conductors enclosed in schedule 80 PVC conduit 8 feet in length entering a trench?

(a) 65 amps   (b) 52 amps   (c) 44 amps   (d) 40 amps

7. What is the ampacity of a #3/0 THWN conductor installed in an ambient temperature of 104°F?

(a) 100 amps   (b) 200 amps   (c) 160 amps   (d) 176 amps

Article 310 Quiz #4 - Open Book

QUIZ #4

8. The ampacity of a copper #10 THWN-2 is ___ when there are three conductors in the conduit and the ambient temperature is 70°F.

(a) 30   (b) 32.4   (c) 35   (d) 41.6

9. The ampacity of a #12 TW conductor when there are not more than three conductors in a raceway and the ambient temperature is 36°C would be ____ amps.

(a) 25   (b) 22   (c) 20.5   (d) 16

10. Determine the allowable ampacity of 13 - #12 THHN conductors in a raceway, when passing through an area where the ambient temperature is 40° C.

(a) 13.65 amps   (b) 15.0 amps   (c) 26.4 amps   (d) 30.0 amps

11. What is the ampacity of four #4/0 THWN copper current carrying conductors in a raceway installed through an ambient temperature of 45° C?

(a) 150.9 amps   (b) 160.1 amps   (c) 163.5 amps   (d) 213.2 amps

12. A 20" length of conduit that separates two cabinets contains 30 current-carrying conductors, the ambient temperature is 27°C. These conductors are to be derated ____.

(a) twice   (b) 45%   (c) 1.08   (d) not required at all

13. The overcurrent protection of a #10 THW conductor, when there are not more than three conductors in a raceway, and the ambient temperature is 28°C, would be ____ amps.

(a) 30   (b) 35   (c) 25   (d) 20

14. Three #8 XHHW conductors are installed in a wet location with an ambient temperature of 45°C. What is the ampacity of this conductor?

(a) 32.8 amps   (b) 41 amps   (c) 45.1 amps   (d) 29 amps

15. What is the ampacity of each of four #8 XHHW copper conductors in a conduit above the dropped-ceiling on a 4-wire, three-phase wye circuit where the load is all flourescent lighting?

(a) 40 amps   (b) 50 amps   (c) 44 amps   (d) 55 amps

ARTICLE 312
Cabinets, Cutout Boxes, and Meter Socket Enclosures

312.1. This article covers the installation and construction of cabinets, cutout boxes, and meter socket enclosures.

Definition: A cabinet is an enclosure that is designed for either surface mounting or flush mounting and is provided with a frame, mat, trim in which a swinging door or doors can be hung.

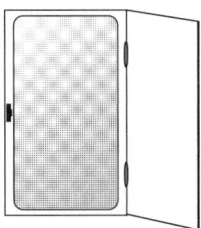

Definition: A cutout box is an enclosure designed for surface mounting that has swinging doors or covers secured directly to and telescoping with the walls of the box proper.

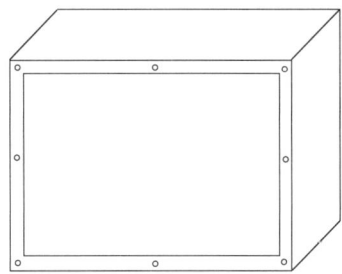

Definition: A meter socket enclosure has an open front and an internal female socket to receive the meter male plug.

  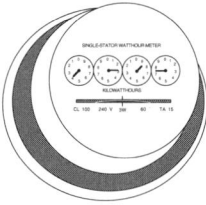 

312.2(A). In damp or wet locations, surface-type enclosures shall be mounted so there is at least 1/4" airspace between the enclosure and the wall.

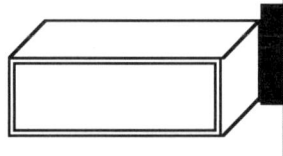

312.3. In walls of concrete, tile, or other noncombustible material, cabinets shall be installed so that the front edge of the cabinet is not set back of the finished surface more than 1/4".

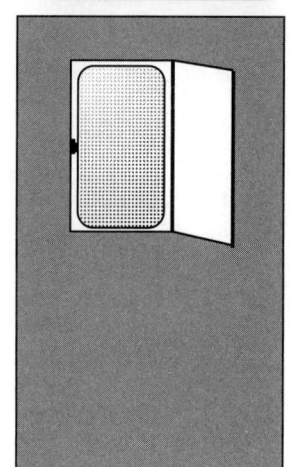

In walls constructed of wood or other combustible material, cabinets shall be flush with the finished surface or project therefrom.

312.4. Plaster, drywall, or plasterboard surfaces that are broken or incomplete shall be repaired so there is no gaps greater than 1/8".

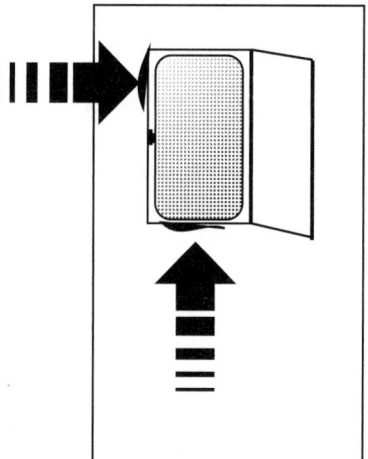

312.5(A). Openings through which conductors enter shall be adequately closed.

312.5(B). Where metal enclosures are installed with messenger wire, open wiring on insulators, or concealed knob-and-tube wiring, conductors shall enter through insulating bushings.

 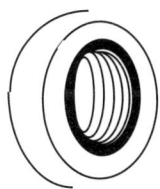

312.5(C). Where cable is used, each cable shall be secured to the enclosure.

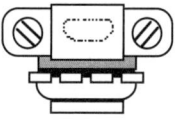

312.6. This section is to ensure safety and effective conductor application by providing enough space to bend conductors within enclosures.

312.6(A). Conductors shall not be deflected within a cabinet or cutout box unless a gutter having a width in accordance with Table 312.6(A) is provided.

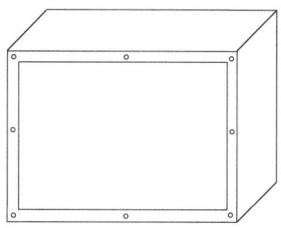

312.6(B1). Table 312.6(A) shall apply where the conductor does not enter or leave the enclosure through the wall opposite its terminal. This is a 90° bend called an "L" bend.

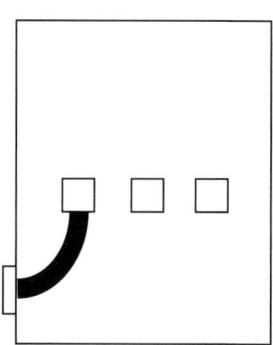

312.6(B2). Table 312.6(B) shall apply where the conductor does enter or leave the enclosure through the wall opposite its terminal. This is called an "S" bend.

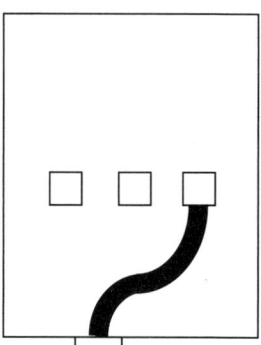

312.6(C). Raceways containing ungrounded conductors #4 or larger that enter a cabinet, box, or raceway, the conductors shall be protected by a substantial fitting providing a smooth rounded insulated surface, unless the conductors are separated by insulation securely fastened.

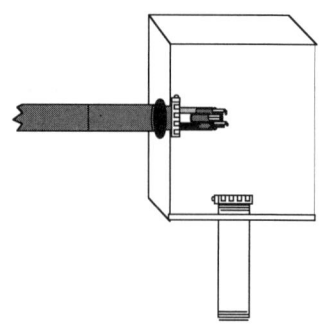

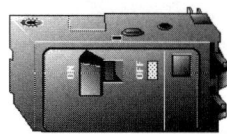

312.7. Cabinets and cutout boxes shall have sufficient space to accommodate all conductors without crowding them.

312.8. Most enclosures for overcurrent devices and/or switches have been designed to accommodate only those conductors intended to be connected to the terminals within. This section states these enclosures must not be used as junction boxes or raceways unless adequate space is provided.

312.9. Cabinets and cutout boxes shall be provided with back-wiring spaces, gutters or wiring compartments.

II. Construction Specifications

312.10(A). Metal enclosures shall be protected against corrosion both inside and out.

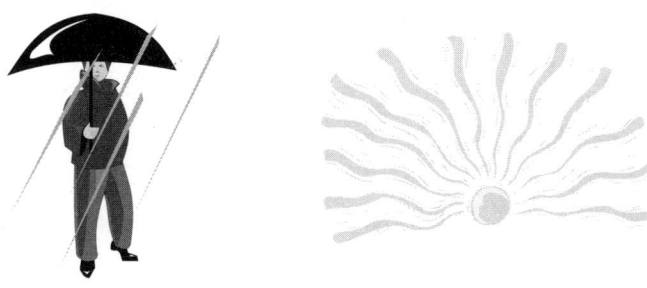

312.10(B). Enclosures constructed of sheet metal shall not be less than .053" (less than 1/16").

1/16" = .0625"

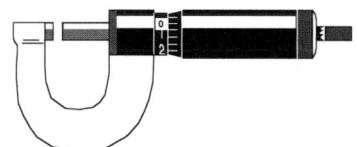

Article 312 Quiz #1 - Open Book

QUIZ #1

1. Enclosures for overcurrent devices in damp or wet locations shall be identified for use in such locations and shall be mounted so there is at least ____ inch air space between the enclosure and the wall.

(a) 1/4 (b) 3/8 (c) 3/4 (d) 1

2. Cabinets and cutout boxes shall be deep enough to allow the closing of the doors when ____ ampere branch circuit panelboard switches are in any position; when combination cutout switches are in any position; or when other single throw switches are opened as far as their construction will permit.

(a) 15 (b) 20 (c) 30 (d) 100

3. A cabinet or cutout box if constructed of sheet steel, the metal thickness shall not be less than ____ inch uncoated.

(a) 0.053 (b) 0.503 (c) 0.040 (d) 1/16"

4. Disregarding exceptions, where ungrounded conductors of ____ or larger enter a raceway in a cabinet, pull box, junction box or auxiliary gutter, the conductor shall be protected by an insulated bushing.

(a) #6 (b) #4 (c) #2 (d) #1/0

5. Metal enclosures shall be protected both in-side and outside against _____.

(a) tampering (b) corrosion (c) wear (d) overfill

6. Cabinets and cutout boxes that contain devices or apparatus connected within the cabinet or box to more than ____ conductors, including those of branch circuits, meter loops, feeder circuits, power circuits, and similar circuits, but not including the supply circuit or continuation thereof, shall have back wiring spaces or one or more side wiring spaces, side gutters, or wiring compartments.

(a) 8 (b) 10 (c) 21 (d) 30

7. A cutout box installed in a wet location shall be ____.

(a) raintight (b) weatherproof (c) waterproof (d) rainproof

TH

Article 312 Quiz #1 - Open Book

QUIZ #1

8. _____ is the distance measured along the enclosure wall from the axis of the centerline of the terminal to a line passing through the center of the opening in the enclosure.

(a) Offset   (b) Radius   (c) Center point   (d) none of these

9. Nonmetallic cabinets in a wet location shall be permitted _____ airspace between concrete, masonry tile or similar wall.

(a) without   (b) with 1/4"   (c) with 1/8"   (d) 1/16"

10. There shall be an air space of at least _____ between walls, back, gutter partition, if of metal, or door of any cabinet, or cutout box and nearest exposed current-carrying parts of devices mounted within the cabinet where the voltage exceeds **251** volts.

(a) 1/4"   (b) 1/2"   (c) 1"   (d) 1 1/2"

TH

ARTICLE 314

Outlet, Device, Pull, and Junction Boxes; Conduit Bodies; Fittings; and Handhole Enclosures

314.1. This article covers all boxes and conduit bodies and their use. It also includes the installation of fittings used in the connection.

Definition: A **conduit body** is a separate portion of a conduit or tubing system that provides access through a removable cover(s) to the interior of the system at a junction of two or more sections of the system or at a terminal point of the system.

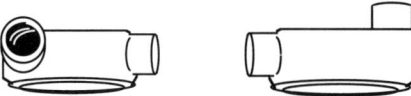

Boxes such as FS and FD are NOT classified as conduit bodies.

Definition: A **fitting** is an accessory such as a locknut, bushing, or other part of a wiring system that is intended primarily to perform a mechanical rather than an electrical function.

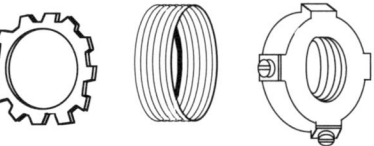

Capped elbows and service-entrance elbows are fittings, NOT conduit bodies, and must NOT contain splices, taps, or devices.

314.2. Round boxes shall not be used where conduits or connectors requiring the use of locknuts or bushings are to be connected to the side of the box. With the side of the box being round and the locknut with a straight shoulder, proper continuity is NOT maintained.

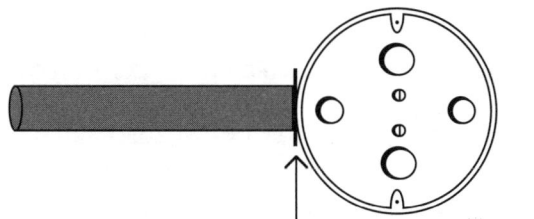
Locknut not making good contact with box

314.3. Nonmetallic boxes are often used in construction along with plastic-coated metal conduits for a corrosion-resistant installation. In the exceptions internal or integral bonding is required in the boxes.

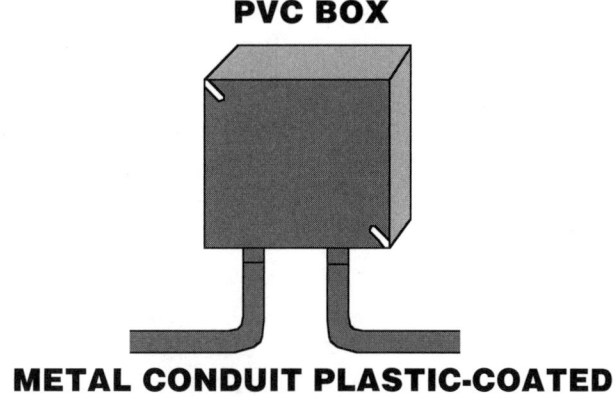

314.4. All metal boxes shall be grounded and bonded.

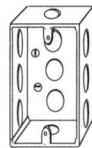 

314.5. Capped elbows and service-entrance elbows shall NOT contain splices, taps, or devices and shall provide free space for all conductors.

II. Installation

314.15. In damp or wet locations, boxes, conduit bodies, and fittings shall be placed or equipped to prevent moisture from entering or accumulating. In wet locations they shall be listed for use in wet locations.

To properly apply the Code must first understand the definitions from Article 100.

Definition: A **damp location** is a location protected from weather and not subject to saturation with water or other liquids but subject to moderate degrees of moisture. Examples of such locations include partially protected locations under canopies, marquees, roofed open porches, etc., and interior locations subject to moderate degrees of moisture, such as some basements, some barns, and some cold storage warehouses.

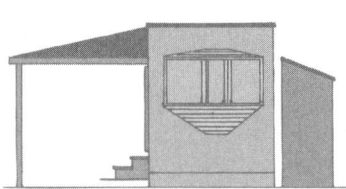

Definition: A **wet location** is a location under ground or in concrete slabs or masonry in direct contact with the earth; in locations subject to saturation with water or other liquids, such as vehicle washing areas; and in unprotected locations exposed to weather.

Definition: **Weatherproof** is constructed or protected so that exposure to the weather will **NOT INTERFERE** with successful operation.

Definition: **Watertight** is constructed so that moisture will **NOT ENTER** the enclosure under specified test conditions.

Weather**PROOF** Rain**PROOF**	**PROOF = WILL NOT INTERFERE**

Water**TIGHT** Rain**TIGHT** Dust**TIGHT**	**TIGHT = WILL NOT ENTER**

314.15

Hazards often occur because of overloading of wiring systems by methods or usage NOT in conformity with the Code. This occurs because initial wiring did not provide for increases in the use of electricity. An initial adequate installation and reasonable provisions for system changes will provide for future increases in the use of electricity.

Limiting the number of wires and circuits in a single enclosure will minimize the effects from a short-circuit or ground fault in one circuit.

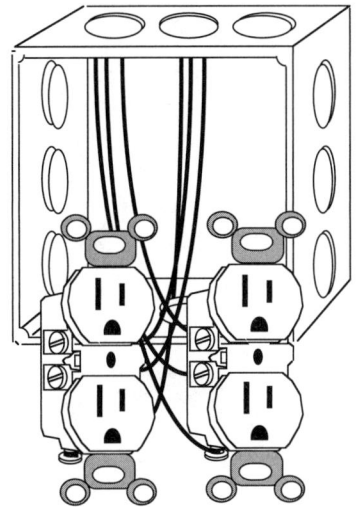

Installing more than the Code maximum permitted conductors in a box has caused accidents and fires. Forcing the receptacles into a crowded box tends to loosen the connections thus resulting in a high resistance fault (heat).

Boxes shall be of sufficient size to provide free space for all enclosed conductors. In no case shall the volume of the box be less than the fill calculation.

Proper calculations in box fill will result in conductors not being jammed into the box causing nicks or damage to the conductor insulation resulting in possible grounds or short circuits.

314.16. In no case shall the volume of the box, as calculated in Table 314.16(A), be less than the fill calculated in Table 314.16(B). This section is in three parts: (A) states the volume of a box (B) states the method for determining how much volume is used by various conductors, devices, etc. (C) applies to conduit bodies only.

•Note: Box fill requirements don't apply to terminal housings supplied with motors or generators.

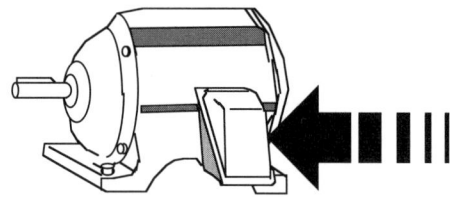

314.16(A). The volume of a box shall be the **total volume** of the assembled sections and, where used, the space provided by plaster rings, domed covers, extension rings, etc.

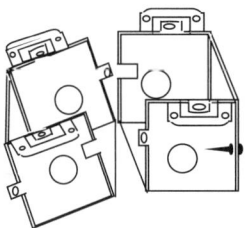 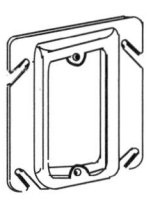 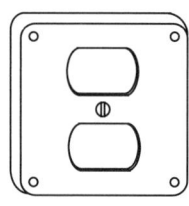 

314.16(B). Box fill is determined by adding together paragraphs (B1 through B5). No allowance shall be required for small fittings such as locknuts and bushings.

314.16(B1). A conductor running through the box shall be counted as one conductor, and each conductor originating outside of the box and terminating inside the box is counted as one conductor. Conductors, no part of which leaves the box, shall not be counted.

A conductor running through the box shall be counted as **one** conductor.

TOTAL 2 CONDUCTORS

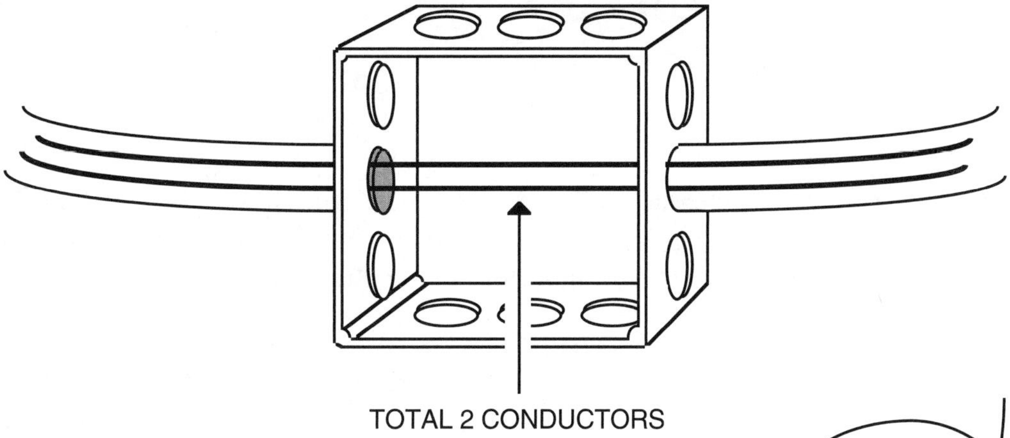

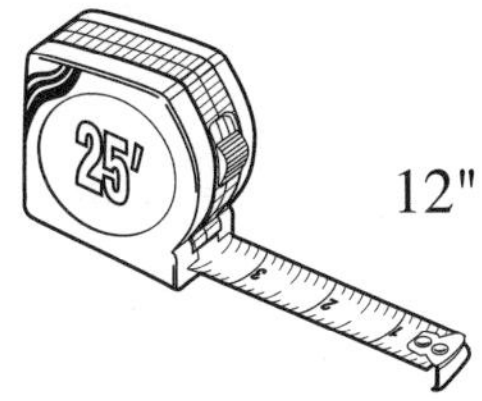

A looped or coiled, unbroken conductor 12" or more in length shall be counted **twice**.

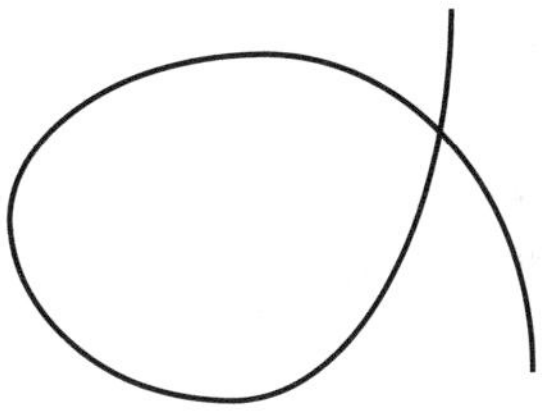

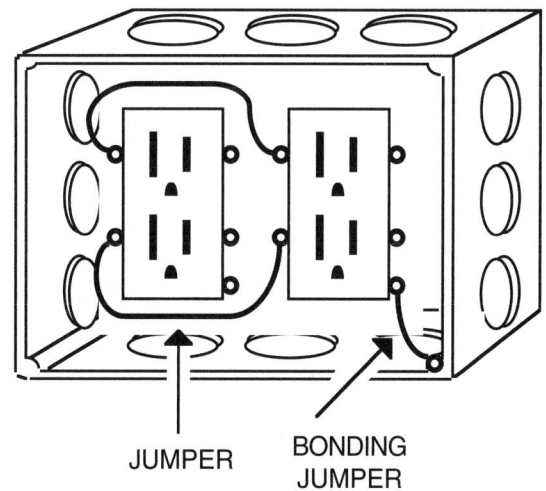

Each conductor originating outside of the box and terminating inside the box is counted as **one** conductor.

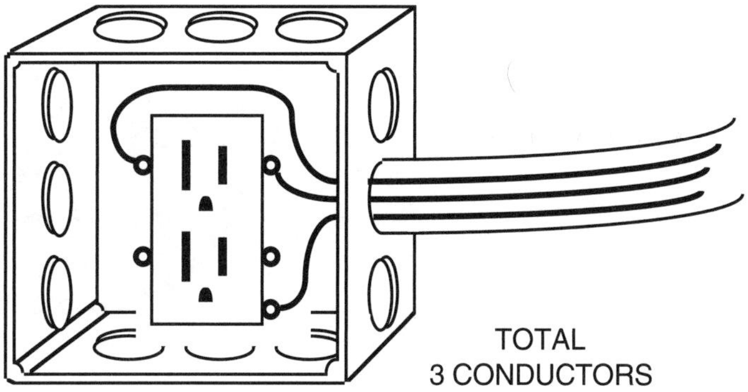

TOTAL 3 CONDUCTORS

Conductors, no part of which leaves the box, shall **not** be counted.

JUMPER   BONDING JUMPER

TH
81

314.16(B1)

314.16(B1) exception: An equipment grounding conductor or conductors or not over four fixture wires smaller than #14, or both, shall be permitted to be omitted from the calculations where they enter a box from a domed fixture and terminate within that box.

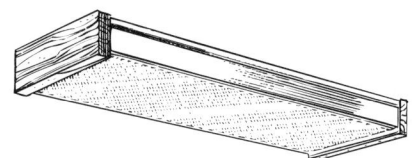

314.16(B2). Where one or more internal cable clamps are present in a box, a **single** volume allownce in accordance with Table 314.16(B) shall be made based on the **largest** conductor present in the box. **No** allowance is required for a cable connector **outside** the box.

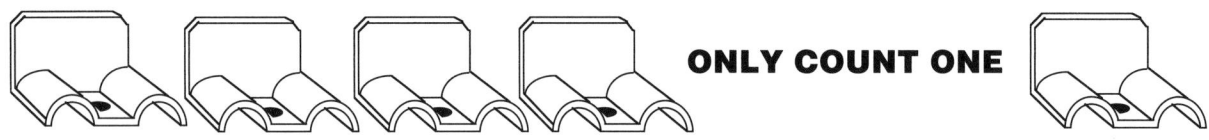

•Note: Do **not** count box connectors, no reduction is required as they are not **internal** cable clamps.

314.16(B3). Where one or more fixture studs or hickeys are present in the box, a **single** volume allowance in accordance with Table 314.16(B) shall be made for **each type of fitting** based on the **largest** conductor present in the box.

314.16(B4). For each yoke or mounting strap containing one or more devices or equipment, a **double volume** allowance in accordance with Table 314.16(B) shall be made for **each** yoke or mounting strap based on the **largest** conductor connected to a device(s) or equipment supported by the yoke or strap. A device or utilization equipment wider than 2 inches shall have a double volume allowance for each gang required for mounting.

•Note: Each **strap** holding a device (switch or receptacle) counts as **two** conductors, if the strap holds a duplex or triplex receptacle, it still counts as **two** conductors.

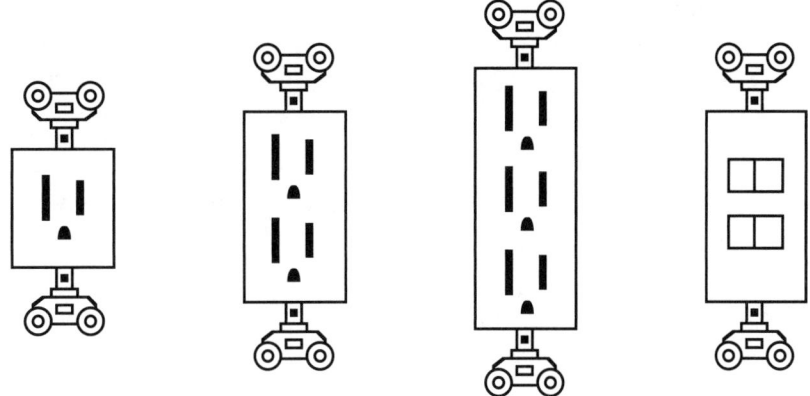

314.16(B5). A deduction of **one** conductor shall be made for one **or more** grounding conductors (green or bare wire) entering a box.

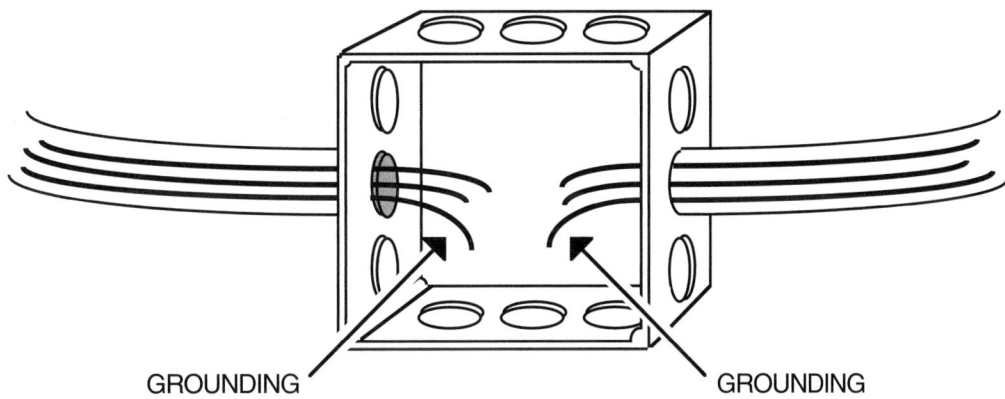

314.16(B5).

Where a second set of equipment grounding conductors, as permitted by Section 250.146(D), is present in the box, then an **additional** deduction of **one** conductor is made.

Section 250.146(D): Where installed for the reduction of electrical noise (electromagnetic interference) on the grounding circuit, a receptacle in which the grounding terminal is purposely insulated from the receptacle mounting means shall be permitted. The receptacle grounding terminal shall be connected to an insulated equipment grounding conductor run with the circuit conductors. This equipment grounding conductor shall be permitted to pass through one or more panelboards without connection to the panelboard grounding terminal bar as permitted in Section 408.40ex., so as to terminate directly at an equipment grounding conductor terminal of the applicable derived system or service.

(FPN): Use of an isolated equipment grounding conductor does not relieve the requirement for grounding the raceway system and outlet box.

In the box shown below with two equipment grounding conductors (count one) and one isolated grounding conductor (count one) you would count a total of **two**.

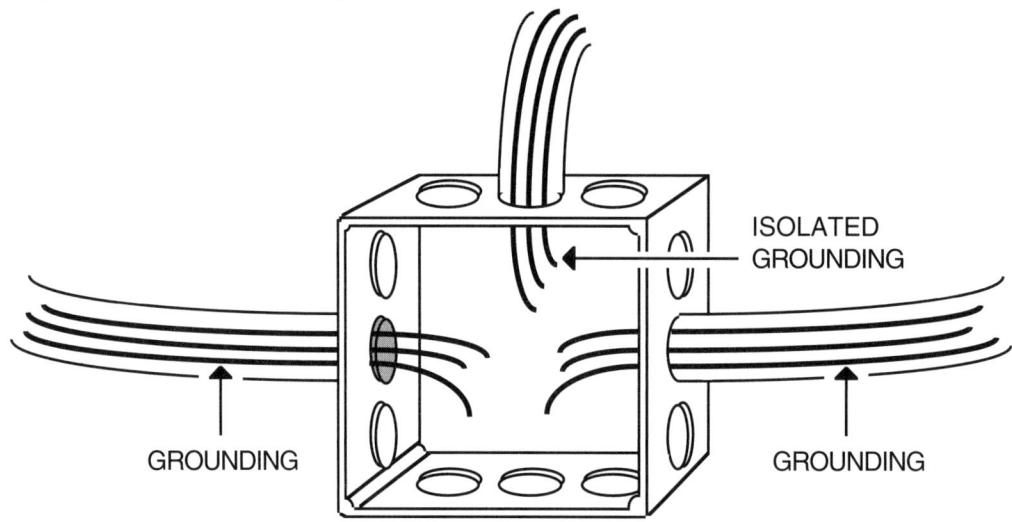

314.16(C). Conduit bodies enclosing #6 conductors or smaller shall have a cross-sectional area not less than **twice** the cross-sectional area of the largest conduit or tubing to which they can be attached.

T. 314.16(A)

Table 314.16(A). When determining the maximum number of conductors permitted in a box, Table 314.16(A) would apply for conductor sizes #18 through #6. Table 314.16(A) shows the number of conductors **all the same size** permitted in a box. But, the number of conductors permitted as shown in Table 314.16(A) represents an **empty** box. If the box contains internal clamps, fixture studs, hickeys, switches or receptacles, the number of conductors shown in Table 314.16(A) would have to be **reduced**.

Table 314.16(A). Metal Boxes

Box Dimension, Inches Trade Size or Type	Min. Cu. In. Cap.	Maximum Number of Conductors*						
		No. 18	No. 16	No. 14	No. 12	No. 10	No. 8	No. 6
4 x 1-1/4 Round or Octagonal	12.5	8	7	6	5	5	5	2
4 x 1-1/2 Round or Octagonal	15.5	10	8	7	6	6	5	3
4 x 2-1/8 Round or Octagonal	21.5	14	12	10	9	8	7	4
4 x 1-1/4 Square	18.0	12	10	9	8	7	6	3
4 x 1-1/2 Square	21.0	14	12	10	9	8	7	4
4 x 2-1/8 Square	30.3	20	17	15	13	12	10	6
4-11/16 x 1-1/4 Square	25.5	17	14	12	11	10	8	5
4-11/16 x 1-1/2 Square	29.5	19	16	14	13	11	9	5
4-11/16 x 2-1/8 Square	42.0	28	24	21	18	16	14	6
3 x 2 x 1-1/2 Device	7.5	5	4	3	3	3	2	1
3 x 2 x 2 Device	10.0	6	5	5	4	4	3	2
3 x 2 x 2-1/4 Device	10.5	7	6	5	4	4	3	2
3 x 2 x 2-1/2 Device	12.5	8	7	6	5	5	4	2
3 x 2 x 2-3/4 Device	14.0	9	8	7	6	5	4	2
3 x 2 x 3-1/2 Device	18.0	12	10	9	8	7	6	3
4 x 2-1/8 x 1-1/2 Device	10.3	6	5	5	4	4	3	2
4 x 2-1/8 x 1-7/8 Device	13.0	8	7	6	5	5	4	2
4 x 2-1/8 x 2-1/8 Device	14.5	9	8	7	6	5	4	2
3-3/4 x 2 x 2-1/2 Masonry Box / Gang	14.0	9	8	7	6	5	4	2
3-3/4 x 2 x 3-1/2 Masonry Box / Gang	21.0	14	12	10	9	8	7	4
FS — Minimum Internal Depth 1-3/4 Single Cover/Gang	13.5	9	7	6	6	5	4	2
FD — Minimum Internal Depth 2-3/8 Single Cover/Gang	18.0	12	10	9	8	7	6	3
FS — Minimum Internal Depth 1-3/4 Multiple Cover/Gang	18.0	12	10	9	8	7	6	3
FD — Minimum Internal Depth 2-3/8 Multiple Cover/Gang	24.0	16	13	12	10	9	8	4

* Where no volume allowances are required by Sections 314.16(B2) through 314.16(B5).

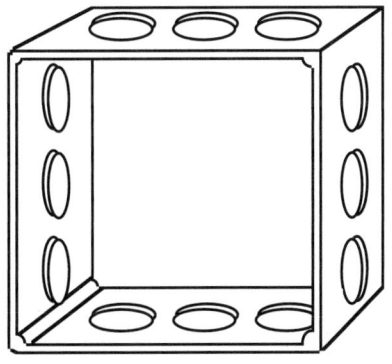

The number of conductors shown in Table 314.16(A), are for an **empty*** box.

* Where no volume allowances are required by Sections 314.16(B2) through 314.16(B5).

TH

Example: Using Table 314.16(A): A 3" x 2" x 2 3/4" device box will hold 6 - #12 conductors. This box will accommodate a maximum of:

A 12-2 with ground romex cable = 3 conductors
cable clamps = 1 conductor
one duplex receptacle = 2 conductors
                                        6 conductors

Now let's reverse the calculation, we know the number of conductors, but need to determine the correct cubic inch box size. Go to Table **314.16(B)**.

Table 314.16(B). Volume Required per Conductor

Size of Conductor	Free Space Within Box for Each Conductor
No. 18	1.50 cubic inches
No. 16	1.75 cubic inches
No. 14	2.00 cubic inches
No. 12	2.25 cubic inches
No. 10	2.50 cubic inches
No. 8	3.00 cubic inches
No. 6	5.00 cubic inches

Table 314.16(B) is a very useful table for everyday box sizing. The electrician should memorize, #14 conductor = 2 cubic inches, and a #12 conductor = 2.25 cubic inches. These two conductors are the most often used in calculating the correct box size using devices. Example, if the electrician is installing #14 conductors, count the conductors, clamps, devices, and multiply the total conductors times 2 cubic inches and this will determine the minimum cubic inch capacity required. Boxes not shown in Table 314.16(A) are required to have the cubic inch capacity marked (314.16(A2)).

Example: Table 314.16(A) shows a 4 11/16" x 1 1/4" square box will hold 11 - #12 conductors. If this box contained three #12-2 with ground nonmetallic sheathed cables, cable clamps, and two duplex receptacles (two straps).

3 - #12 black conductors = 3 conductors
3 - #12 white conductors = 3 conductors
3 - #12 bare conductors = 1 conductor
3 - cable clamps = 1 conductor
2 - duplex receptacles = 4 conductors
                                     12 conductors

12 - #12 conductors x 2.25 cubic inches = 27 cubic inch box required, a 4 11/16" x 1 1/4" square box at 25.5 cubic inches would be a **violation**.

T. 314.16(B)

Example: Using mixed size conductors. The box shown below contains two #12-2 with ground nonmetallic sheathed cables to a duplex receptacle, and one #14-2 with ground nonmetallic sheathed cable to a switch. The box contains cable clamps. What is the cubic inch capacity required?

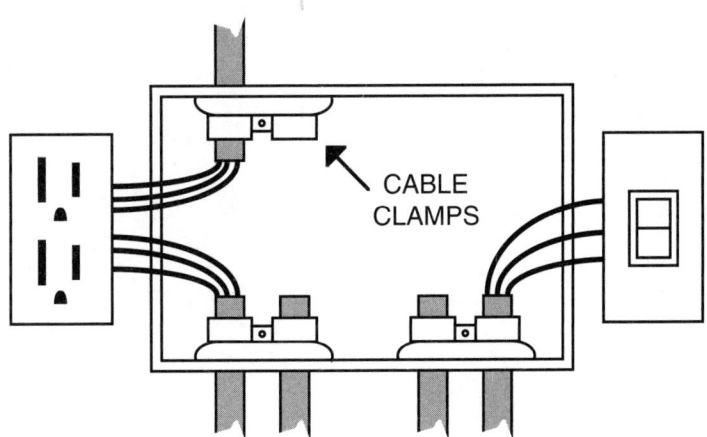

Solution:

2 - #12 black conductors = 2 conductors
2 - #12 white conductors = 2 conductors
2 - #12 bare conductors = 1 conductor
1 - receptacle strap   = 2 conductors
2 - cable clamps   = 1 conductor
                           8 - #12 conductors = 8 x 2.25 cubic inches = 18 cubic inches

1 - #14 black conductor = 1 conductor
1 - #14 white conductor = 1 conductor
1 - switch strap   = 2 conductors
1 - #14 bare conductor = 0 counted as a #12 (370.16b5)
1 - cable clamp   = 0 counted as a #12 (370.16b2)
                          4 - #14 conductors = 4 x 2 cubic inches = 8 cubic inches

18 cubic inches + 8 cubic inches = **26 cubic inch box required minimum**.

Table 314.16(A) and Table 314.16(B) show conductor sizes **through #6**. For conductor sizes **#4 and larger** 314.28 is used for calculations.

314.17. Conductors entering boxes shall be protected from abrasion.

314.17(A). Openings through which conductors enter shall be adequately closed.

314.17(B). Requires cables or raceways to be secured to all metal boxes, conduit bodies, or fittings by threaded connections, connector devices, or internal box clamps.

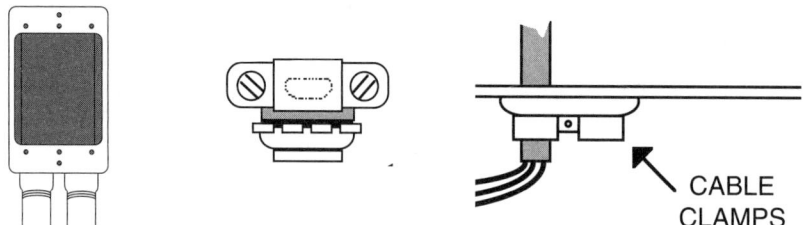

314.17(C). Requires that a nonmetallic box must have a temperature rating at least equal to the lowest-temperature-rated conductor entering the box.

Where NM cable is connected to nonmetallic boxes, the cable must enter through a knockout (KO) opening provided for NM cable, and not through a hole made at any point on the box. At least 1/4" of the cable sheath must be brought inside the box.

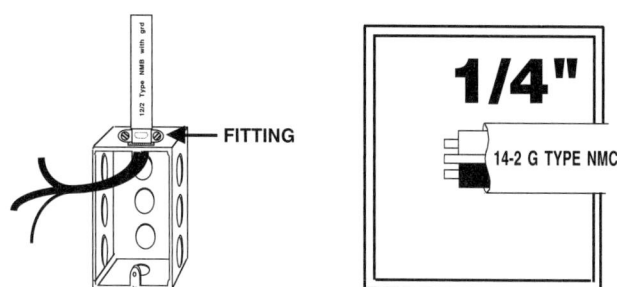

Exception: Where NM cable or UF cable is used with **single gang** boxes not larger than 2 1/4" x 4" mounted in walls or ceilings, and where the cable is fastened within 8" of the box measured along the sheath and where the cable extends through a cable knockout not less than 1/4", securing the cable to the box shall not be required. Multiple cable entries shall be permitted in a **single** cable knockout opening.

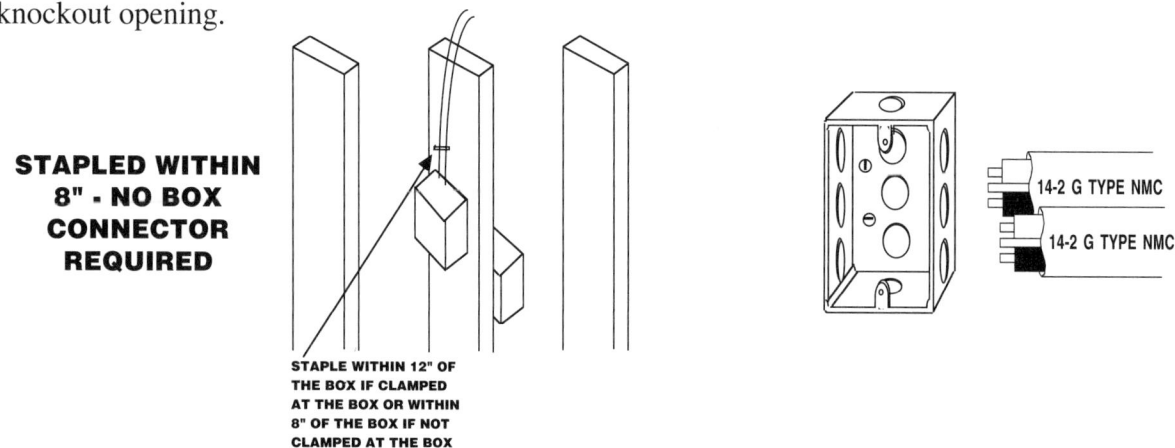

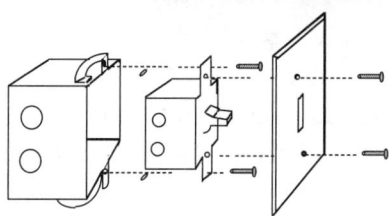

314.19. If the screws used for attaching the receptacles and switches to boxes were used also for mounting the boxes, a poor mechanical job would result, since the boxes would be insecurely held whenever the devices were not installed and the screws loosened for adjustment of the switch or receptacle position.

314.20. In walls or ceilings with a surface of concrete, tile, gypsum, plaster, or other **noncombustible** material, boxes employing a flush-type cover or faceplate shall be installed so that the front edge of the box, plaster ring, extension ring will not set back of the finished surface more than **1/4"**.

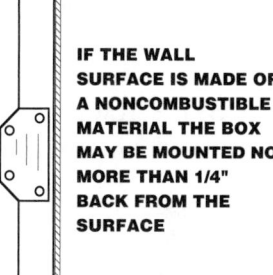

IF THE WALL SURFACE IS MADE OF A NONCOMBUSTIBLE MATERIAL THE BOX MAY BE MOUNTED NO MORE THAN 1/4" BACK FROM THE SURFACE

In walls and ceilings constructed of wood or other **combustible** surface material, boxes, etc. shall be **flush** with the finished surface or project therefrom.

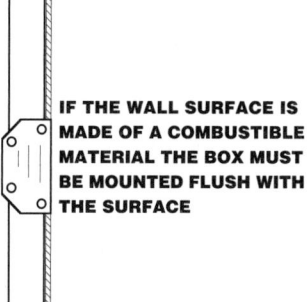

IF THE WALL SURFACE IS MADE OF A COMBUSTIBLE MATERIAL THE BOX MUST BE MOUNTED FLUSH WITH THE SURFACE

314.21. Plaster, drywall, or plasterboard surfaces that are broken or incomplete around boxes employing a flush-type cover or faceplate shall be repaired so there will be no gaps or open spaces greater than **1/8"** at the edge of the box. This is the reason inspectors don't allow square or hexagonal boxes in ceilings without mud rings.

314.22. The extension ring is secured to the box by two screws passing through ears attached to the box.

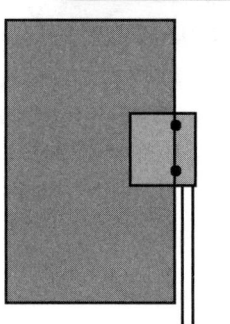

314.23. The Code requires all boxes, conduit bodies and fittings to be fastened in their installed position.

314.23(B1). Screws shall not pass through the box unless exposed threads in the box are protected using approved means to avoid abrasion of conductor insulation.

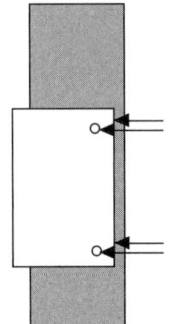

Nails through the box into a wood stud mounting nails must not be more than 1/4" from back of box

314.23(B2). Metal braces shall be protected against corrosion and formed from metal that is not less than .020" thick uncoated. Wood braces shall have a cross section not less than 1" x 2". Wood braces in wet locations shall be treated for the conditions.

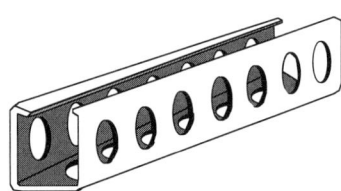 

314.23(C). A box mounted in a finished surface shall be rigidly secured by clamps, anchors, or fittings identified for the application.

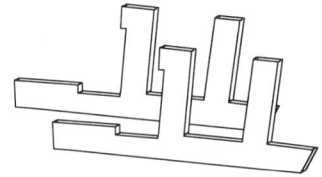

314.23(D1). An enclosure shall be fastened to framing members by mechanical means such as bolts, screws, or rivets, or by the use of clips or other securing means identified for the use with the type of ceiling framing member(s) and enclosure(s) employed.

314.23(F). Boxes that contain **devices** and are not over 100 cubic inches in size and have threaded entries or hubs shall be considered adequately supported where two or more **conduits are threaded** wrenchtight into the box hubs and each conduit is supported within 18" of the box.

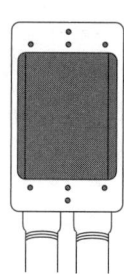

This section says "where the **conduits** are threaded wrenchtight". It doesn't say where the *fittings* are threaded wrenchtight. Rigid metal or intermediate metal conduit is threaded, not PVC.

As I walk through city parks and other outdoor areas that have receptacles it's very common to see the box supported by two PVC conduits from below grade. In some cases I've even seen a single PVC conduit supporting the box.

Below grade PVC is the best choice to use for soil conditions. But the box is NOT considered supported by this type of raceway. To meet the Code the *box* would have to be supported by another means such as bolting it to a piece of kindorf channel.

314.23(H). This section permits a pendant box (such as one containing a START-STOP button) to be supported from a multiconductor cable using a strain-relief connector threaded into the hub on the box.

314.24. No box **without** enclosed devices or utilization equipment shall have an internal depth of less than **1/2"**. Boxes intended to enclose flush devices shall have an internal depth of not less than **15/16"**.

314.25. Each box shall have a cover, or faceplate except electric-discharge lighting fixtures surface mounted over concealed outlet, pull, or junction boxes and designed not to be supported solely by the outlet box shall be provided with suitable openings in the back of the fixture to provide access to the wiring in the box.

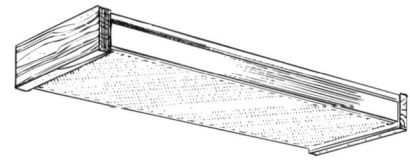

314.25(A). Nonmetallic boxes shall be arranged so the grounding conductor can be connected to any fitting or device that requires grounding.

The nonmetallic box shown below has a **metal** cover, this cover is required to be grounded.

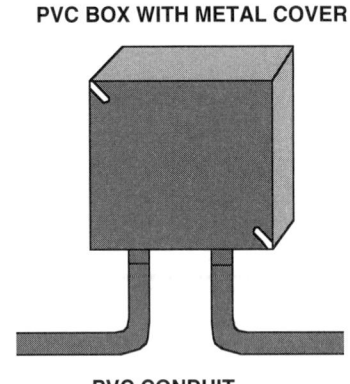

314.27(B). Boxes or fittings shall be permitted to support lighting fixtures weighing **50 pounds** or less. A lighting fixture that weighs more than 50 pounds shall be supported independently of the outlet box unless the outlet box is listed and marked for the maximum weight to be supported.

314.27(C). This section requires floor boxes to be completely suitable for the particular way in which they are used. Adjustable floor boxes can be installed in every type of floor construction.

314.27(D). A ceiling paddle fan must not be supported from a ceiling box, unless the box is UL listed as suitable as the sole support means for a fan. The vibration of ceiling fans places severe dynamic loads on the screw attachment points of boxes.

The minimum height of a paddle fan is not found in the electrical Code. The **Mechanical Code** states: Rotary fans without fan blade protection shall provide for not less than 8' of clearance from the finished floor level to the bottom side of the unprotected fan blades.

The exception is for fan blades of low speed residential type ceiling fans installed *within dwelling units* shall be located at least 6' 8" from the finished floor.

DWELLING UNITS
6' 8"

COMMERCIAL
8'

314.28(A). Minimum size. For raceways 3/4 inch trade size or larger, containing conductors of #4 or larger, and for cables containing conductors #4 or larger, the minimum dimensions of pull or junction boxes installed in a raceway or cable run shall comply with the following:

314.28(A1). In straight pulls the length of the box shall not be less than **eight times** the trade diameter of the largest raceway.

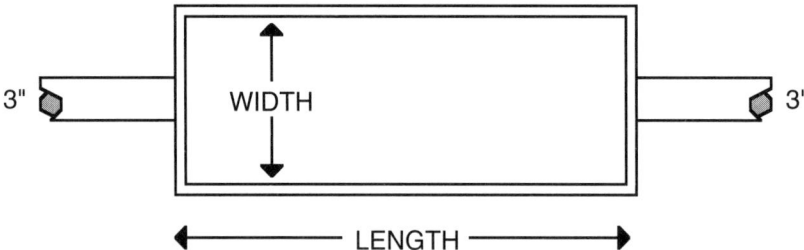

LENGTH = 3" conduit x 8 = 24" minimum.

WIDTH - The box must be wide enough to provide proper installation of the conduit locknuts and bushings within the box.

Example: Straight pull, what is the minimum length of this pull box?

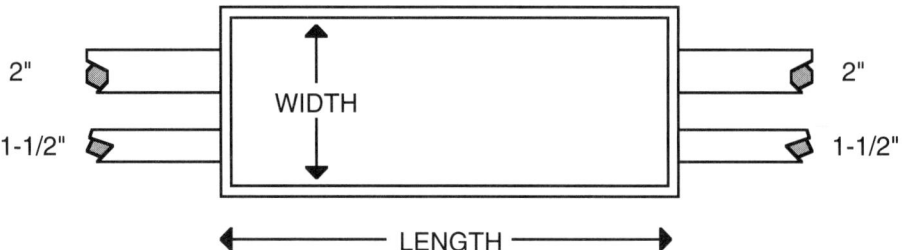

LENGTH = Largest raceway 2" x 8 = 16" minimum length.

WIDTH = Width necessary for locknuts and bushings.

314.28(A2). Where angle or U pulls or splices are made, the distance between each raceway entry inside the box and the opposite wall of the box shall not be less than six times the trade diameter of the largest raceway. This distance shall be increased for additional entries by the amount of the maximum sum of the diameters of all other raceway entries in the same row on the same wall of the box. Each row shall be calculated individually, and the single row that provides the maximum distance shall be used.

The distance between raceway entries enclosing the same conductor shall not be less than six times the trade diameter of the larger raceway.

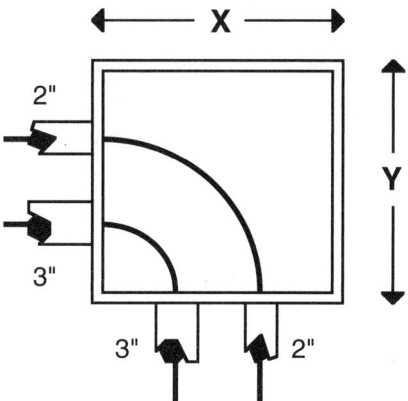

Sizing the angle pull box:

Starting with dimension "**X**", we are calculating the distance from the **same wall** (the wall with the conduit enclosing the conductors in an angle pull) to the **opposite wall** (of the angle pull).

This distance shall not be less than **six** times the trade diameter of the **largest** raceway (6 x 3" conduit = 18") **plus** the diameters of all other raceway entries in any one row on the **same wall** of the box. 6 x 3" = 18" **plus** 2" conduit = 20".   Dimension "**X**" = 20" **minimum**.

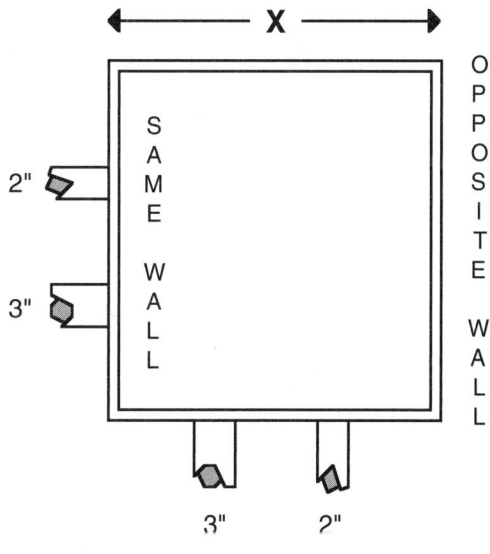

Next calculate dimension "Y":

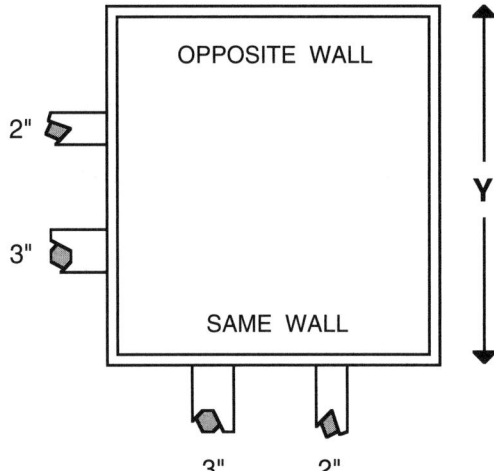

Largest raceway on **same wall** (3" x 6 = 18") **plus** all other raceways on the **same wall** (2").
3" x 6 = 18" + 2" = 20".   Dimension "**Y**" = **20" minimum**.

Example: Calculate dimension "**Z**".

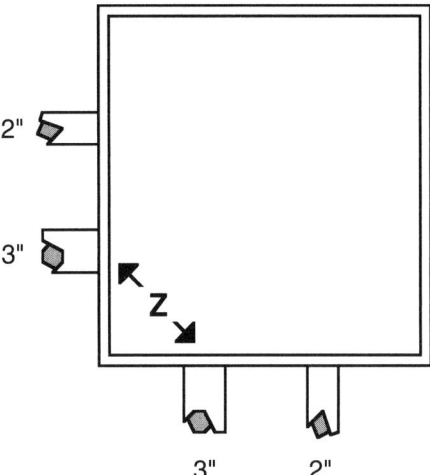

The distance between raceway entries enclosing the same conductor shall not be less than **six times** the trade diameter of the larger raceway.

Solution: 3" conduit x 6 = 18".   Dimension "**Z**" = **18" minimum**.

314.28(A2)

Example: Calculate dimension "**X**" in a **U Pull**.

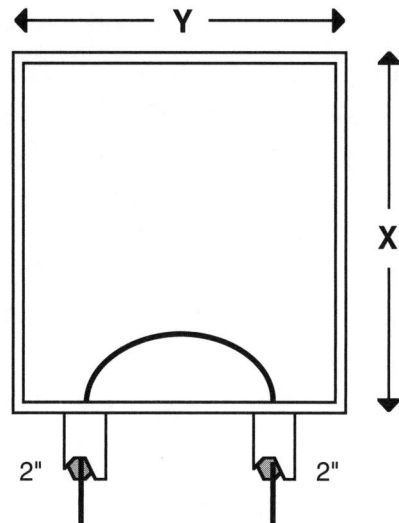

Solution: 2" conduit x 6 = 12" + 2" = 14". Dimension "**X**" = **14" minimum**.
Dimension "**Y**" = width necessary for locknuts and bushings.

Example: Calculate the distance between raceways in a **U Pull**.

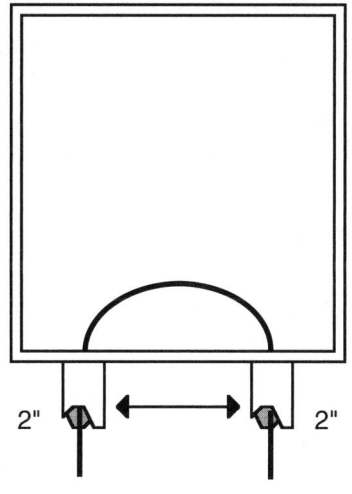

Solution: 2" conduit x 6 = **12" minimum distance between raceways**.

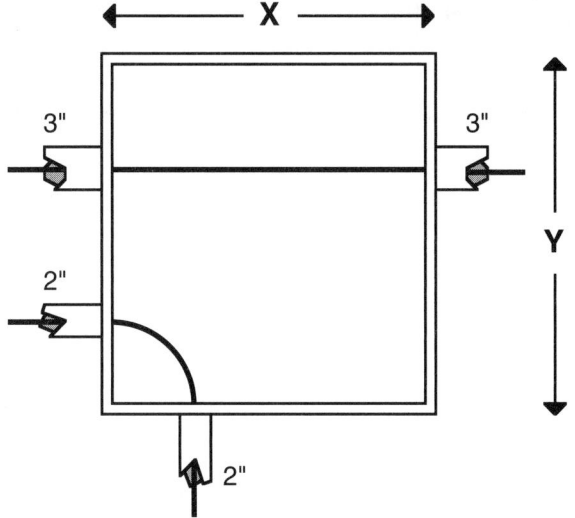

Example: Combination of a straight pull and an angle pull in the same box. Calculate dimension "**Y**".

Solution: Same wall = 2" conduit x 6 = 12" plus all other entries on the **same wall**, there are none. Dimension "**Y**" = **12**" **minimum**.

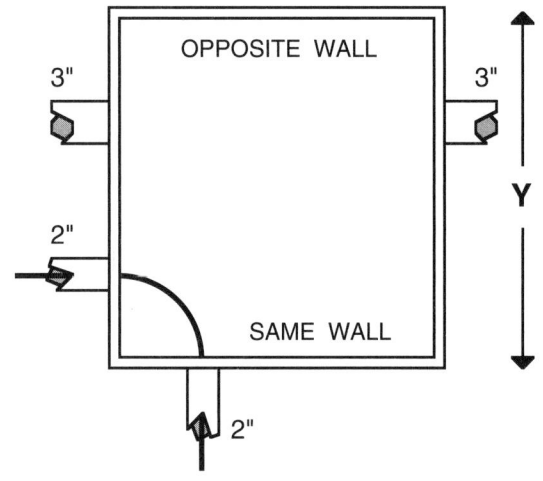

Example: Calculate dimension "**X**".

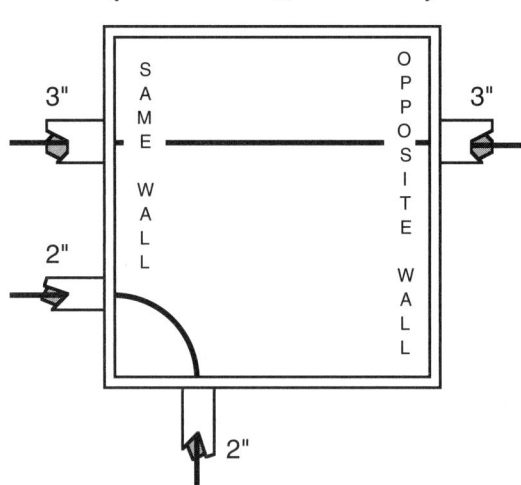

Solution: Same wall = 2" conduit x 6 = 12" plus 3" = 15". But, we also have a straight pull in dimension "X", straight pull = 3" conduit x 8 = 24". Dimension "**X**" = **24**" **minimum**.

TH
98

314.29. Boxes, conduit bodies, and **handhole enclosures** shall be installed so that the wiring contained in them can be rendered accessible without removing any part of the building or, in underground circuits, without excavating sidewalks, paving, earth or other substance that is used to establish the finished grade.

III. Construction Specifications

314.40(A). Metal boxes, conduit bodies, and fittings shall be corrosion resistant or shall be well-galvanized, enameled, or otherwise properly coated inside and out to prevent corrosion.

314.40(D). A means shall be provided in each metal box for the connection of an equipment grounding conductor. The means shall be permitted to be a tapped hole or equivalent.

Where a grounding conductor enters a box it shall be connected to a grounding screw (this screw can't be used for any other purpose) or by a device suitable for use (ground clip).

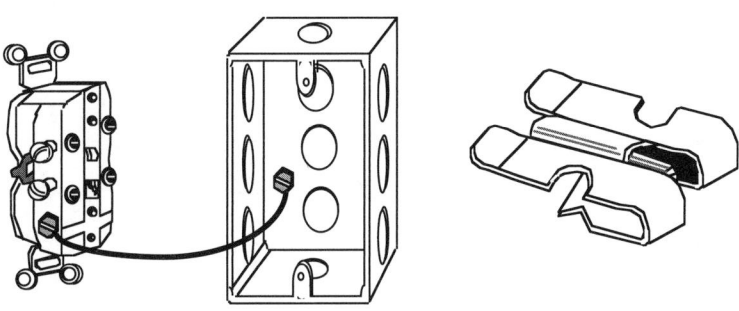

IV. Pull and Junction Boxes for Use on Systems Over 600 Volts

314.71(A). For **straight pulls** the length of the box shall not be less than **48 times** the outside diameter, over sheath, of the largest shielded or lead-covered conductor or cable entering the box. The length shall not be less than 32 times the outside diameter of the largest nonshielded conductor or cable.

314.71(B)

314.71(B).For angle or U pulls Distance to the opposite wall. The distance between each cable or conductor entry inside the box and the opposite wall of the box shall not be less than **36 times** the outside diameter, over sheath, of the largest cable or conductor.

314.72(E). Boxes shall be closed by suitable covers fastened in place. Covers for boxes shall be permanently marked "DANGER - HIGH VOLTAGE - KEEP OUT."

QUIZ #1

Article 314 Quiz #1 - Open Book

1. In straight pulls, the length of the box shall be not less than _____ times the trade diameter of the largest raceway.

(a) 4   (b) 6   (c) 8   (d) 12

2. Where a permanent barrier is installed in a pull box, each section is considered as _____.

(a) permanent barriers are not allowed   (b) a separate box
(c) 60% of the box   (d) the same box

3. Plaster, drywall or plasterboard surfaces that are broken or incomplete shall be repaired so there will be no gaps or open spaces greater than _____ inch at the edge of the fitting or box.

(a) 1/16   (b) 1/8   (c) 3/16   (d) 1/4

4. What is the minimum thickness of metal for a 6" x 4" x 3 1/4" box?

(a) .0625"   (b) .0747"   (c) 15 MSG   (d) 16 MSG

5. The distance between a cable or conductor entry and its exit from the box shall be not less than _____ times the outside diameter, over sheath, of that cable or conductor, 1000 volt system.

(a) 6   (b) 18   (c) 36   (d) 48

6. Angle pull dimensional requirements apply to junction boxes only when the size of conductor is equal to or larger than _____.

(a) #0   (b) #4   (c) #3/0   (d) #6

7. _____ boxes shall not be used where conduits or connectors requiring the use of locknuts or bushings are to be connected to the side of the box.

(a) Round   (b) Shallow   (c) Device   (d) Gang

8. Where NM cable is used, the cable assembly, including the sheath, shall extend into the box no less than _____.

(a) 1/2"   (b) 3/4"   (c) 1/4"   (d) 1"

Article 314 Quiz #1 - Open Book

QUIZ #1

9. Conduit bodies shall have a cross-sectional area at least ____ that of the largest conduit to which they are connected, #6 conductors and smaller.

(a) 100% (b) twice (c) 40% (d) 75%

10. Enclosures supported by suspended ceiling systems shall be fastened to the framing member by mechanical means such as ____.

I. clips identified for use   II. screws   III. rivets   IV. bolts

(a) I only (b) II only (c) II and IV only (d) I, II, III and IV

11. A switch box installed in a tiled wall may be recessed ____ behind the finished wall.

(a) 1/4" (b) 3/8" (c) 1/2" (d) not at all

12. Fixtures shall be supported independently of the outlet box where the weight exceeds ____ pounds.

(a) 60 (b) 50 (c) 40 (d) 30

13. The number of #12 conductors permitted in a 3" x 2" x 1 1/2" deep device box is ____.

(a) 6 (b) 5 (c) 4 (d) 3

14. When counting the number of conductors in a box, a conductor running through the box is counted as ____ conductor(s).

(a) one (b) two (c) zero (d) none of these

15. A luminaire (fixture) supported by a single condit shall not exceed ____ in any horizontal direction from the point of conduit entry.

(a) 4" (b) 6" (c) 8" (d) 12"

Article 314   Quiz #2 - Open Book

QUIZ #2

1. A 3" x 2" x 2" device box is how many cubic inches?

(a) 12   (b) 14   (c) 10   (d) 8

2. Where nonmetallic sheathed cable is used with boxes no larger than ___ mounted in walls or ceilings and where the cable is fastened within 8 inches of the box, securing the cable to the box shall not be required.

(a) 2 1/4" x 4"   (b) 2/12" x 4"   (c) 2" x 4"   (d) 1 1/4" x 4"

3. Of the following, ___ box may be used for a floor receptacle.

(a) a 4 11/16" x 1 1/4" square metal box with device ring listed for the purpose
(b) a 3" x 2" x 2 1/2" metal device box with device ring listed for the purpose
(c) a box listed specifically for this application
(d) any of these

4. A means shall be provided in each metal box over 100 cubic inches for the connection of an equipment grounding conductor. The means shall be permitted to be ___.

I. a tapped hole   II. the cover screw   III. a screw used to mount the box

(a) I only   (b) II only   (c) I and II only   (d) I, II, or III

5. When sizing a pull box for a straight pull of # 4/3 Romex, the length of the box shall not be less than ____ times the trade diameter of the raceway.

(a) 4   (b) 6   (c) 8   (d) 10

6. Which answer best completes the following sentence describing the Code requirements for the use of short radius capped elbow type conduit bodies containing conductors smaller than #6? Capped elbow type conduit bodies ____.

(a) are not permitted by the Code   (b) may be used to enable the installation of the raceway
(c) may contain devices   (d) may contain splices and taps

7. An installation requires a device box with a capacity of 10.25 cubic inches. What is the minimum size box allowed?

(a) 2" x 2" x 3"   (b) 3" x 2" x 2 1/4"   (c) 3" x 2" x 2"   (d) 2" x 3" x 3"

TH
103

QUIZ #2

Article 314 Quiz #2 - Open Book

8. Outlet boxes mounted in non-combustible walls or ceilings must be mounted so that they will be set back not more than a maximum of ____ from the finished surface.

(a) 1/8"   (b) 1/4"   (c) 1/2"   (d) 3/4"

9. Metal covers shall be of the same material as the box with which they are used, or they shall be lined with firmly attached insulating material not less than ____ thick.

(a) 1/32"   (b) 1/16"   (c) 1/8"   (d) .06"

10. Outlet boxes intended to enclose devices flush with the wall surface shall have an internal depth not less than ____.

(a) 1/2"   (b) 3/4"   (c) 15/16"   (d) 1"

11. According to the National Electrical Code, electrical junction boxes shall be installed so that the wiring contained in the box ____.

(a) cannot be removed
(b) is visible at all times
(c) is always readily accessible
(d) can be rendered accessible without removing any part of the building

12. Where necessary, a shallow outlet box not less than ____ inches deep may be used.

(a) 1/2   (b) 3/4   (c) 1   (d) 1 1/4

13. Where pull and junction boxes are used one or more sides of any pull box shall be _____.

(a) blocked   (b) solid   (c) welded   (d) removable

14. When combinations of conductors enter a box, which conductor size shall be used when utilizing the volume deductions permitted for fittings and devices?

(a) Total   (b) Smallest   (c) Largest   (d) Average

15. Threaded boxes not over 100 cubic inches, that contain devices, shall be considered to be adequately supported if two or more circuits are threaded into the box wrenchtight and on the same side and if each conduit is supported within ____ inches of the box.

(a) 36   (b) 30   (c) 24   (d) 18

Article 314 Quiz #3 - Open Book

QUIZ #3

1. Wood braces used in structural mounting of boxes shall have a cross-section not less than nominal ____.

(a) 3/4" x 1 1/2"   (b) 1" x 1 1/2"   (c) 1" x 2"   (d) 3/4" x 2"

2. The volume of a wiring enclosure (box) shall be the total volume of the ____, and, where used, the space provided by plaster rings, domed covers, extension rings, etc., that are marked with their volume in cubic inches, or are from boxes the dimensions of which are listed in Table 314.16a.

(a) enclosure   (b) outlet   (c) assembled sections   (d) none of these

3. For straight pulls, the length of the box shall be not less than ____ the outside diameter, over sheath, of the largest conductor or cable entering the box on systems over 600 volts.

(a) 8 times   (b) 6 times   (c) 36 times   (d) 48 times

4. Where NM cable or underground feeder and branch circuit cable is used with boxes no larger than a nominal size 2 1/4" x 4" mounted in walls and where the cable is fastened within ____ inches of the box measured along the sheath and where the sheath extends into the box no less than 1/4", securing the cable to the box shall not be required.

(a) 8   (b) 10   (c) 12   (d) 24

5. Which of the following is permitted to support a lighting fixture weighing over 50 pounds?

**(a) The screwshell of a lampholder.
(b) A box or fitting that is listed for the weight to be supported.
(c) An outlet box.
(d) Fixture wires #14 and larger.**

6. Which of the following statements about junction boxes is/are true?

I. All shall have a cover   II. All over 6' in length shall have conductors cabled or racked

(a) I only   (b) II only   (c) both I and II   (d) neither I nor II

Article 314 Quiz #3 - Open Book

QUIZ #3

7. A junction box used in a system rated 1000 volts shall have a marking on the box of ____.

(a) Caution   (b) Danger   (c) Do Not Open   (d) Danger High-Voltage Keep Out

8. Enclosures that are not over 100 cubic inches in size and which have two conduits supported within three feet on either side of the enclosure and the enclosure does not contain devices or support fixtures shall not be required to have the enclosure supported if the conduits are ____.

(a) rigid nonmetallic conduits
(b) threaded into hubs identified for the purpose
(c) installed with locknuts inside and outside enclosure
(d) shoulders of fittings outside and locknuts inside the box

9. Outlet boxes mounted in combustible walls or ceilings must be mounted so they will be ____ the finished surface.

(a) set back not more than 1/8" from
(b) set back not more than 1/4" from
(c) set back not more than 1/2" from
(d) flush or project from

10. Handhole covers shall require the use of tools to open, or they shall weigh over ____ pounds.

(a) 25   (b) 50   (c) 75   (d) 100

11. A wall-mounted fixture weighing not more than ____ pounds shall be permitted to be supported on other boxes or plaster rings that are secured to other boxes, provided the fixture or its supporting yoke is secured to the box with no fewer than two #6 or larger screws.

(a) 2   (b) 3   (c) 4   (d) 6

12. A #16 conductor is ____ cubic inch.

(a) 1.5   (b) 1.75   (c) 2   (d) 2.25

QUIZ #4

Article 314   Quiz #4   -   Open Book

1. What size octagon box is required for 4 - #12 and 3 - #14 conductors?

(a) 1 1/4"   (b) 1 1/2"   (c) 2"   (d) 2 1/8"

2. A conduit body contains the following conductors. Three #12 THHN conductors running through the fitting. Two #12 THHN conductors which enter the fitting and are spliced in the fitting to two #12 THHN conductors which leave the fitting. What is the minimum cubic inch capacity that the manufacturer must have marked on the conduit body?

(a) 13.50 cubic inches   (b) 15.75 cubic inches   (c) 16.5 cubic inches   (d) 18 cubic inches

3. What size box is required for the following?

1 - #14 ungrounded conductor (black)
1 - #14 grounded conductor   (white)
1 - #14 grounding conductor   (green)
2 - #14 fixture wires

(a) 4 cubic inch   (b) 6 cubic inch   (c) 8 cubic inch   (d) 10 cubic inch

4. What is the minimum dimension for "X" in the box shown below?

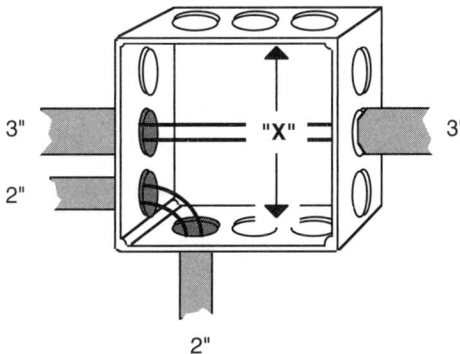

(a) 10"   (b) 12"   (c) 24"   (d) 26"

Article 314 Quiz #4 - Open Book

5. A two gang metal box containing nonmetallic cable clamps along with a switch and receptacle is installed in the kitchen of a dwelling unit. The switch is connected to a piece of #14 from a 15 amp circuit and the receptacle is connected to a piece of #12 on a 20 amp circuit. The wiring method is nonmetallic sheathed cable with a ground. The minimum cubic inch capacity box permitted by Code is ____ cubic inches.

(a) 21.5   (b) 22   (c) 23   (d) 24

6. What is the minimum cubic inch allowed for the box shown below? The box contains three cable clamps, two - #12-2 w/grd romex cables to the duplex receptacle and one- #12-2 w/grd romex cable to the single-pole switch.

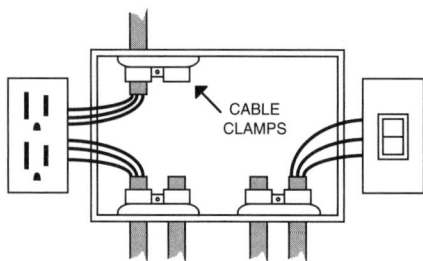

(a) 34 cu.in.   (b) 31.5 cu.in.   (c) 27 cu.in   (d) none of these

7. The volume required for two #12 TW grounding conductors and two #12 TW conductors in a box would be ____ cubic inches.

(a) 9   (b) 6.75   (c) 6   (d) 4.5

8. The size of the pull box shown to the right should not be less than ____.

(a) 12" x 14"
(b) 16" x 18"
(c) 22" x 22"
(d) 24" x 24"

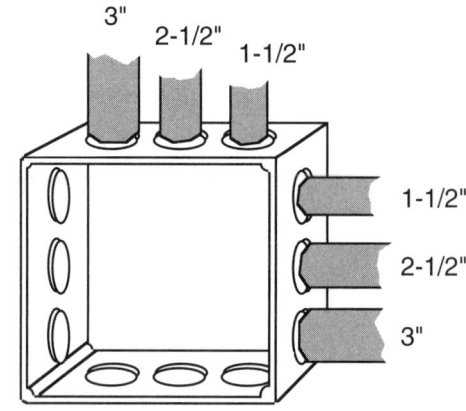

Article 314   Quiz #5 - Open Book

QUIZ #5

1. What is the minimum cubic inch capacity necessary to contain 2 pieces of #14-2 and one piece of #12-2 romex with ground, assuming the box has cable clamps.

(a) 14 cubic inch   (b) 15 cubic inch   (c) 16 cubic inch   (d) 17 cubic inch

2. What is the cubic inch capacity required for a device box containing one duplex receptacle, cable clamps and two #12-2 with ground nonmetallic sheathed cables (romex)?

(a) 13.5 cu.in.   (b) 15.75 cu.in.   (c) 16 cu.in.   (d) 18 cu.in.

3. How many #12 conductors can you install in a 3" x 2" x 2 1/2" device box containing cable clamps and a duplex receptacle?

(a) 5   (b) 4   (c) 3   (d) 2

4. A metal device box contains cable clamps, six #12 conductors, and one single-pole switch. Which of the following is the minimum size box permitted?

(a) 12 cubic inch   (b) 13 1/2 cubic inch   (c) 15 cubic inch   (d) 20.25 cubic inch

5. How many #12 conductors are permitted in a 3" x 2" x 1 1/2" box?

(a) 5   (b) 4   (c) 3   (d) 2

Article 314 Quiz #5 - Open Book

QUIZ #5

6. What size box is required for the twelve #10 THW conductors listed below?

4 - #10 THW (black)
4 - #10 THW (white)
4 - #10 THW (green)

(a) 27.5 cubic inch   (b) 30 cubic inch   (c) 22.5 cubic inch   (d) 20.25 cubic inch

7. When counting the number of conductors in a box, a conductor running through the box is counted as ____ conductor(s).

(a) not counted   (b) one   (c) two   (d) count only if ungrounded

8. The box shown to the right:

X = ____ inches

Y = ____ inches

Z = ____ inches

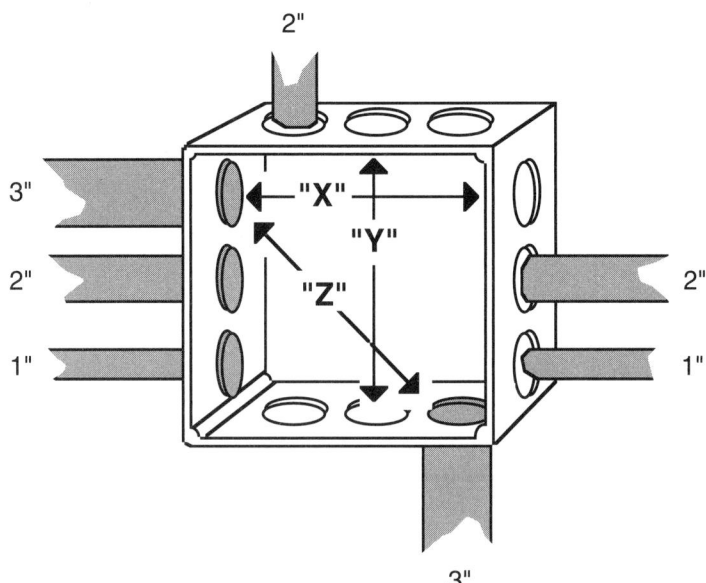

ARTICLE 320

Armored Cable Type AC

320.1. Type AC cable sometimes called *BX* has the conductors installed in a flexible metal type of conduit and along with the insulated conductors, a thin strip of bare metal is installed in contact with the flexible metal conduit the full length for grounding and to lower the total resistance in the cable.

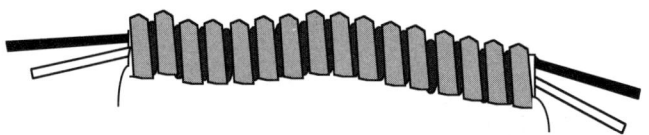

II. Installation

320.10. Uses Permitted. Type AC cable shall be permitted as follows:

(1) For feeders and branch circuits in both exposed and concealed work
(2) In cable trays
(3) In dry locations
(4) Embedded in plaster finish on brick or other masonry, except in damp or wet locations
(5) To be run or fished in the air voids of masonry block or tile walls where such walls are not exposed or subject to excessive moisture or dampness

320.12. Uses Not Permitted. Type AC cable shall not be used as follows:

(1) Where subject to physical damage
(2) In damp or wet locations
(3) In air voids of masonry block or tile walls where such walls are exposed or subject to excessive moisture or dampness
(4) Where exposed to corrosive fumes or vapors
(5) Embedded in plaster finish on brick or other masonry in damp or wet locations

320.15. This section requires AC cable to closely follow the surface of the building. Securing to the bottom of a joist is permitted where not subject to physical damage.

320.17. AC cable shall be protected in accordance with 300.4 where installed through or parallel to framing members.

300.4(A1). This section requires that the outer edge of bored holes for cables or conduit be no more than 1 1/4 inches from the outer edge in wooden joists, rafters, studs or other wood members. In a standard 2" x 4" stud this is in most cases is not possible, so a provision is made for protection to prevent nails or screws from damaging the conductors to be installed if the hole is less than 1 1/4 inches from the outer edge. This protection can be a steel plate at least 1/16 inch thick, a bushing must be used in steel studs, and the protection must be of the appropriate length and width to cover the area of the wiring.

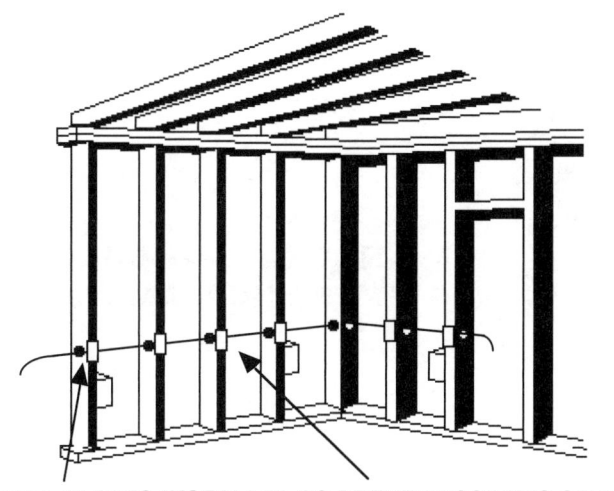
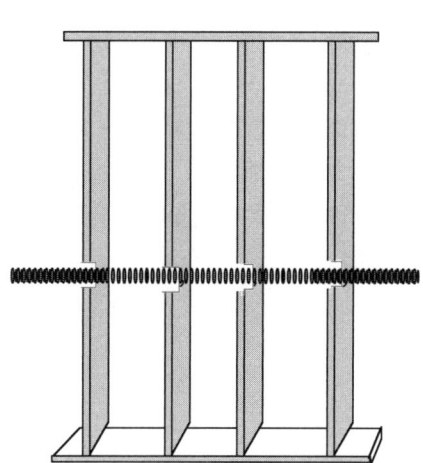

NAIL PLATES INSTALLED TO PREVENT SCREWS OR NAILS FROM DAMAGING THE CONDUCTORS

300.4(A2) Conduit or cable is permitted to be laid in notches in wood studs, joists and rafters if protected by steel nail plates at least 1/16 inch thick and the notches do not cause any weakening.

300.4(D). When cables or raceways are installed parallel to joists, rafters, or studs the cable or raceway must be installed so that it is not less than 1 1/4 inches from the nearest edge where nails or screws may be driven. If this 1 1/4 inch distance cannot be maintained, then steel plates or metal sleeves must be used.

320.23(A). In Accessible Attics. Where run across the top of floor joists, or within 7' of floor or floor joists across the face of rafters or studding, in attics roof spaces that are accessible, the cable shall be protected by substantial guard strips that are at least as high as the cable.

Where this space is not accessible by permanent stairs or ladders, protection shall only be required within 6' of the nearest edge of the scuttle hole or attic entrance.

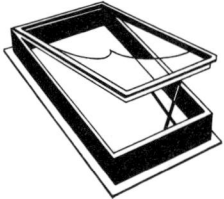

320. 24. The radius of the curve of the inner edge of any bend shall not be less than 5 times the diameter of the AC cable.

NOT LESS THAN 5 TIMES THE DIAMETER

320.30(A). AC cable shall be supported and secured by staples, cable ties, straps, hangers, or similar fittings, designed and installed so as not to damage the cable.

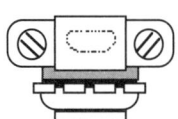 

320.30(B). AC cable shall be secured within 12" of every box, cabinet, or fitting and at intervals not exceeding 4 1/2' where installed on or across framing members.

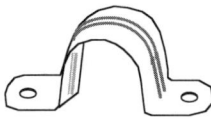

320.30(C). Horizontal runs of AC cable installed in wooden or metal framing members shall be considered supported where such support does not exceed 4 1/2' intervals.

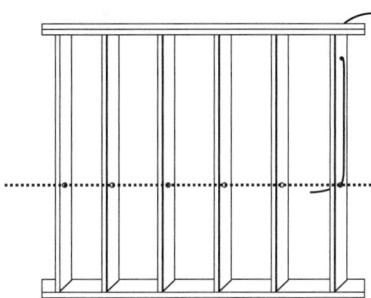

320.30(D). AC cable shall be permitted to be unsupported where the cable complies with any of the following:

(1) Is fished between access points through concealed spaces in finished buildings or structures and supporting is impracticable
(2) Is not more than 2' in length at terminals where flexibility is necessary
(3) Is not more than 6' in length from the last point of cable support to the point of connection to a lighting fixture or other electrical equipment and the cable and point of connection are within an accessible ceiling

320.40. When connecting AC cable to a box or other equipment, it is necessary to cut and remove the armor the appropriate length for the conductors to be terminated. An anti-short bushing is required when the armor is removed to prevent the conductors from being damaged. This bushing slips between the exposed conductors and the metal armor. Type AC cable can be cut with a hacksaw by cutting one of the spirals and twisting the armor slightly to remove the armor. Extreme care must be taken when using a hacksaw to cut the armor to prevent damaging the conductors inside. Special cable cutters are available to cut the armor at just the right depth. These cutters will not damage the conductors.

320.80(A). AC cable must have 90°C rated insulation, but it must be loaded to no more than the 60°C value shown in Table 310.16. Although it is permissible to use the 90°C current value shown in Table 310.16 for the purposes of derating, the actual load carried must be no greater than the current value shown for the particular size and conductor material.

III. Construction Specifications

320.100. AC cable shall have an armor of flexible metal tape and shall have an internal bonding strip of copper or aluminum in intimate contact with the armor for its entire length.

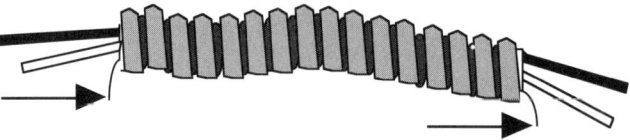

320.108. AC cable is required to provide an adequate path for fault current as required by 250.4(A)(5) or (B)(4) to act as an equipment grounding conductor. This is accomplished by the #16 aluminum bonding strip that runs the length of the cable's sheath. This bonding strip shorts out the high impedance of the coiled metal jacket and provides a UL listed ground path.

ARTICLE 322

Flat Cable Assemblies Type FC

322.2. FC cable is a flat assembly with 3 or 4 parallel #10 special stranded copper conductors. The assembly is installed in an approved U-channel surface metal raceway with one side open. Tap devices can be inserted anywhere along the raceway. Pin-type contacts penetrate the insulation of the cable assembly and contact the multistranded conductors.

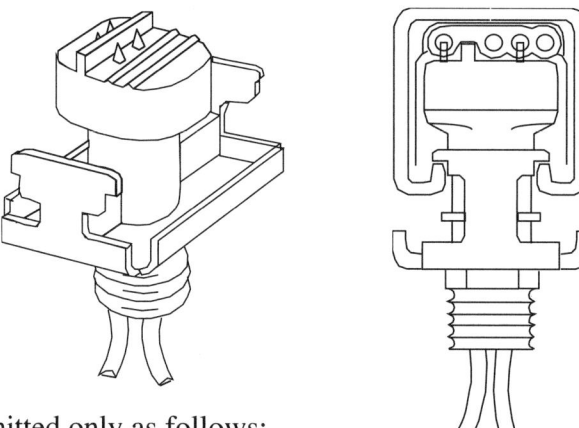

II. Installation

322.10. Flat cable assemblies shall be permitted only as follows:

(1) As branch circuits to supply suitable tap devices for lighting, small appliances, or small power loads. The rating of the branch circuit shall not exceed 30 amps.
(2) Where installed for exposed work.
(3) In locations where they will not be subjected to physical damage. Where a flat cable assembly is installed less than 8' above the floor or fixed working platform, it shall be protected by a cover identified for the use.
(4) In surface metal raceways identified for the use. The channel portion of the surface metal raceway systems shall be installed as complete systems before the flat cable assemblies are pulled into the raceways.

322.12. Flat cable assemblies shall not be used as follows:

(1) Where subject to corrosive vapors unless suitable for the application
(2) In hoistways or on elevators or escalators
(3) In any hazardous (classified) location
(4) Outdoors or in wet or damp locations unless identified for the use

322.30. Flat cable assemblies shall be supported by means of their special design features, within the surface metal raceways

322.56(B). Taps shall be made between any phase conductor and the grounded conductor or any other phase conductor by means of devices and fittings identified for the use. Tap devices shall be rated at not less than 15 amps, or more than 300 volts to ground, and shall be color-coded in accordance with 322.120(C).

III. Construction

322.100. Flat cable assemblies shall consist of 2, 3, 4, or 5 conductors.

322.104. Flat cable assemblies shall have special stranded #10 copper conductors.

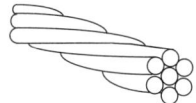

322.120(B). The grounded conductor shall be identified by a white or gray marking throughout its length.

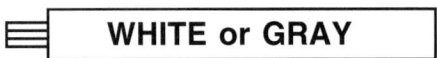

322.120(C). Terminal blocks shall have distinctive and durable markings for color or word coding. The grounded conductor section shall have a white marking. The next adjacent section of the terminal block shall have a black marking. The next section shall have a red marking. The final or outer section, opposite the grounded conductor section shall have a blue marking.

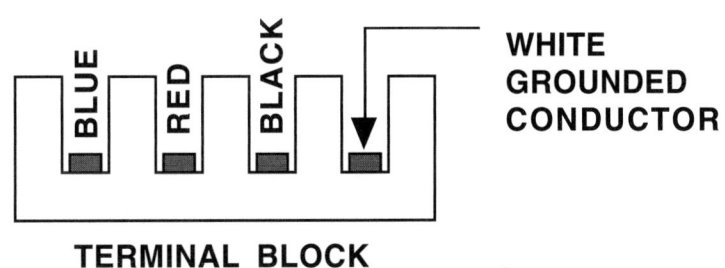

ARTICLE 324

Flat Conductor Cable FCC

324.1. Under carpet wiring to floor outlets eliminates any need for core drilling of concrete floors. FCC wiring offers versatile supply to floor outlets for power and communication. The flat cable is inconspicuous under carpet squares.

324.2. For 120 volt power, the flat cable contains three flat, black, white and green #12 copper conductors for 20 amp circuits. Telephone circuits use flat, 3-pair, #26 gauge conductors. Data connection circuit use flat coaxial cable that is only .09" high.

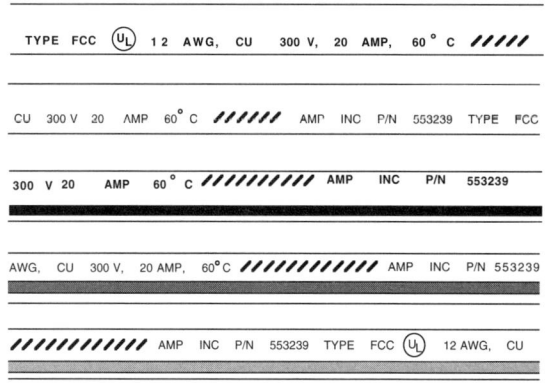

II. Installation

324.10. Uses Permitted. FCC systems shall be permitted both for general-purpose and appliance branch circuits and for individual branch circuits.

324.10(B1). Voltage between ungrounded (hot) conductors shall not exceed 300 volts. Voltage between ungrounded (hot) and the grounded (white) conductor shall not exceed 150 volts.

324.10(B2). General-purpose and appliance branch circuits shall not exceed 20 amps. Individual branch circuits shall not exceed 30 amps.

324.10(C). FCC systems shall be permitted on hard floors.

324.10(F). Materials used for floors heated in excess of 86°F shall be identified as suitable for use at these temperatures.

324.10(G). Any portion of an FCC system with a height above the floor level of .090" shall be tapered or feathered at the edges to floor level.

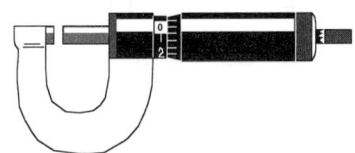

1/16" = .0625"

324.12. Uses NOT permitted.

(1) Outdoors or in wet locations

(2) Where subject to corrosive vapors

(3) In any hazardous location

(4) In residential, school, and hospital buildings

324.18. Not more than two FCC cables run may be crossed over each other at any one point. To prevent lumping under the floor carpets.

324. 42. All receptacles, receptacle housings and self-contained devices used with the FCC system shall be identified for this use and shall be connected to the FCC cable and metal shields. Connection from any grounding conductor of the FCC cable shall be made to the shield system at each receptacle.

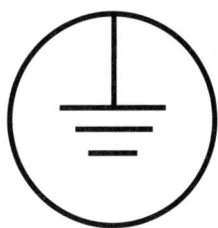

III. Construction

324.100(A). FCC cable shall be listed for use with the FCC system and shall consist of 3, 4, or 5 flat copper conductors, one of which shall be an equipment grounding conductor.

324.120. FCC cable shall be clearly marked on both sides at intervals not over 24" with the information required by 310.11(A) and the following:

(1) Material of conductors
(2) Maximum temperature rating
(3) Ampacity

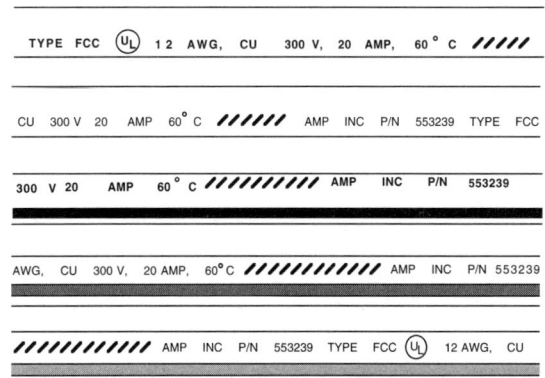

ARTICLE 326

Integrated Gas Spacer Cable Type IGS

326.2. IGS cable is a factory assembly of one or more conductors, each individually insulated and enclosed in a loose fit, nonmetallic flexible conduit as an integrated gas spacer cable rated 0 through 600 volts.

The cable system has the advantage of lower first cost for materials and low installation cost. It eliminates the need for field pulling of cables into conduits and eliminates the cost of assembly of conduit in the field. The system may be directly buried, plowed in, or bored in for further savings, It is a cable and conduit system.

A tough natural-gas-approved pipe is used as the conduit. When it is pressurized, it will withstand much abuse. The gas pressure keeps out moisture and serves to monitor the cable for damage by insects or mechanical damage that can lead to future failure. The gas pressure can even be attached to an alarm to sound a loss of pressure or to trip a CB for hazardous locations. Even on dig-ins, the gas serves to warn the diggers. The gas prevents combustion and burning or cable failure. The SF_6 gas is a nontoxic, odorless, tasteless, and will not support combustion. It acts to put a fire out.

II. Installation

326.10. IGS cable shall be permitted for use underground, including direct burial in the earth, as the following:

(1) Service-entrance conductors
(2) Feeder or branch-circuit conductors

326.12. IGS cable shall NOT be used as interior wiring or be exposed in contact with buildings.

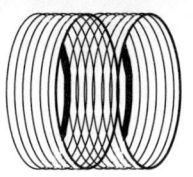

326.24. Where the coilable nonmetallic conduit and cable is bent for installation purposes or is flexed or bent during shipment or installation, the radii of bends measured to the inside of the bend shall not be less than specified in Table 326.24.

326.26. A run of IGS cables between pull boxes or terminations shall not contain more than the equivalent of four quarter bends (360° total), including those bends located immediately at the pull boxes or terminations.

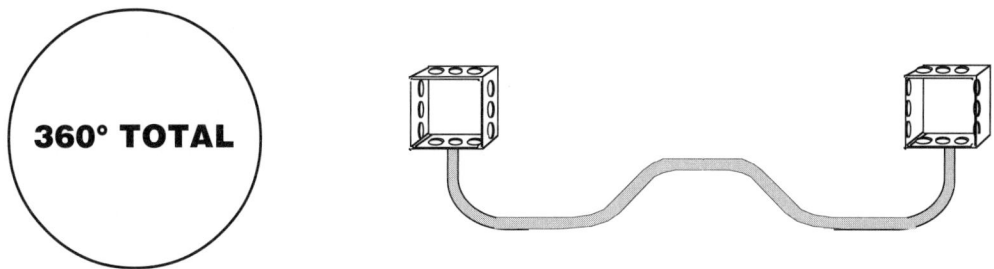

326.80. The ampacity of IGS cable shall not exceed the values shown in Table 326.80.

III. Construction Specifications

326.104. The conductors shall be solid aluminum rods, laid in parallel, consisting of one to nineteen 1/2" diameter rods. The minimum size shall be 250 kcmil, maximum size 4750 kcmil.

326.112. The insulation shall be dry kraft paper tapes and pressurized sulfur hexafluoride gas SF_6 both approved for electrical use. The nominal gas pressure shall be 20 pounds per square inch. The thickness of the paper spacer shall be as specified in Table 326.112.

ARTICLE 328

Medium Voltage Cable Type MV

328.2. MV cable is a single or multiconductor solid dielectric insulated cable rated 2001 volts or higher.

They are single or multiconductor, aluminum or copper, with solid extruded dielectric insulation and may have an extruded jacket, metallic covering or combination of both over the single conductors or over the assembled conductors in a multiconductor power cable.

All insulated conductors rated higher than 8000 volts have electrostatic shielding. Cables rated 5000 or 8000 volts may be shielded or nonshielded.

Nonshielded cables are intended for use where conditions of maintenance and supervision ensure that only competent individuals service and have access to the installation.

Shielded cables are marked "MV-90" and are suitable for use in wet or dry locations at 90°C.

II. Installation

328.10. MV cable shall be permitted for use on power systems rated up to 35,000 volts as follows:

(1) In wet or dry locations
(2) In raceways
(3) In cable trays as in 392.3, 392.6(F), 392.8, and 392.12
(4) Direct buried per 300.50
(5) In messenger-supported wiring in accordance with Part II of Article 396
(6) As exposed runs in accordance with 300.37

328.12. MV cable shall NOT be used as follows:

(1) Where exposed to direct sunlight, unless identified for the use.

328.80. The ampacity shall be determined by Table 310.60. In cable trays per 392.13.

III. Construction Specifications

328.100. MV cables shall have copper, aluminum, or copper-clad aluminum conductors and shall comply with Table 310.13(C) and Table 310.13(D) or Table 310.13(E).

TH

ARTICLE 330

Metal-Clad Cable
MC

330.2. MC cable is a factory assembly of one or more insulated circuit conductors with or without optical fiber members enclosed in an armor of interlocking metal tape, or a smooth or corrugated metallic sheath. Also includes Type ALS (aluminum-sheathed) and Type CS (copper sheathed).

MC cable armor is much heavier the Armored AC cable.

II. Installation

330.10(A). MC cable shall be permitted as follows:

(1) For services, feeders, and branch circuits
(2) For power, lighting, control, and signal circuits
(3) Indoors or outdoors
(4) Exposed or concealed
(5) To be direct buried where identified for such use
(6) In cable tray where identified for such use
(7) In any raceway
(8) As aerial cable on a messenger
(9) In hazardous locations as permitted
(10) In dry locations and embedded in plaster finish on brick or other masonry except in damp or wet locations
(11) In wet locations where any of the following conditions are met:
    (a) The metallic covering is impervious to moisture.
    (b) A lead sheath or moisture-impervious jacket is provided under the metal covering.
    (c) The insulated conductors under the metallic covering are listed for use in wet
        locations and a corrosion resistant jacket is provided over the metallic sheath.
(12) Where single-conductor cables are used, all phase conductors, and, where used, the neutral conductor shall be grouped together to minimize induced voltage on the sheath.

330.10(B). MC cable shall be permitted to be installed in compliance with Parts II and III of Article 725 and 770.133 as applicable with the following:

(1) MC cable installed in cable tray shall comply with 392.3, 392.4, 392.6, and 392.8 through 392.13.

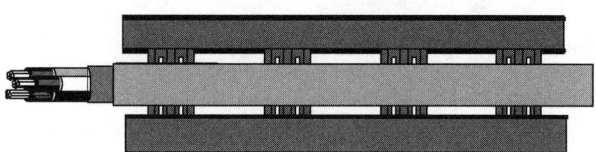

(2) Direct-buried cable shall comply with 300.5 or 300.50, as appropriate.

(3) MC cable installed as service-entrance cable shall be permitted.

(4) MC cable installed outside of buildings or Structures or as aerial cable shall comply with 225.10, 396.10, and 396.12.

330.12. MC cable shall NOT be used under either of the following conditions:

(1) Where subject to physical damage

(2) Where exposed to any of the destructive corrosive conditions in (a) or (b), unless the metallic sheath or armor is resistant to the conditions or is protected by material resistant to the conditions:

(a) Direct burial in earth or embedded in concrete unless identified for direct burial

(b) Exposed to cinder fills, strong chlorides, caustic alkalis, or vapors of chlorine or of hydrochloric acids

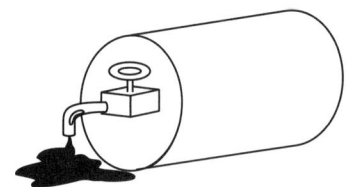

330.24(A). Bending radius for smooth sheath:

Radius shall not be less than:
(a) 10 times the outside diameter for cables with an outside diameter of 3/4" or less.

(b) 12 times the outside diameter for cables with an outside diameter over 3/4" but not over 1 1/2".

(c) 15 times the outside diameter for cables with an outside diameter over 1 1/2"

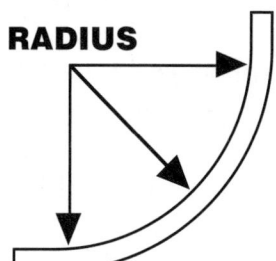

330.24(B). Interlocked-type armor or corrugated sheath the bending radius shall be not less than 7 times the external diameter of the metallic sheath.

330.24(C). For shielded conductors the bending radius shall be not less than 12 times the overall diameter of one of the individual conductors or 7 times the overall diameter of the multiconductor cable.

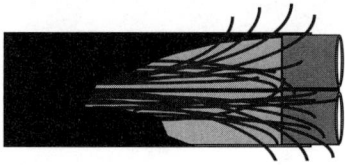

330.30(B). Cables shall be secured each 6 feet.

Articles 320 - 330 Quiz #1 - Open Book

QUIZ #1

1. FCC carpet squares that are adhered to the floor shall be attached with ____.

(a) tacking strip   (b) release-type adhesive   (c) glue   (d) none of these

2. Armored cable installed in thermal insulation shall have conductors rated at ____. The ampacity of the cable installed in these applications shall be that of 60 degree C conductors.

(a) 60 degrees C   (b) 194 degrees F   (c) 75 degrees C   (d) 90 degrees F

3. Type ____ is a single or multiconductor solid dielectric insulated cable rated 2001 volts or higher.

(a) MI   (b) NM   (c) MC   (d) MV

4. Power feed, grounding connection, and shield system connection between the FCC system and other wiring systems shall be accomplished in a ____.

(a) transition assembly   (b) raceway   (c) trench   (d) none of these

5. Tap devices used in FC assemblies shall be rated at not less than ____ amps or more than 300 volts, and they shall be color-coded in accordance with the requirements of 322.120(C).

(a) 20   (b) 15   (c) 30   (d) 40

6. Lengths of not more than ____ of AC cable at terminals where flexibility is necessary does not have to be supported.

(a) 28"   (b) 2'   (c) 30"   (d) 3'

7. A protective layer which is installed between the floor and type FCC flat conductor cable to protect the cable from physical damage and may or may not be incorporated as an integral part of the cable is the ____.

(a) transition assembly   (b) outer sheath   (c) bottom shield   (d) header

8. The minimum size copper conductor permitted in metal-clad cable is ____.

(a) #18   (b) #16   (c) #14   (d) #12

Articles 320 - 330 Quiz #1 - Open Book

QUIZ #1

9. FCC cable connections shall use connectors identified for their use, such that ____ against dampness and liquid spillage are provided.

I. sealing   II. insulation   III. electrical continuity

(a) I only   (b) II only   (c) III only   (d) I, II and III

10. Flat cable assemblies may be installed ___.

I. for small power loads outdoors, not subject to physical damage
II. as tap devices for lighting and small appliances
III. for small power loads in hoistways

(a) I only   (b) II only   (c) I and III only   (d) I, II, and III

11. When installing a type FCC system under carpet squares, not more than ___ crossings of cable runs shall be permitted at any one point.

(a) 1   (b) 2   (c) 4   (d) 5

12. Materials used for floors heated in excess of 30°C or ____ shall be identified for use at these temperatures.

(a) 76°F   (b) 80°F   (c) 86°F   (d) 90°F

13. Medium voltage cable insulation is rated for voltages ___ volts and higher.

(a) 150   (b) 600   (c) 1000   (d) 2001

14. The nominal gas pressure for IGS cable insulation shall be ____ pounds per square inch gage.

(a) 5   (b) 10   (c) 15   (d) 20

15. The grounded conductor of Type FC cable shall be identified throughout its length by means of a distinctive and durable _____ marking.

(a) white   (b) black   (c) blue   (d) green

Articles 320 - 330 Quiz #2 - Open Book

QUIZ #2

1. Unsupported runs of armored cable shall be permitted to be unsupported where the cable is not more than ____ inches at terminals where flexibility is necessary.

(a) 24   (b) 30   (c) 36   (d) 48

2. Type ____, a flat cable assembly, is an assembly of parallel conductors formed intergrally with an insulating material web specifically designed for field installation in surface metal raceway.

(a) FCC   (b) FC   (c) TC   (d) SNM

3. Type AC cable shall be permitted for branch circuits and feeders in ____.

I. concealed work   II. exposed work   III. hazardous locations

(a) I, II and III   (b) II and III only   (c) I and III only   (d) I and II only

4. Voltage between the hot (ungrounded) conductors on FCC cable shall not exceed ____ volts.

(a) 50   (b) 300   (c) 150   (d) 600

5. Type ____ cable is a factory assembly of one or more conductors, each individually insulated and enclosed in a metallic sheath of interlocking tape, or a smooth or corrugated tube.

(a) MI   (b) AC   (c) MC   (d) MV

6. Which of the following may **not** be used in damp or wet locations?

(a) AC armored cable   (b) EMT   (c) open wiring   (d) rigid steel conduit

7. Type FCC cable shall be clearly and durably marked with ____.

I. material of conductors   II. maximum temperature rating   III. ampacity

(a) I only   (b) II only   (c) III only   (d) I, II and III

Articles 320 - 330 Quiz #2 - Open Book

QUIZ #2

8. The ampacity of a #250 kcmil IGS cable is ____ amperes.

(a) 119   (b) 168   (c) 215   (d) 255

9. Type FCC cable wiring system is designed for installations under ____.

(a) tile   (b) carpet   (c) carpet squares   (d) concrete

10. Nonmetallic sheath cable: If the attic is **not** accessible by stairs or permanent ladder, the cable needs to be protected only within ____ feet of a scuttle hole.

(a) 2   (b) 3   (c) 6   (d) 10

11. All type FCC cable connections shall use connectors identified for their use, installed such that ____ against dampness and liquid spillage are provided.

I. electrical continuity   II. insulation   III. sealing

(a) I only   (b) II only   (c) III only   (d) I, II and III

12. Armored cable installed in thermal insulation shall have conductors rated at ____. The ampacity of cable installed in these applications shall be that of 60 degree C conductors.

(a) 60 degrees C   (b) 194 degrees F   (c) 75 degrees C   (d) 90 degrees F

13. Type MV cables shall not be used unless identified for the use ____.

I. in cable trays   II. where exposed to direct sunlight

(a) I only   (b) II only   (c) both I and II   (d) neither I nor II

14. Type ____ cable consists of three or more flat copper conductors placed edge-to-edge and separated and enclosed within an insulating assembly.

(a) NMC   (b) AC   (c) MI   (d) FCC

15. When a flat cable assembly is installed less than ____ feet from the floor, it shall be protected by a metal cover identified for the use.

(a) 8   (b) 10   (c) 12   (d) 15

ARTICLE 332

Mineral-Insulated, Metal-Sheathed Cable Type MI

332.2. MI cable is in a single-conductor construction from #16 AWG through #4/0 AWG, two-and three-conductor from #16 AWG through #4 AWG, four-conductor from #16 AWG through #6 AWG, and seven-conductor #16, #14, #12, and #10 AWG. The exterior sheath may be of copper or alloy steel.

MI cable is the Rolls Royce of the wiring methods.

Insulation between conductors and from conductors to sheath is compressed magnesium oxide. The intent of this cable was to provide a wiring material which would be completely non-combustible, thus eliminating the fire hazards resulting from faults or excessive overloads on circuits. The cable is constructed entirely of inorganic materials. The conductors, sheath, and protective armor are of metal. The insulation which is highly compressed magnesium oxide is extremely stable at high temperatures (fusion temperature of 2800°C).

II. Installation

332.10. Uses permitted includes general use as services, feeders, and branch circuits in exposed and concealed work, in dry and wet locations, for underplaster extensions and embedded in plaster, masonry, concrete, or fill, for underground runs, or where exposed to weather, continuous moisture, oil, or other conditions not having a deteriorating effect on the metallic sheath.

The maximum operating temperature for general use (determined by present standard terminations is 185°F.
The cable itself is recognized for 482°F in special applications.

332.12. Use NOT permitted. MI cable has good resistance to corrosion, but acid soils may damage the copper sheath. Direct burial with an outer plastic or neoprene jacket would ensure protection

332.17. MI cable shall be protected in accordance with 300.4 where installed through or parallel to framing members.

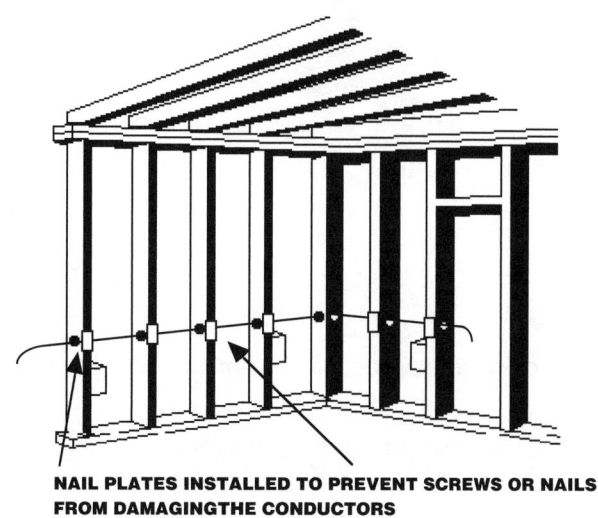

NAIL PLATES INSTALLED TO PREVENT SCREWS OR NAILS FROM DAMAGING THE CONDUCTORS

332.24. Bends shall be made so the cable is not damaged. The radius of the inner edge of any bend shall not be less than 5 times the external diameter of the sheath for cable not more than 3/4" diameter. 10 times the external diameter of the sheath for cable greater than 3/4" but not more than 1" in external diameter.

When bending a 90° stub we are in effect making a bend 1/4 of 360° or 1/4 of a circle.

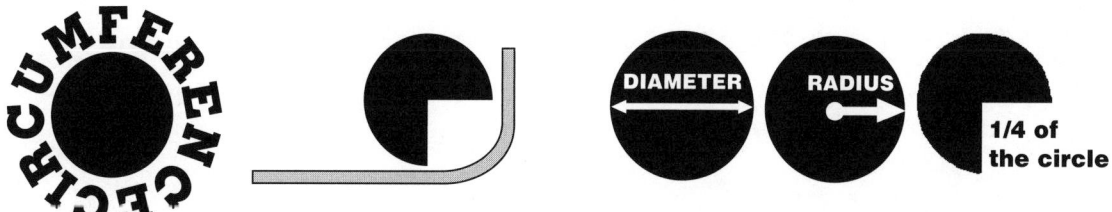

332.30. MI cable shall be supported at intervals not exceeding 6'.

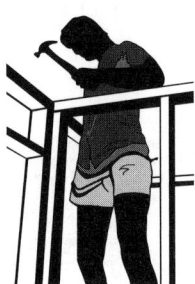

332.40(B). Where MI cable terminates, an end seal fitting shall be installed immediately after stripping to prevent the entrance of moisture into the insulation.

III. Construction

332.104. Conductors shall be of solid copper, nickel, or nickel-coated copper.

332.108. Where the outer sheath is made of copper, it shall provide an adequate path to serve as an equipment grounding. Where the outer sheath is made of steel, a separate equipment grounding conductor shall be provided.

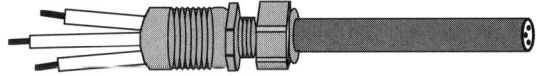

ARTICLE 334

Nonmetallic-Sheathed Cable: Types NM, NMC, and NMS

334.2. Nonmetallic-Sheathed cable is a factory assembly of two or more insulated conductors enclosed within an overall nonmetallic jacket.

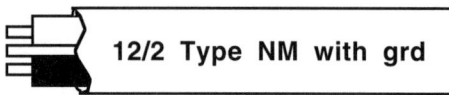

NM cable is the most popular used cables for wiring branch circuits and feeders in residential buildings. Called "Romex" by an electrician.

The NM cable has an overall covering of fibrous or plastic material which is flame-retardant and moisture-resistant.

Type NMC is similar, but the overall covering is also fungus-resistant and corrosion-resistant.

The letter "C" indiates corrosion-resistant.

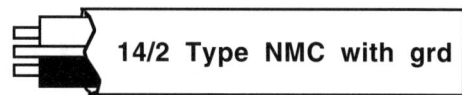

Type NMS is the same as NM cable. It is a hybrid cable containing power, signaling, communication - voice/data/video- and even optical fiber cable. NMS is the multifunction smart house cable that provides for security, convenience, etc. in a residence.

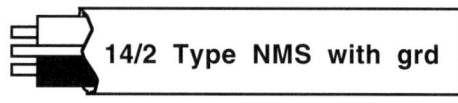

II. Installation

•Author's note: The Code for many years stated basically that NM cable could be used to wire any building up to 3 stories as long as it wasn't a hazardous location, place of assembly (100 or more people), motion picture studio, storage battery room, hoistway, service cable, or embedded in concrete.

I could wire my office, the 7-Eleven store, etc. in "romex" per the Code. I could never understand why "local Codes" prohibited wiring a commercial building in "romex". The reply I was given is that it was UNSAFE! If it was unsafe the National Electrical Code would not permit it!

This is the best part, the employee responsible for the "local" rule works at the desk from 8am to 5pm in a "safe" wiring method of steel conduit, then goes home and sleeps in the dark hours of the night in his home wired in the so-called unsafe "romex"??

The point I would mention is that NM cable has a solid copper equipment grounding conductor to carry the "UNSAFE" fault current to the circuit breaker to open the circuit. Whereas, the Electrical Metallic Tubing (thinwall) is assembled using compression and set-screw connections that over the years I have seen numerous applications where the connecting fittings had pulled apart leaving NO path for the fault current to open the circuit.

334.10. This cable may be used for concealed or exposed wiring in any kind of building or structure. One-family, two-family, multifamily, and other structures.

But for multifamily or other buildings or structures, the use of NM cable is permitted ONLY if these locations meet the requirements of Type III, IV, or V construction (Annex E).

334.10(4). May be used in cable trays in structures permitted to be Types III, IV, or V where the cables are identified for the use.

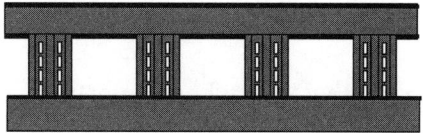

334.10(A2). Type NM cable can be installed or fished in air voids in masonry block or tile walls.

334.12. Uses not permitted.

334.12(A). Now the use of NM cable is regulated by the type of construction. It may be used if the structure is a Type III, IV, or V construction.

Annex E   Types of Construction

The five different types of construction can be summarized briefly as follows (also see Table E.2):

Type I is a Fire-Resistive construction type. All structural elements and most interior elements are required to be noncombustible. Interior, nonbearing partitions are permitted to be 1 or 2 hour rated. For nearly all occupancy types, Type I construction can be of unlimited height.

Type II construction has 3 categories, Fire-Resistive, One-Hour Rated and Non-Rated. The number of stories permitted for multifamily dwellings varies from 2 for Non-Rated and 4 for One-Hour Rated to 12 for Fire-Resistive construction.

Type III construction has 2 categories ,One-Hour Rated and Non-Rated. Both categories require the structural framework and exterior walls to be of noncombustible material. One-Hour Rated construction requires all interior partitions to be one-hour rated. Non-Rated construction allows nonbearing interior partions to be of non-rated construction. The maximum permitted number of stories for multifamily dwellings, and other structures is 2 for Non-Rated and 4 for One-Hour Rated.

(continued next page)

Type IV is a single construction category which provides for heavy timber construction. Both the structural framework and the exterior walls are required to be noncombustible except that wood members of certain minimum sizes are allowed. This construction type is seldom used for multifamily dwellings but, if used, would be permitted to be 4 stories high.

Type V construction has two categories, One-Hour Rated and Non-Rated. One-Hour Rated construction requires a minimum of one-hour rated construction throughout the building. Non-Rated construction allows nonrated interior partitions with certain restrictions. The maximum permitted number of stories for multifamily dwellings and other structures is 2 for Non-Rated and 3 for One-Hour Rated.

Defining the type of construction has caused problems for electrical personnel as they cannot readily establish if the structure is a Type III which allows the use of NM cable or is the building a Type II which prohibits the use. The designer and building department will make this judgement.

334.12(A)

Table E.1 Fire Resistance Ratings (in hours) for Type 1 through Type 5 Construction

	Type I		Type II			Type III		Type IV	Type V	
	443	332	222	111	000	211	200	2HH	111	000
Exterior Bearing Walls- Supporting more than one floor, columns, or other bearing walls..	4	3	2	1	0^1	2	2	2	1	0^1
Supporting one floor only...........	4	3	2	1	0^1	2	2	2	1	0^1
Supporting a roof only................	4	3	1	1	0^1	2	2	2	1	0^1
Interior Bearing Walls- Supporting more than one floor, columns, or other bearing walls..	4	3	2	1	0	1	0	2	1	0
Supporting one floor only...........	3	2	2	1	0	1	0	1	1	0
Supporting a roof only................	3	2	1	1	0	1	0	1	1	0
Columns- Supporting more than one floor, columns, or other bearing walls..	4	3	2	1	0	1	0	H^2	1	0
Supporting one floor only...........	3	2	2	1	0	1	0	H^2	1	0
Supporting a roof only................	3	2	1	1	0	1	0	H^2	1	0
Beams, Girders, Trusses, Arches- Supporting more than one floor, columns, or other bearing walls..	4	3	2	1	0	1	0	H^2	1	0
Supporting one floor only...........	3	2	2	1	0	1	0	H^2	1	0
Supporting a roof only................	3	2	1	1	0	1	0	H^2	1	0
Floor Construction	3	2	2	1	0	1	0	H^2	1	0
Roof Construction	2	1 1/2	1	1	0	1	0	H^2	1	0
Exterior Nonbearing Walls[3]	0^1	0^1	0^1	0^1	0^1	0^1	0^1	0^1	0^1	0^1

▨ Those members shall be permitted to be of approved combustible material.

Source: Table 3.1 from NFPA 220, *Standard on Building Construction,* 1999
[1]See A-3-1 in NFPA 220.
[2]"H" indicates heavy timber members; see text for requirements.
[3]Exterior nonbearing walls meeting the conditions of acceptance of NFPA 285, *Standard Method of Test for Evaluation of Flammabilty Characteristics of Exterior Non-Load-Bearing Wall Assemblies Containing Combustible Components Using the Intermediate-Scale, Multistory Test Apparatus,* shall be permitted to be used.

334.12(A)

Table E.2 Maximum Number of Stories for Types V, IV, and III Construction

Construction Type	Maximum Number of Stories Permitted
V Non-Rated	2
V Non-Rated, Sprinklered	3
V One-Hour Rated	3
V One-Hour Rated, Sprinklered	4
IV Heavy Timber	4
IV Heavy Timber, Sprinklered	5
III Non-Rated	2
III Non-Rated, Sprinklered	3
III One-Hour Rated	4
III One-Hour Rated, Sprinklered	5

334.12(A). Uses NOT permitted.

(2) Exposed in dropped or supended ceilings in other than one-and-two family and multifamily dwellings

(3) As service entrance cable

334.12(A). Uses NOT permitted.

(4) In commercial garages having hazardous locations as defined in 511.3

(5) In theaters and similar locations unless it is installed in buildings or portions thereof that are not required to be of fire-rated construction per the building code

(6) In motion picture studios

(7) In storage battery rooms

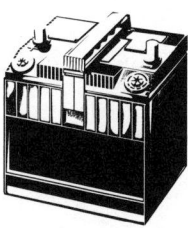

(8) In hoistways or on elevators or escalators

(9) Embedded in concrete

(10) In hazardous locations except where permitted

334.15(B). Where passing through a floor, the cable shall be enclosed in rigid metal conduit, intermediate metal conduit, electrical metallic tubing, Schedule 80 PVC, or other approved means.

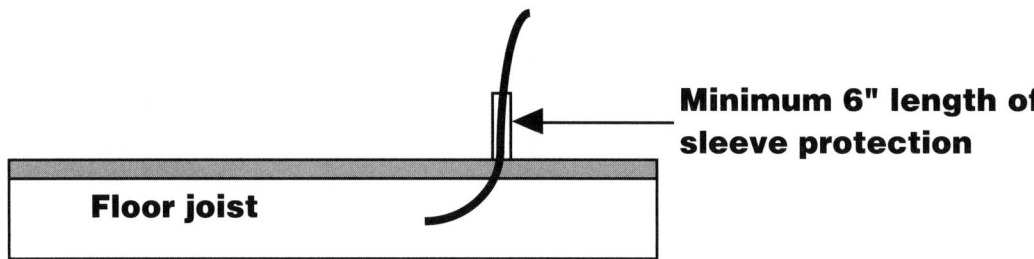

334.15(C). Where cable is run at angles with joists in unfinished basements and crawl spaces, it shall be permissible to secure cables not smaller than two #6 AWG or three #8 AWG directly to the lower edges of the joists. Smaller cables shall be run through bored holes in joists or on running boards.

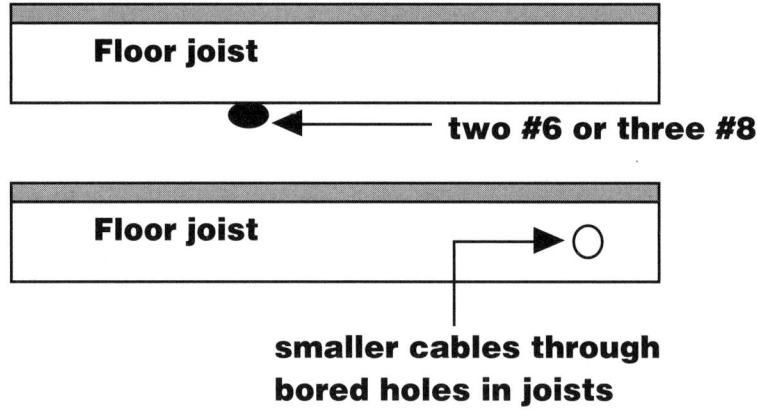

334.24. Bends in NM cable shall be made so the cable is not damaged. The radius of the curve of the inner edge of any bend shall not be less than 5 times the diameter of the cable.

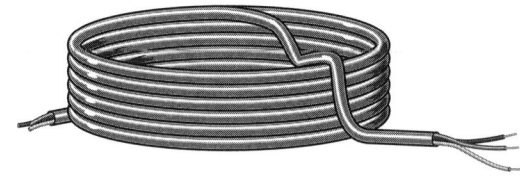

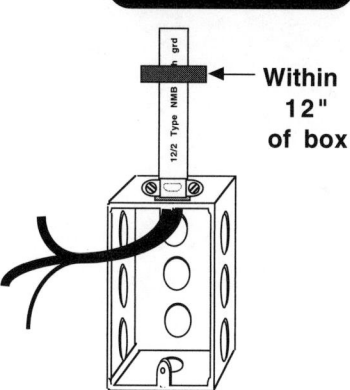

334.30. NM cable shall be supported and secured within 12" of every box and not exceeding 4 1/2' on the cable length.

334.80. The ampacity of NM cable shall be for a 60°C temperature rating. The 90°C required insulation rating ampacity can be used for derating purposes, provided the final derated ampacity does not exceed that for a 60°C rated conductor.
   Table 310.15(B2a) shall apply to cables bundled passing through a bored hole in wood framing.

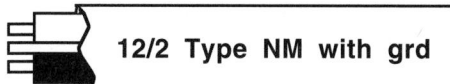

AMPACITY 60°C
INSULATION RATING 90°C

III. Construction Specifications

334.104. NM cable conductors shall be sizes #14 through #2 copper, or #12 through #2 aluminum or copper-clad aluminum.

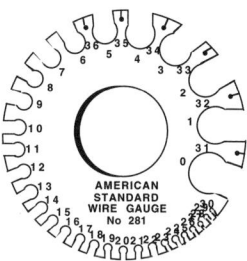

334.108. NM cable shall contain an insulated, covered, or bare equipment grounding conductor.

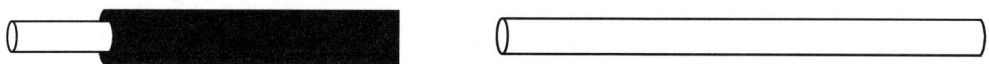

ARTICLE 336

Power and Control Tray Cable Type TC

336.2. Type TC cable is a factory assembly of two or more insulated conductors, with or without associated bare or covered grounding conductors, under a nonmetallic sheath.

II. Installation

336.10. TC cable shall be permitted:

(1) For power, lighting, control, and signal circuits

(2) In cable trays

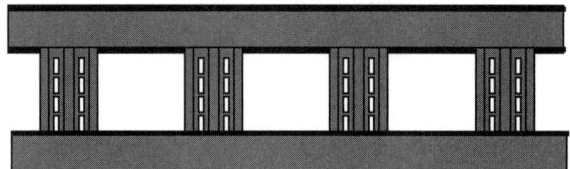

(3) In raceways

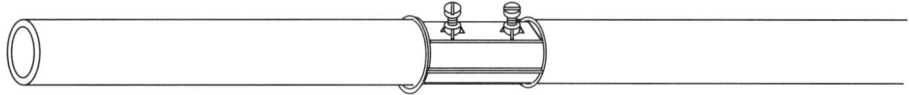

(4) Outdoors supported by a messenger wire

336.10. TC cable shall be permitted:

(5) For Class 1 circuits per Article 725 Parts II and III

(6) For non-power-limited fire alarm circuits if conductors comply with 760.49

(7) In industrial establishments where conditions of maintenance and supervision ensure that only qualified persons service the installation

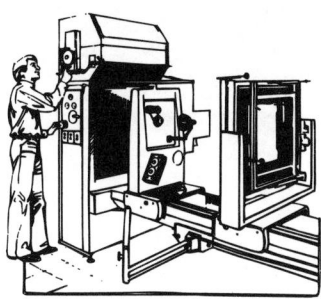

(8) In wet locations the cable shall be resistant to moisture and corrosive agents

336.12

336.12. TC cable shall NOT be installed or used:

(1) Where it will be exposed to physical damage

(2) Installed outside a raceway or cable tray, except as permitted 336.10(7)

(3) Where exposed to the direct rays of the sun, unless sunlight resistant

(4) Direct buried, unless identified for such use

336.24. Bends in TC cable shall not damage the cable. The minmum bending radius for cable without metal shielding is:

(1) Four times the overall diameter for cables 1" or less in diameter

(2) Five times the overall diameter for cables larger than 1" but not more than 2" in diameter

(3) Six times the overall diameter for cables larger than 2" in diameter

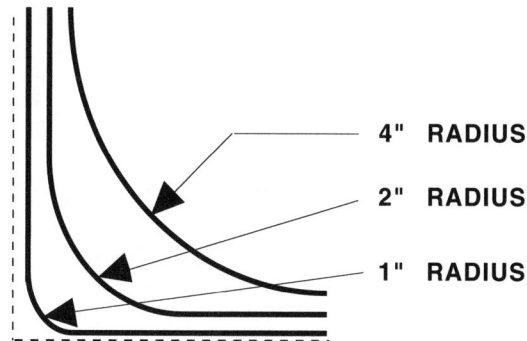

Type TC cables with metallic shielding shall have a minimum bending radius of not less than 12 times the cable overall diameter.

336.80. TC cable ampacity shall be determined by 392.11 for #14 and larger conductors, according to 402.5 for #18 through #16 conductors where installed in cable trays, and according to 310.15 when installed in raceways or messenger supported.

III. Construction Specifications

336.104. TC cable shall be in sizes #18 to #1000 kcmil copper, nickel, or nickel coated copper and sizes #12 through #1000 kcmil aluminum or copper-clad aluminum.

336.116. The outer jacket shall be flame-retardant, nonmetallic material.

ARTICLE 338

Service-Entrance Cable Types SE and USE

338.2. SE cable can be a single conductor or multiconductor assembly provided with or without an overall covering.

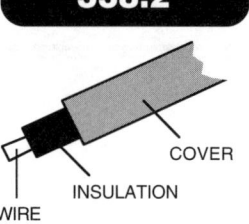

Type SE service-entrance cable has a flame-resistant, moisture-resistant covering.

SE cable

Type USE service-entrance cable, identified for underground use by the letter "U" has a moisture-resistant covering, but not required to have a flame-retardant covering.

USE cable

Type SER cable, the letter "R" is for round. Generally three XHHW insulated conductors and one bare conductor. Colors black, red, blue and the bare is used as a neutral.

SER cable

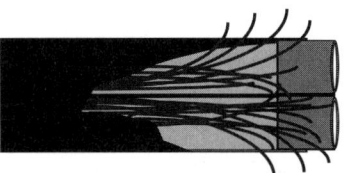
Only the grounded conductor is permitted to be bare

II. Installation

338.10. USE used for sevice laterals shall be permitted to emerge from the ground outside at terminations in meter bases or other enclosures where protected in accordance with 300.5(D).

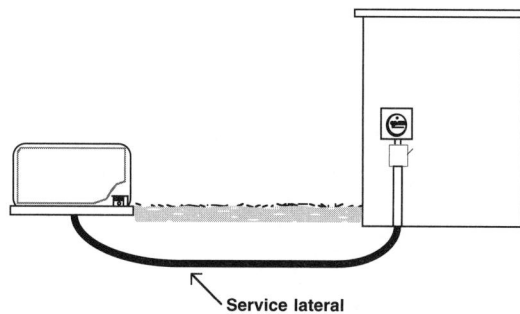
Service lateral

338.10(B2). SE cable shall be permitted for use where the insulated conductors are used for circuit wiring and the uninsulated conductor is used only for equipment grounding purposes.

Exception: Uninsulated conductors shall be permitted as a grounded conductor in accordance with 250.32, 250.140, and 225.30 through 225.40.

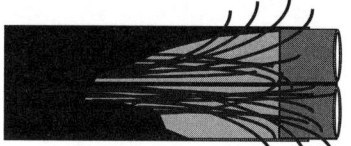

338.12. Uses **Not** Permitted for SE & USE Cable.

338.24. Bends in SE and USE cable shall be made so that the radius of the curve of the inner edge of any bend, during or after installation, shall not be less than 5 times the diameter of the cable.

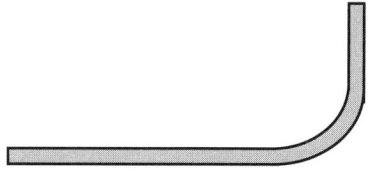

To bend is to have or take a turn, change, or deviation from a straight line without sharps breaks or angularity.

III. Construction

338.100. USE, cabled, single-conductor for underground use shall be permitted to have a bare copper conductor cabled with the assembly.

Type SE or USE containg two or more conductors shall be permitted to have one conductor uninsulated.

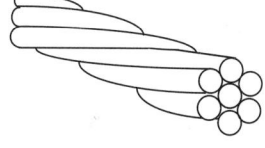

ARTICLE 340

Underground Feeder and Branch Circuit Cable Type UF

340.2. UF cable provides an economical wiring system for wet and corrosive installations. This is the cable buried underground at your residence to the post light.

A factory assembly of one or more insulated conductors with an integral or an overall covering of nonmetallic material suitable for direct burial in earth.

II. Installation

340.10(1). For underground requirements follow section 300.5.

When conduit or cable listed for direct burial are installed underground, they must be buried to a depth so that it is unlikely to be damaged by someone digging in the area at a later date. The depth requirements vary according to the type of raceway or cable. Rigid non-metallic conduit will not be damaged by someone trenching with a shovel but UF cable might be, so UF cable must be buried deeper than PVC conduit.

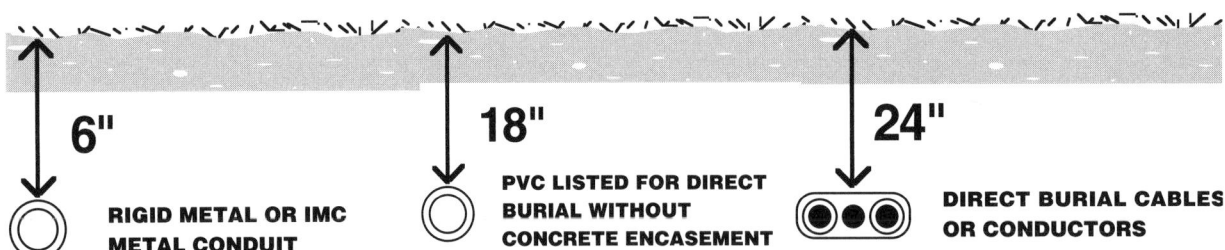

Table 300.5: Residential branch circuits rated 120 volts or less with GFCI protection and maximum overcurrent protection of 20 amps UF cable can be buried 12".

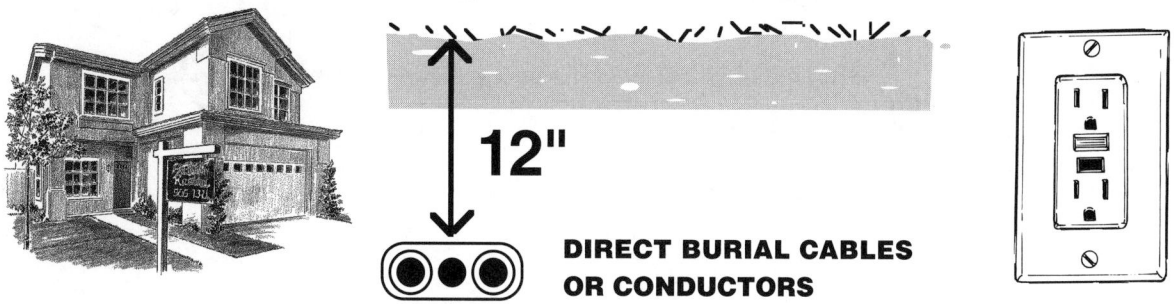

300.5(C). When underground cables are installed under a building they shall be installed in a raceway. The required raceway must extend beyond the outside walls of the building.

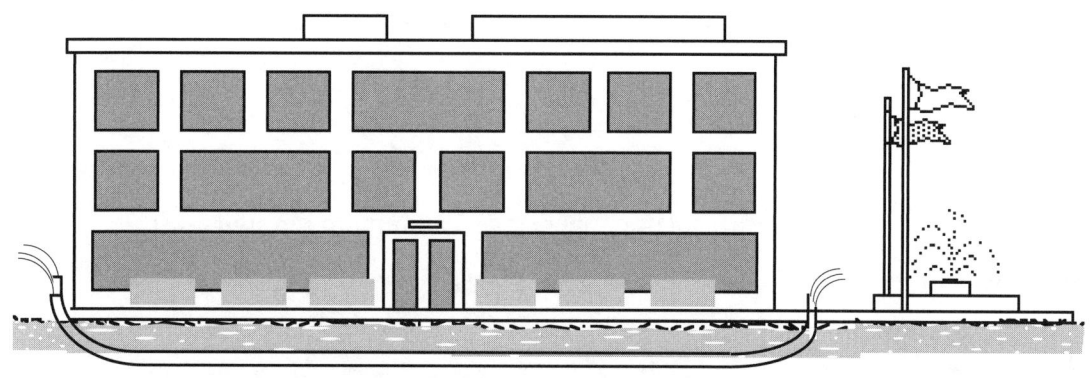

A CABLE INSTALLED UNDER A BUILDING MUST BE IN A RACEWAY

300.5(D1) Where direct buried conductors and cables emerging from grade and specified in columns 1 and 4 of Table 300.5 shall be protected by enclosures or raceways from the burial depth to at least 8 feet above the ground. This protection shall not be required to be more than 18 inches below grade level.

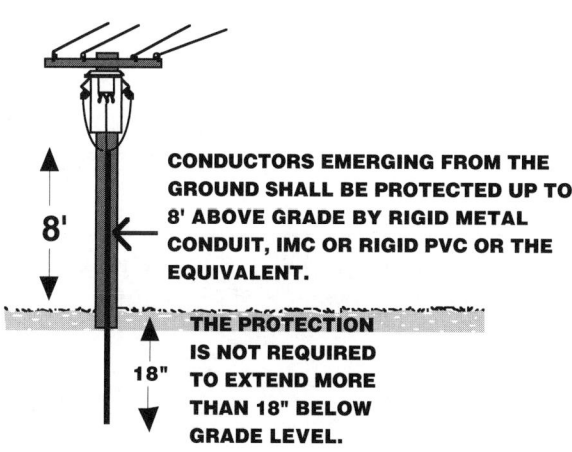

340.12. Uses NOT permitted are basically the same as NM cable (romex). UF cable is NOT permitted to be exposed to the sun, unless identified as sunlight resistant.

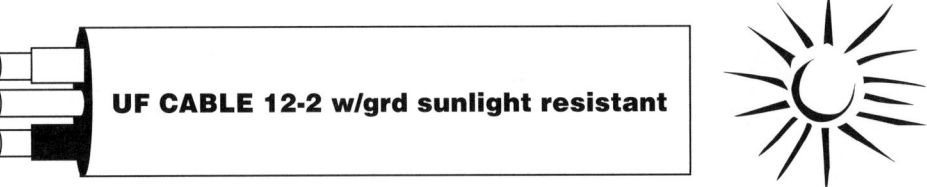

340.24. The bending radius of UF is the same as romex, 5 times the diameter of the cable.

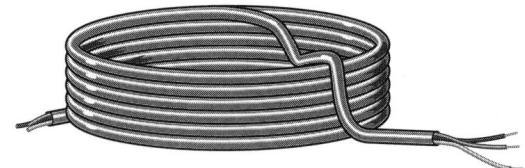

III. Construction Specifications

340.104. UF conductors shall be sizes #14 copper or #12 aluminum through #4/0.

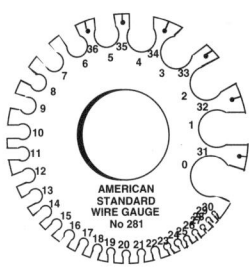

340.112. UF shall have a moisture-proof insulation. Where used as a substitute wiring method for NM cable (romex), the conductor insulation shall be rated 90°C.

340.116. The overall covering shall be flame retardant; moisture, fungus, and corrosion resistant; and suitable for direct burial in earth.

Articles 332 - 340 Quiz #1 - Open Book

QUIZ #1

1. Nonmetallic sheath cable must be supported within ____ of a metal box.

(a) 6"   (b) 12"   (c) 24"   (d) 48"

2. Which of the following statements about MI cable is correct?

(a) it may be used in any hazardous location
(b) it may be mounted flush on a wall in a wet location
(c) it shall be supported every 10 feet
(d) a single run of cable shall not contain more than four quarter bends

3. The ampacity of type UF cable shall be that of ____ conductors.

(a) 60°F   (b) 75°C   (c) 140°C   (d) 60°C

4. UF cable is not permitted in ____.

(a) storage battery rooms   (b) commercial garages
(c) motion picture studios   (d) all of these

5. ____ cable shall be flame-retardant, moisture-resistant, fungus-resistant, and corrosion-resistant.

(a) MI   (b) USE   (c) NMC   (d) NM

6. MI cable has ____.

(a) solid copper conductors
(b) outer sheath to provide mechanical protection
(c) an adequate path for grounding purposes
(d) all of these

7. Type UF cable shall be permitted for interior wiring in ____ locations.

I. dry   II. wet   III. corrosive

(a) I only   (b) I or II   (c) I or III   (d) I, II or III

TH
164

QUIZ #1

Articles 332 - 340 Quiz #1 - Open Book

8. The ampacity of types NM and NMC cable shall be that of ____ conductors.

(a) 60° C   (b) 75° C   (c) 90° C   (d) 140° C

9. The radius of the inner edge of any bend shall not be less than ____ times the diameter of the metallic sheath of MI cable and not more than 3/4" in external diameter.

(a) 5   (b) 3   (c) 8   (d) 10

10. Which of the following is **true** concerning type NM cable?

**(a) it may be installed where exposed to corrosive fumes
(b) it may be fished in air voids in masonry block or tile walls
(c) it may be embedded in masonry, concrete, or plaster
(d) it may be covered with plaster, adobe, or similar finish**

11. Type SE service-entrance cables shall be permitted in interior wiring systems where all of the circuit conductors of the cable are of the ____ type.

I. rubber-covered   II. thermoplastic   III. metal

(a) I and II only   (b) II only   (c) II and III only   (d) I, II and III

12. NM cable passing through a floor shall be enclosed in a conduit extending at least ____ above the floor.

(a) 6"   (b) 8"   (c) 12"   (d) 18"

Articles 332 - 340 Quiz #2 - Open Book

QUIZ #2

1. SE cable used to supply ____ shall not be subject to conductor temperatures in excess of the temperature specified for the type of insulation involved.

(a) lighting   (b) appliances   (c) motors   (d) generators

2. Type UF cable shall be permitted for ____.

(a) service entrance cable   (b) embedded in concrete
(c) direct burial   (d) hoistways

3. Which of the following statements about the protection of nonmetallic sheathed cable from physical damage is/are correct?

I. When passing through a floor the cable shall be enclosed in a pipe or conduit extending at least 6 inches above the floor.
II. When run across the top of the floor joists in an accessible attic, the cable shall be protected by guard strips.

(a) I only   (b) II only   (c) both I and II   (d) neither I nor II

4. Nonmetallic sheathed cable, NMC, must be supported at intervals not exceeding ____.

(a) 4'   (b) 4 1/2'   (c) 6'   (d) none of these

5. Type UF cable is manufactured in sizes #14 through # ___ copper.

(a) 4/0   (b) 4   (c) 6   (d) 10

6. Disregarding any exceptions, Type MI cables shall not be permitted to be used ____.

(a) where exposed to oil and gasoline
(b) where exposed to destructive corrosive conditions
(c) where embedded in plaster or concrete whether above or below grade
(d) In any of the above conditions

7. Bending of nonmetallic sheathed cable shall not be less than ____ the radius of the inner edge of the cable.

(a) 2 times the diameter of   (b) 3 times the circumference of
(c) 4 times the circumference of   (d) 5 times the diameter of

Articles 332 - 340 Quiz #2 - Open Book

QUIZ #2

8. Types NM, NMC, and NMS cables shall **NOT** be used as follows _____.

(a) in exposed work.
(b) as service-entrance cable.
(c) fished in voids in masonry blocks
(d) on the outside walls of masonry block or tile

9. Type TC cables with metallic shielding shall have a minimum bending radius of not less than ___ times the cable overall diameter.

(a) ten (b) twelve (c) twenty four (d) thirty six

10. For general wiring, ____ type cable containing one or more conductors is approved for direct burial in earth.

(a) THW (b) USE (c) THHW (d) THHN

11. Disregarding any exceptions, Type UF cable shall be permitted to be ____.

(a) used in hoistways
(b) used as service entrance cable
(c) used in storage battery rooms
(d) buried directly in the earth for use underground

12. Use of UF cable is permitted ____.

(a) where embedded in poured concrete
(b) in theaters
(c) for wiring in wet locations
(d) as service entrance conductors

TH

QUIZ #3

Articles 332 - 340 Quiz #3 - Open Book

1. Power and control tray cable can be installed ____.

I. as open cables on brackets or cleats   II. in cable trays in hazardous locations

(a) I only   (b) II only   (c) both I and II   (d) neither I nor II

2. NM cable insulation rating shall be ____.

(a) 60°C   (b) 75°C   (c) 90°C   (d) 104°F

3. The overall covering of UF cable shall be ____.

I.   suitable for direct burial in the earth
II. flame-retardant
III. moisture, fungus and corrosion resistant

(a) III and II only   (b) I only   (c) I and III only   (d) I, II and III

4. Type USE service entrance cable, identified for underground use in a cabled assembly, may have a ____ concentric.

(a) bare copper   **(b) covered metal**
(c) bare aluminum   **(d) covered**

5. Which of the following statements about MI cable is correct?

(a) it may be used in any hazardous location
(b) a single run of cable shall not contain more than the equivalent of 4 quarter bends
(c) it shall be securely supported at intervals not exceeding 10 feet
(d) it may be mounted flush on supporting surfaces in a wet location

6. The overall covering for type NMC cable shall be ____.

I.   flame retardant
II. moisture resistant
III. fungus resistant
IV. corrosion resistant
V.   all of these

(a) II and III   (b) I and III   (c) II, III and IV   (d) V

QUIZ #3

Articles 332 - 340 Quiz #3 - Open Book

7. ____ of insulating material shall be permitted to be used without boxes in exposed cable wiring.

I. Switch devices   II. Outlet devices   III. Tap devices

(a) I only   (b) II only   (c) III only   (d) I, II and III

8. If SE or USE cable consists of two or more conductors, one shall be permitted to be ____.

(a) insulated   (b) green   (c) tagged   (d) uninsulated

9. MI cable shall be permitted ____.

I.   as feeders and branch circuits
II. for wet and dry locations
III. for concealed or exposed

(a) I only   (b) II only   (c) III only   (d) I, II and III

10. The temperature limitation of MI cable is based on the ____.

(a) ambient temperature   (b) conductor insulation
(c) insulating materials used in the end seal   (d) none of these

11. The power conductors in type NMS cable are manufactured in sizes ____.

(a) #14 - #6   (b) #14 - #4   (c) #14 - #2   (d) #12 - #2

12. Type UF cable shall be permitted ____.

(a) in a theater
(b) in commercial garages
(c) where embedded in poured concrete
(d) for interior wiring in wet or corrosive locations

ARTICLE 342

Intermediate Metal Conduit Type IMC

342.2. IMC has a wall with less thickness than rigid metal conduit, but has a thicker wall than EMT. IMC uses the same threading method and standard fittings for rigid metal conduit and has the same general application rules as rigid metal conduit. It has about 25% less steel than rigid metal which makes it lighter in weight.

By the IMC wall being thinner the inside diameter allows for more conductor fill. Table C4 allows four #6 XHHW conductors in a 3/4" IMC. Wheareas a 3/4" rigid metal conduit in Table C8 allows only three #6 XHHW conductors due to the smaller inside diameter.

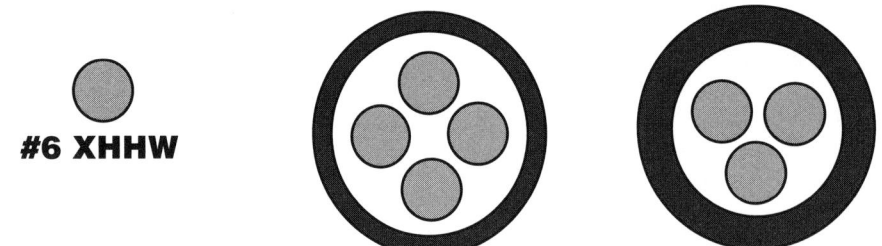

II. Installation

342.10(B). IMC, elbows, couplings, and fittings shall be permitted to be installed in concrete, in direct contact with the earth, or in areas subject to severe corrosive influences where protected by corrosion protection and judged suitable for the condition.

342.14. Where practicable, dissimilar metals in contact anywhere in the system shall be avoided to eliminate the possibility of galvanic action.

Aluminum fittings and enclosures shall be permitted to be used with IMC. Tests have established that aluminum fittings and enclosures create no difficulty when used with steel raceways.

342.20. IMC is permitted to be installed in sizes 1/2" to 4" trade size.

FPN: See 300.1(C) for the metric designator and trade sizes.

Table 300.1(C)

Metric Designator	Trade Size
12	3/8"
16	1/2"
21	3/4"
27	1"
35	1 1/4"
41	1 1/2"
53	2"
63	2 1/2"
78	3"
91	3 1/2"
103	4"
129	5"
153	6"

Note. The metric designators and trade sizes are for identification purposes only and are not actual dimensions.

342.24. The radius of the curve of any field bend to the centerline of the conduit shall not be less than indicated in Table 2, Chapter 9.

Table 2 Radius of Conduit and Tubing Bends

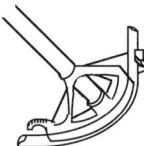

Conduit or Tubing Size	One Shot and Full Shoe Benders	Other Bends
Trade Size	Inch	Inch
1/2"	4"	4"
3/4"	4 1/2"	5"
1"	5 3/4"	6"
1 1/4"	7 1/4"	8"
1 1/2"	8 1/4"	10"
2"	9 1/2"	12"
2 1/2"	10 1/2"	15"
3"	13"	18"
3 1/2"	15"	21"
4"	16"	24"
5"	24"	30"
6"	30"	36"

342.26. There shall not be more than the equivalent of four quarter bends (360° total) between pull points.

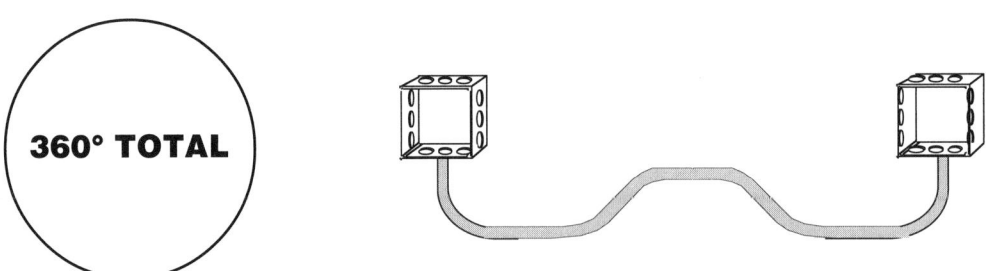

342.28. All cut ends shall be reamed or otherwise finished to remove rough edges.

Where conduit is threaded in the field, a standard cutting die with a taper of 1 in 16 (3/4" taper per foot) shall be used.

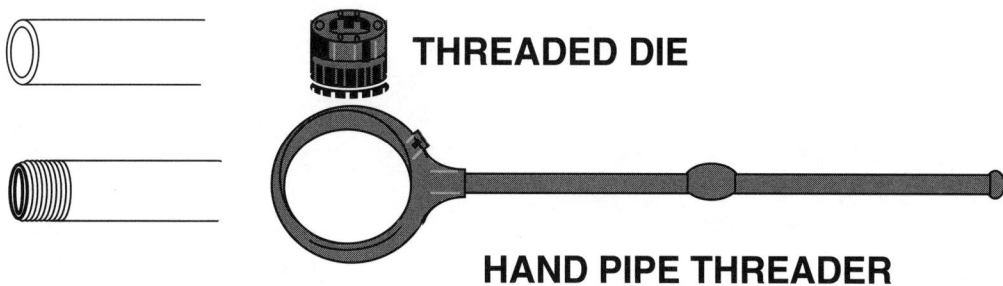

342.30(B). Conduit is to be clamped within 3 feet of a box and every 10 feet in length.

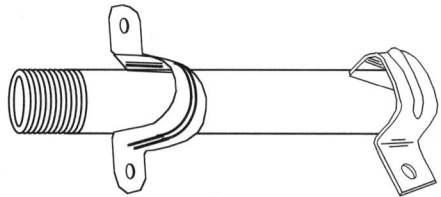

342.30(C). IMC is permitted to be unsupported (clamped) if it is an unbroken length without a coupling not more than 18 inches long and without oversized, concentric or eccentric knockouts.

III. Construction Specifications

342.130. Standard length of IMC is 10 feet, including attached coupling, both ends threaded.

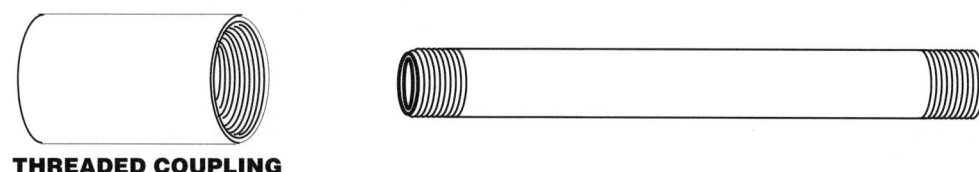

ARTICLE 344

Rigid Metal Conduit Type RMC

344.2. Rigid conduit is the same dimensions as standard water pipe. The *heavier wall* makes rigid conduit a better choice for mechanical protection from abuse. It is treated to make the inside wall smooth and coated outside to protect against corrosion. When plated with zinc during the galvanizing process is where it gets its name; *galvanized conduit*. Plastic covered rigid conduit is used in the industry around corrosive fumes.

GALVANIZED RIGID STEEL

Metallic conduits provide mechanical protection as well as making the conductors accessible. Since rigid conduit is threaded, various threaded fittings are used in its installation.

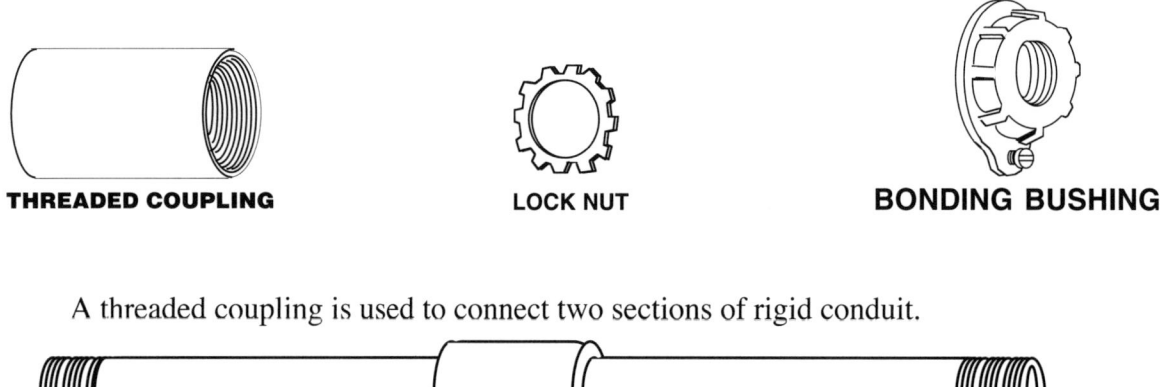

THREADED COUPLING **LOCK NUT** **BONDING BUSHING**

A threaded coupling is used to connect two sections of rigid conduit.

A locknut is used on each side of a wall on the box to secure the conduit to the box.

Rigid steel conduit looks like water pipe but it is softer to make bending easier. It has a 60% thicker wall than E.M.T. and provides the most protection for the conductors. Nails cannot be driven through rigid steel conduit. Rigid steel conduit is manufactured in sizes 1/2" to 6".

A rigid steel conduit system is more expensive than E.M.T. and is used where cost is not a major factor and the conditions require more protection than is provided with E.M.T., such as in hazardous locations where any spark must be totally confined inside the conduit to prevent ignition of gasoline fumes, or in an area where the conduit may be subject to damage such as a truck driving over it.

Rigid steel conduit is threaded on the job, in most instances, but compression and set screw fittings are available.

Set screw and compression type fittings for rigid steel conduit are more expensive and are generally used only when it is not practical to thread the conduit, such as a stub-up too close to a wall.

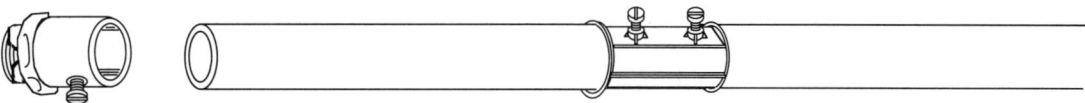

THREADED COUPLING   THREADED RIGID ALUMINUM CONDUIT

Rigid aluminum conduit is used often where more protection is required than is provided by E.M.T. and in highly corrosive areas. Rigid aluminum conduit is manufactured in sizes 1/2" to 6".

Rigid aluminum conduit weighs the same as thinwall E.M.T. conduit even though the wall thickness of the aluminum is much greater. Its light weight and ease of installation and resistance to corrosion is well suited for certain applications.

In installations in poured concrete, care must be taken to ensure that the concrete mixture does not contain calcium chloride which is sometimes used to speed up the concrete setting process. Chloride can lead to the disintegration of aluminum in a short period of time. Without the chloride in the concrete, a limited chemical reaction on the conduit surface forms a self-stopping coating which prevents corrosion for the life of the structure.

Rigid aluminum is threaded in the field in most installations but set screw and compression fittings are available. Care should be taken not to mix steel fittings with aluminum conduit or galvanic action can occur.

344.24. Bends. The radius of the curve of any field bend to the centerline of the conduit shall not be less than indicated in Table 2, Chapter 9.

Don't confuse the hickey with the roll-type hand bender. Both are used to bend conduit by hand, but in totally different ways. The roll-type bender supports the walls of the conduit and provides a bending radius that conforms to the Code requirements.

The hickey is used for rigid conduit only and the person holding the handle must form the bend as well as the radius as the bender is applied. This must be done in such a manner so as not to flatten or kink the conduit. The hickey is used somewhat like the hydraulic bender as you make segment bends. Several segment 10° bends are made to complete the bend at the proper radius. Hickeys should not be used to bend EMT because very little support is given to the walls of the conduit.

It would require nine 10° segment bends to make a 90° stub-up bend.

Effective hand bending with a hickey type bender is limited to 1/2", 3/4", and 1" rigid conduit. All bends made with a *hickey* bender should be made on the floor.

344.30(B)

344.30(B). Rigid metal conduit shall be supported with one of the following:

(1) Supported at intervals not exceeding 10 feet

(2) The distance between supports for straight runs of conduit shall be permitted with Table 344.30(B2) provided the conduit is made up of *threaded* **couplings**

Table 344.30(B2) Supports for Rigid Metal Conduit

Conduit Size	Maximum Distance Between Rigid Metal Conduit Supports
Trade Size	Feet
1/2" - 3/4"	10'
1"	12'
1 1/4" - 1 1/2"	14'
2" - 2 1/2"	16'
3" and larger	20'

•Note: Table 344.30(B2) can be used if the conduit is THREADED.

Example: If made up with threadless couplings, a 1" rigid metal conduit shall be supported at least every ____ feet.

(a) 6   (b) 8   (c) 10   (d) 12

The key word is **"threadless"** couplings. Section 344.30(B1) states a conduit shall be supported at least every 10'. 344.30(B2) states if made up with **threaded** couplings, you can use Table 344.30(B2) for supports and extend to 12'.

With threaded conduit and couplings the conduit wall has more self supporting strength than with compression or set screw threadless fittings.

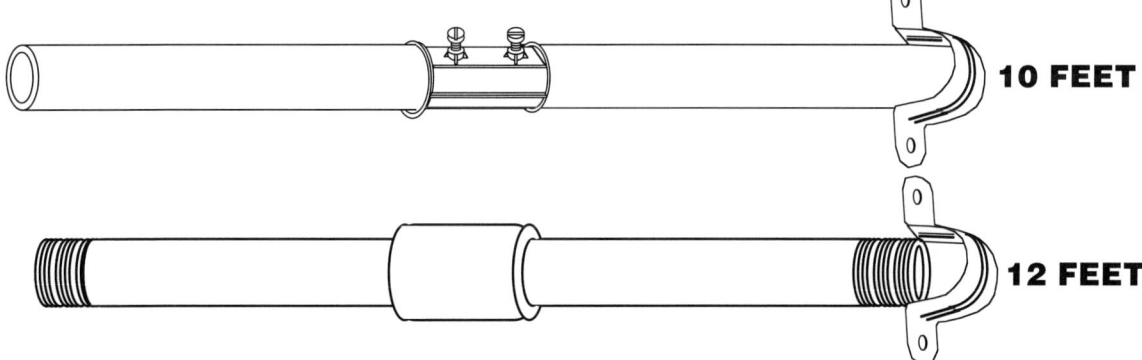

344.30(C). Rigid metal conduit is permitted to be unsupported if it is an unbroken length without a coupling not more than 18 inches long and without oversized, concentric or eccentric knockouts.

ARTICLE 348

Flexible Metal Conduit Type FMC

348.2. FMC is a raceway of circular cross section made of helically wound, formed, interlocked metal strip. Known to the electrician as "flex" or "greenfield".

Flexible metal conduit, is used whenever a connection is made to a type of *adjustable* equipment, such as a drive belt motor or equipment that may vibrate in use.

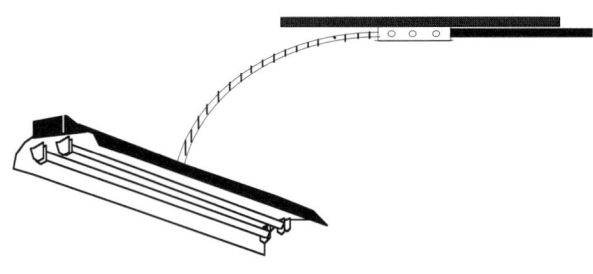

Flexible metal conduit is used often for *fixture whips*. Fixture whips are 4 to 6 feet in length and are used to connect light fixtures to a junction box such as in a suspended ceiling. This is done often in commercial buildings. The above ceiling wiring is installed with EMT or another wiring method to a junction box. The fixture whip is installed from the junction box to the light fixture.

II. Installations

348.10. FMC shall be permitted to be used in exposed and concealed locations.

348.12. FMC shall NOT be used in the following:

(1) In wet locations

(2) In hoistways, other than permitted in 620.21(A1)

(3) In storage battery rooms

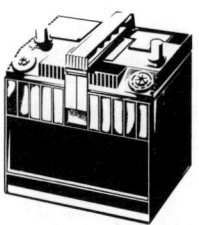

(4) In any hazardous location except as permitted by other articles in the NEC®.

(5) Where exposed to materials having a deteriorating effect on the insulated conductors, such as oil or gasoline

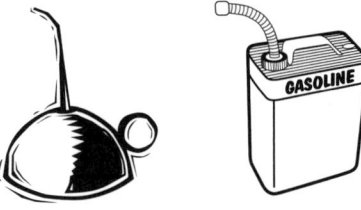

(6) Underground or embedded in concrete

(7) Where subject to physical damage

348.20. Flexible metal conduit minimum size is 1/2", trade size 3/8" is permitted for:

(1) To enclose the stranded leads of motors to the junction box

(2) In lengths not to exceed 6 feet for any of the following:
a. For utilization equipment
b. As part of a listed assembly
c. For tap conductors to light fixtures per 410.67(C)

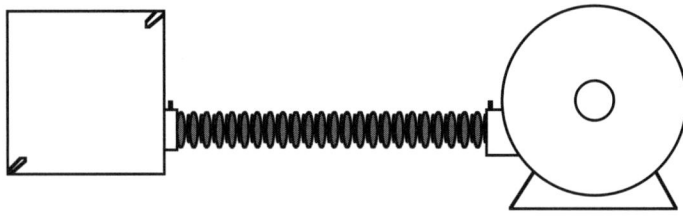

(3) For manufactured wiring systems per 604.6(A)

(4) In hoistways per 620.21(A1)

(5) As part of a listed assembly to connect wired light fixture sections per 410.137(C)

348.22. The number of conductors installed in 3/8" FMC shall not exceed the number permitted in Table 348.22.

348.60. Grounding and Bonding. Where used to connect equipment where flexibility is required after installation, an equipment grounding conductor shall be installed.

Where flexibility is not required after installation, FMC shall be permitted to be used as an equipment grounding conductor when installed per 250.118(5).

Listed flexible metal conduit (greenfield) and listed flexible metal tubing can be used as an equipment grounding conductor if the conditions listed are met:

Flexible Metal Conduit - Flexible Metal Tubing

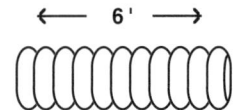

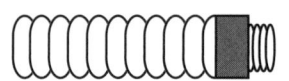
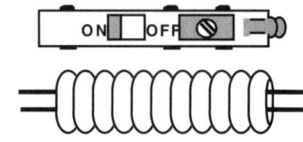

Length shall not exceed 6 feet **Fittings must be listed for grounding** **Protected at 20A or less**

348.60

Any length of flex can be used in a circuit, but when the flex is longer than 6 feet it must contain an **internal** equipment grounding conductor (no longer called a bonding jumper). The equipment grounding conductor is sized from Table 250.122 based on the overcurrent device (fuse or breaker).

The length in the **ground return path** can not exceed 6 feet.

The sketch shown below would be in violation with the two pieces of flex (2' and 5') that equal a total of 7 feet in the ground return path.

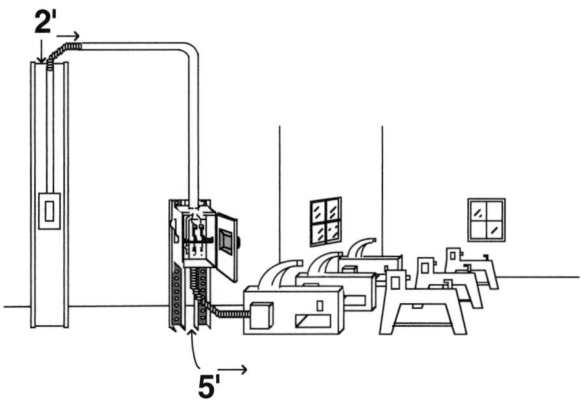

Where required or installed, equipment grounding conductors shall be installed per 250.134(B).

The equipment grounding where installed with a raceway, cable, or cord must be contained **within** the same raceway, cable or cord. For AC equipment it is a **violation** to install the equipment grounding conductor outside of the conduit. By containing the conductors together the circuit will have a minimum AC inductive reactance because of the mutual cancellation of the magnetic fields around the conductors.

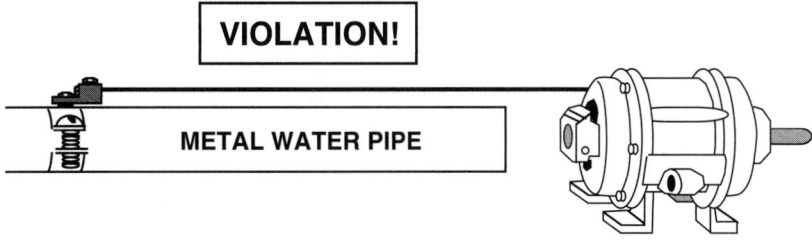

Where required or installed, equipment bonding jumpers shall be installed per 250.102.

The equipment bonding jumper shall be permitted to be installed inside or outside of a raceway or enclosure. Where installed on the outside of a conduit or enclosure it shall not exceed 6 feet in length. As shown in the example with the expansion coupling, sometimes it is impossible to install the bonding jumper inside of the conduit. Where installed inside of a raceway, the equipment bonding jumper shall comply with 250.148, which requires maintaining continuity and connection to a grounding screw. Section 250.119 requires a grounding conductor to be bare or green in color.

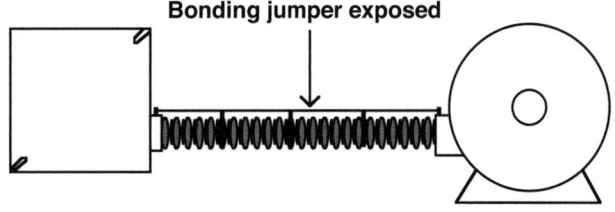

ARTICLE 350

Liquidtight Flexible Metal Conduit Type LFMC

350.2. Liquidtight (called sealtight in the industry) is a raceway of circular cross section having an outer liquidtight, nonmetallic, sunlight-resistant jacket over an inner flexible metal core.

Liquidtight flexible metal conduit is another type of flexible metal conduit, which has a *thermoplastic outer jacket* that is liquidtight. This type is used to connect equipment that is located outside and may vibrate in use such as an air conditioning compressor at a house or apartment.

II. Installation

350.10. Liquidtight shall be permitted to be used exposed or concealed in locations as follows:

(1) Where conditions of installation, operation, or maintenance require flexibility or protection from liquids, vapors, or solids.

(2) As permitted in hazardous locations where specifically approved.

(3) For direct burial where listed and marked for the purpose.

350.12. Liquidtight shall NOT be used:

(1) Where subject to physical damage.

(2) Where any combination of ambient and conductor temperature produces an operating temperature in excess of that for which the material is approved.

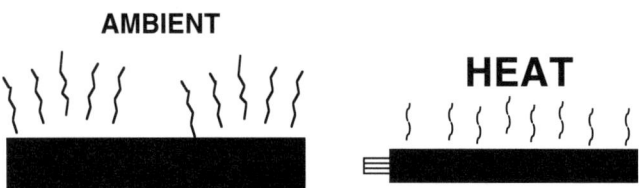

•Note: Most of the Code sections on bends, grounding, securing for liquidtight flexible metal conduit follow the Code rules as Article 348 for flexible metal conduit.

ARTICLE 352

Rigid Polyvinyl Chloride Conduit Type PVC

352.2. The PVC conduits include fiber conduit, rigid polyvinyl chloride, polyethylene conduit, and styrene conduit.

Polyvinyl chloride or PVC, as the electrcian calls it, is used generally for underground wiring as it has excellent moisture and corrosion resistance.

Except for hazardous locations and for support of fixtures, rigid PVC can generally be used wherever rigid metal conduit is allowed.

Polyvinyl choloride (PVC) conduit is manufactured in two types commonly used in residential, commercial, and industrial installations in sizes 1/2" to 6". The required color for electrical PVC conduit is *grey* and water PVC pipe is white.

Rigid schedule 40 is used underground and in walls, ceilings and floors where not exposed to physical damage.

SCHEDULE 40 PVC

Rigid schedule 80 is used where more protection from physical damage is required, such as protecting conductors running up a pole.

SCHEDULE 80 PVC (heavy wall)

II. Installation

352.10. Above ground applications of PVC conduit must be Schedule 40 or Schedule 80 PVC conduit, which is the only PVC conduit listed for above ground use.

352.12. It should be remembered that PVC conduit is NOT permitted in ducts, plenums, and other air handling spaces per 300.22.

Only MI cable, MC cable, EMT, flexible metal tubing, Flexible metal conduit not over 4', IMC, or rigid metal conduit without nonmetallic covering shall be installed in ducts or plenums specifically fabricated to transport environmental air.

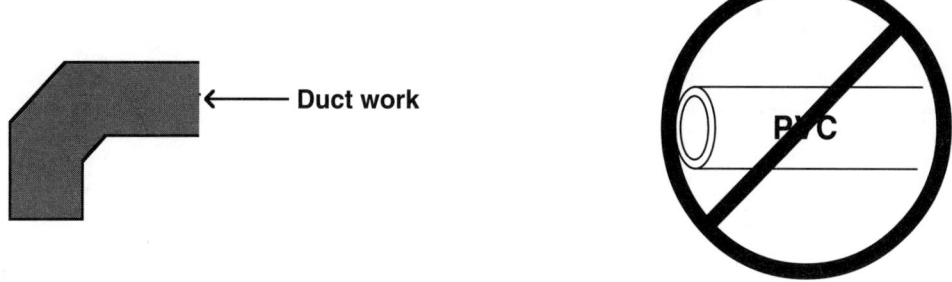

•Generally speaking it has been made clear that the Code panel oppose nonmetallic wiring methods in ducts and plenums, except for nonmetallic cable assemblies that are specially listed for such use. Using PVC would not propagate a fire, it would contribute to the smoke and provide additional flammable material in the air duct.

352.12(B). PVC is NOT permitted to support light fixtures or other equipment.

352.30(A). PVC shall be securely fastened within 3 feet of each box. PVC listed for securing at other than 3 feet shall be installed within its listing.

352.30(B). PVC shall be suppported as required in Table 352.30.

Table 352.30 Support of Rigid Polyvinyl Chloride Conduit

Conduit Size	Maximum Spacing Between Supports
1/2" - 1"	3'
1 1/4" - 2"	5'
2 1/2" - 3"	6'
3 1/2" - 5"	7'
6"	8'

352.30(C). PVC conduit is permitted to be unsupported (clamped) if it is an unbroken length without a coupling not more than 18 inches long and without oversized, concentric or eccentric knockouts.

352.44. Expansion fittings shall be provided to compensate for thermal expansion and contraction where the length change, in accordance with Table 352.44, is expected to be 1/4" or greater in a straight run between scurely mounted boxes, etc.

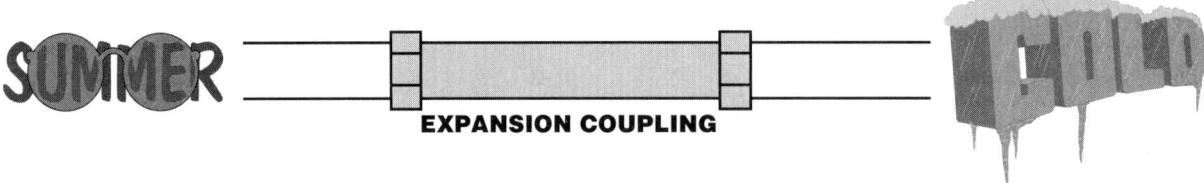

352.60. Where equipment grounding is required, a separate equipment grounding conductor shall be installed in the conduit.

III. Construction Specifications

352.100. PVC above ground, shall be flame retardant, resistant to impact and crushing, resistant to distortion from heat, and resistant to low temperature and sunlight effects.

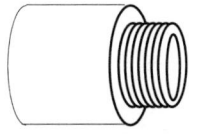
MALE ADAPTER

PVC COUPLNG

PVC male adapters (connectors) are used to connect the conduit to a box, etc.

The fittings (connectors, couplings) are glued to the PVC using a solvent-cement which will *weld* the PVC fittings to the PVC conduit. The area to be glued must be clean and dry.

PVC glue is specially formulated for this purpose and has a shelf life. Moisture destroys PVC glue, the lid must be promptly replaced after use and the conduit and fittings must be clean and dry before applying the glue.

PVC couplings are used to connect two pieces of conduit together.

Polyvinyl choloride (PVC) conduit is shipped in 10 foot lengths with one coupling per length.

PVC can be bent without using bending tools. PVC can be bent by heating, forming the bend, and then cooling the conduit with cold water. An open flame should n*ever* be used to heat PVC.

HEAT GUN

A heat gun using hot-air is used, but the simplest is a "hot box", which has electric heating elements and rollers to help heat the conduit all around the place where the bend is to be made. 2" and larger sizes require internal support during bending, which can be provided by plugging the ends before heating. The expanded, heated air inside prevents the walls from collapsing while soft.

PVC can be cut several ways. Most often a hacksaw with a fine tooth blade is used.

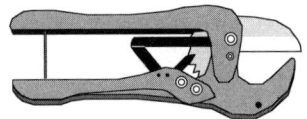 A special PVC cutting tool is also a very easy way to cut the conduit.

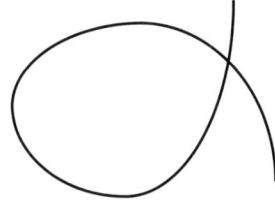 I have even used a nylon string in tight places to cut the PVC. By see-sawing the string back and forth, the friction created actually cuts the plastic conduit.

After cutting the PVC the ends should be reamed both inside and outside.

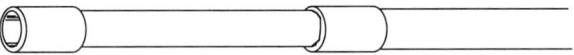

ARTICLE 353

High Density Polyethylene Conduit Type HDPE Conduit

353.2. This was a new Article in the 2005 Code. HDPE conduit was in the previous Code in Tables C10 and C10(A) for conduit fill. It was shown in the Tables along with PVC Schedule 40 with the same wire fill.

HDPE is a nonmetallic raceway of circular cross section in discrete lengths or in continuous lengths from a reel.

II. Installation

353.10. HDPE conduit is permitted in direct burial installations in earth or concrete or above ground where encased in not less than 2 inches of concrete.

353.12. HDPE conduit shall NOT be used under the following conditions:

(1) Where exposed

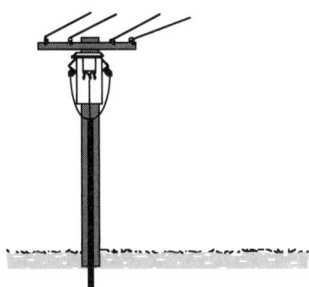

(2) Within a building

(3) In hazardous locations, except as permitted by other articles of the NEC®.

(4) Where subject to ambient temperatures in excess of 122°F unless listed otherwise

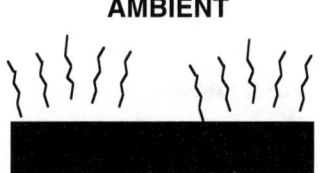

(5) For conductors or cables operating at a temperature higher the the HDPE conduit listed operating temperature rating

Exception: Conductors or cables rated at a temperature higher than the HDPE conduit listed temperature rating shall be permitted to be installed in HDPE conduit, provided they are not operated at a temperature higher than the HDPE conduit listed temperature rating.

353.20(A). HDPE conduit smaller than 1/2" shall NOT be used.

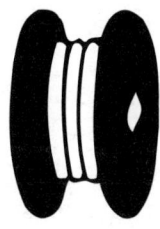

353.20(B). HDPE conduit larger than 6" shall NOT be used.

353.24. Bends shall be permitted to be made manually without auxiliary equipment, and the radius of the curve to the centerline of such bends shall not be less than shown in Table 354.24.

Table 354.24 Minimum Bending Radius for Nonmetallic Underground Conduit with Conductors (NUCC)

Conduit Size	Minimum Bending Radius
1/2"	10"
3/4"	12"
1"	14"
1 1/4"	18"
1 1/2"	20"
2"	26"
2 1/2"	36"
3"	48"
4"	60"

353.60. Where equipment grounding is required, a separate equipment grounding conductor shall be installed in the conduit.

III. Construction Specifications

353.100. HDPE conduit shall be composed of high density polyethylene that is resistant to moisture and chemical atmospheres. It shall be of sufficient strength to withstand abuse, such as impact and crushing, in handling and during installation. Where direct buried, without encasement in concrete, it shall be capable of withstanding continued loading that is likely encountered after installation.

ARTICLE 354

Nometallic Underground Conduit with Conductors Type NUCC

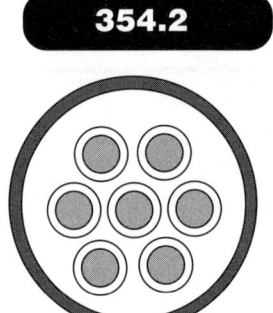

354.2. NUCC is a factory assembly of conductors or cables inside a nonmetallic, smooth wall conduit with a circular cross section.

The conduit comes with the conductors installed.

II. Installation

NUCC basically follows the same rules as HDPE for uses permitted, not permitted, size, bends, etc.

III. Construction Specifications

354.100(A). NUCC is an assembly that is provided in continuous lengths shipped in a coil, reel, or carton.

354.100(C). Conductors and cables used in NUCC shall be listed and comply with 310.8(C). Conductors of different systems shall be in accordance with 300.3(C).

With the exception of solar photovoltaic systems, the conductors of different systems such as direct current and alternating current 600 volts or less may be installed in the same raceway, cable, or wiring enclosure if all of the conductors have an insulation rating at least equal to the highest voltage of any conductor.

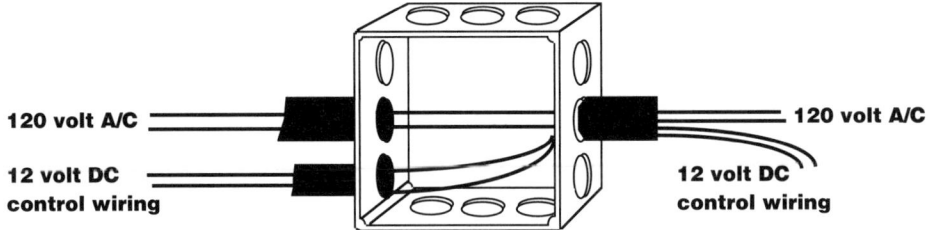

ARTICLE 355

Reinforced Thermosetting Resin Conduit Type RTRC

355.2. A rigid nonmetallic conduit with integral or associated couplings, connectors, and fittings for the installation of electrical conductors and cables.

II. Installation

355.10. The use of RTRC shall be permitted:

(A) In walls, floors, and ceilings.

(B) In locations subject to severe corrosive influences (300.6) and where subject to chemicals for which the materials are specifically approved.

(C) In cinder fill.

(D) Wet locations

(E) Dry and Damp Locations.

(F) Exposed

(G) Underground

(H) Support of Conduit bodies not larger than the largest trade size of an entering raceway.

355.12. RTRC shall **NOT** be used:

(A) In any hazardous location, except as permitted by other articles of the NEC®.

(B) Support of luminaires.

(C) Where subject to physical damage unless identified for such use.

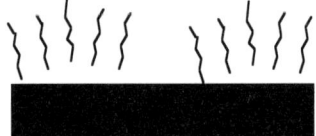

(D) Where subject to ambient temperatures in the excess of 122°F.

(E) For conductors or cables operating at a temperature higher than RTRC listed operating temperature rating.

ARTICLE 356

Liquidtight Flexible Nonmetallic Conduit Type LFNC

356.2. LFNC is a raceway of circular cross section of various types:

(1) A smooth seamless innercore and cover bonded together and having one or more reinforcement layers between the core and covers, designed as Type LFNC-A

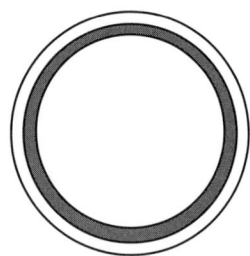

(2) A smooth inner surface with integral reinforcement within the conduit wall, designated as Type LFNC-B

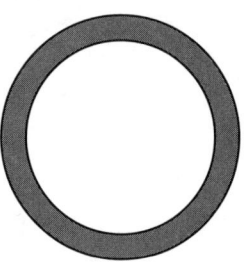

(3) A corrugated internal and external surface without integral reinforcement within the conduit wall, designated as Type LFNC-C

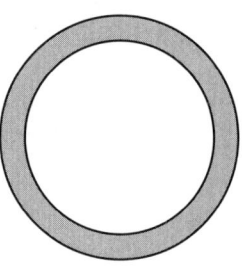

Liquidtight flexible nonmetallic conduit is used extensively in *outdoor applications*. When used outdoors it must be listed for use in direct sunlight and must be listed and marked as suitable for outdoor use. Liquidtight flexible nonmetallic conduit does not provide the same physical protection for the conductors and liquidtight flexible metal conduit.

356.10(4). LFNC may be used exposed or concealed and also direct buried in earth if listed and marked for the purpose.

356.12(3). It must NOT be used in any individual length over 6' long unless special approval is given because the required degree of flexibility necessitates a longer length. Grounding requires a conductor within or outside the flex.

356.20. Although 1/2" is the smallest size of LFNC, **(A1)** notes that 3/8" LFNC may be used for motors with detached junction boxes.

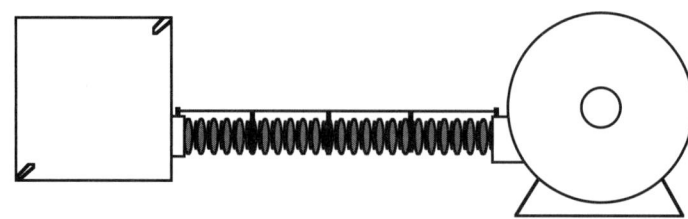

ARTICLE 358

Electrical Metallic Tubing Type EMT

358.2. EMT is an unthreaded thinwall raceway of circular cross section designed for the physical protection and routing of conductors and cables and for use as an equipment grounding conductor when installed utilizing appropriate fittings. EMT is generally made of steel (ferrous) with protective coatings or aluminum (nonferrous).

The most popular raceway is the E.M.T. called *thinwall* conduit by the electrician.

It is light in weight and can be bent easy. It is not threaded. The wall is too thin to have threads.

II. Installation

It comes in 10 foot lengths from 1/2" to 4". It must be supported every 10 feet and within 3 feet of a box.

358.28. Always cut EMT with a hack saw having a blade with 32 teeth to the inch. This will provide a smooth cut. After the cut, ream the ends to remove any burrs or sharp edges that would cut the insulation on the wires being installed.

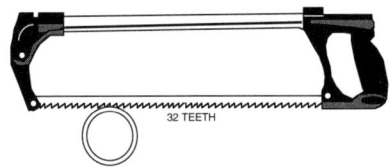

358.30(A). Conduit is to be clamped within 3 feet of a box and every 10 feet in length.

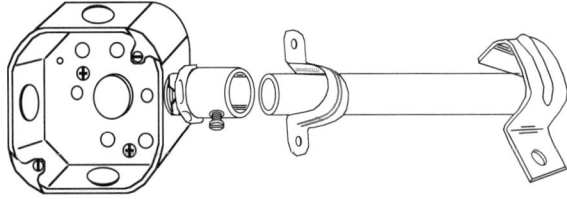

358.30(C). EMT is permitted to be unsupported (clamped) if it is an unbroken length without a coupling not more than 18 inches long and without oversized, concentric or eccentric knockouts.

Electrical Metallic Tubing is widely used in commercial and industrial buildings and a limited amount of residential work. It is lightweight (2.95 pounds for a 10 foot length of 1/2 inch E.M.T. compared to 8.2 pounds for a 1/2 inch rigid steel conduit of the same length). It is easier and faster to install for indoor and outdoor wiring than rigid steel conduit. In earlier times, rigid steel conduit installed in interior walls of buildings was a time consuming laborious operation because each piece is hand threaded. Because of its light weight and easy to install fittings, E.M.T. has become the steel conduit system to use except for special applications that may require the use of rigid steel conduit.

358.42. All joints and connections are made with a threadless fitting. Most popular are the compression or set-screw fittings. There is also a threadless fitting that requires an indenting tool to indent the fitting in one position.

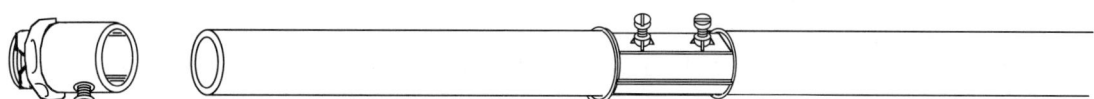

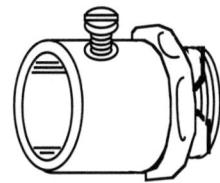

SET SCREW CONNECTOR USED TO CONNECT THE TUBING TO A BOX ETC.

Set screw type fittings are generally easier and faster to install. This type of fitting is not raintite and cannot be used in wet locations. The set screw is firmly tightened against the wall of the inserted tubing providing a firm connection which also provides a continuous grounding path.

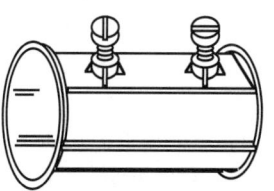

SET SCREW COUPLING USED TO CONNECT TWO PIECES OF CONDUIT TOGETHER

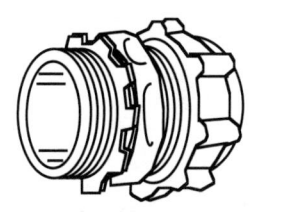

COMPRESSION CONNECTOR USED TO CONNECT THE TUBING TO A BOX ETC.

Compression type fittings, when tightened, compress tightly against the wall of the conduit and provide a tight seal and may be used in wet locations. Each end of a coupling and one end of a connector has a male thread, and a split compression ring in the center, the outer ring is screwed onto the threaded end, compressing the split ring for a tight fit.

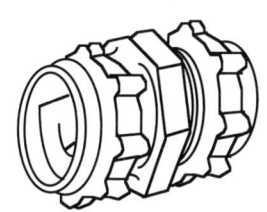

COMPRESSION COUPLING USED TO CONNECT TWO PIECES OF CONDUIT TOGETHER

358.60. EMT shall be permitted as an equipment grounding conductor.

Editor's note: I personally have disagreed with this section over the years. I feel an equipment grounding conductor should be installed within the raceway. Over the years I have seen far too many incidents where the compression or set-screw couplings have pulled apart leaving NO path for the return of the fault current to the circuit breaker.

It is very important that EMT be installed with the proper listed fittings, but also, the raceway must be installed in a workmanlike manner. Even then, there is no guarantee as the years go by that a person may accidentally damage the raceway causing a fitting to have a loose connection thus losing the proper equipment grounding connection required. I would hope that all local codes would may it a requirement to install a equipment grounding conductor. Remember the National Electrical Code is the *minimum* requirement, you can always improve on it.

Conduit provides mechanical protection to protect conductors, permits easy wiring modifications.

If a metal raceway is being used as the equipment grounding conductor, bending the conduit is better than using several condulet fittings. Each joint is a possible loose connection in the required effective grounding path to carry the heavy fault currents.

Many electricians assume that the conduit is used essentially for mechanical protection and do not realize the likelihood of *sparking* when the conduit is called upon to carry fault current.

Where metal raceway is used as the equipment grounding path, couplings, bushings, set-screws, and locknuts should be checked to see that they are tight and properly seated. Any metal raceway used as the equipment grounding path should be examined carefully for rigid mounting and secure joints. Metal conduit is part of the electrical circuit, therefore the joints must be tight and clean to carry the large current under accidental fault conditions.

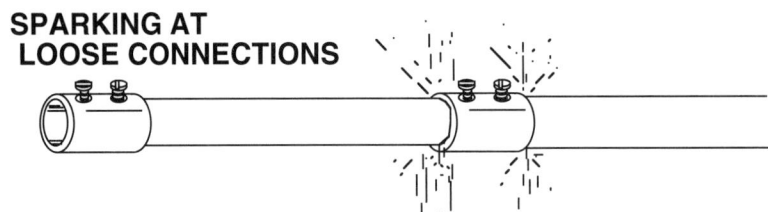

358.60

The Code places no restriction on the *length* of metal conduit. It must have continuity as well as the required conductivity to pass enough current to open the breaker or blow the fuse under a fault condition.

Joints in conduits and raceways require *special* consideration to avoid a shower of sparks and accompanies a fire hazard during a fault condition.

Some electricians know better but are careless in their work and this results in loosely assembled conduit systems which will definitely throw sparks if they are called upon to carry fault currents.

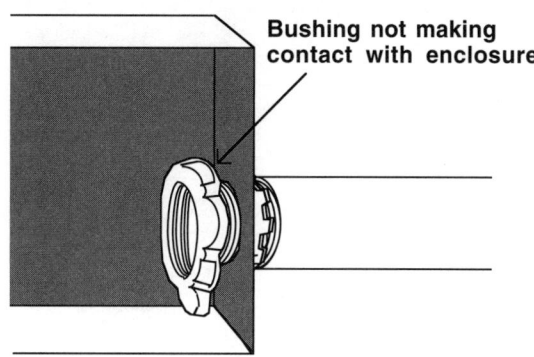

The reason the conduits are to be cut square is in some cases the metal conduit is being used as the equipment grounding conductor to carry the heavy fault currents. If the conduits are not cut square you have less metal contact area with the coupling and heavy arcing can occur at this point.

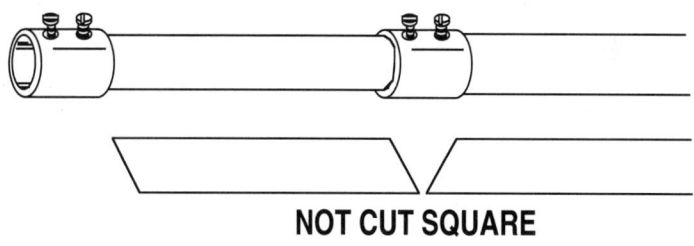

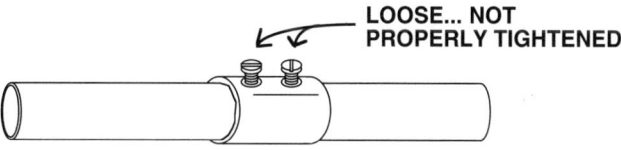

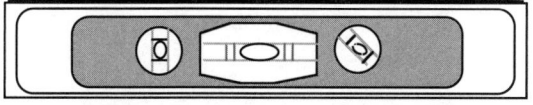

A level is used to ensure the conduit system is installed plumb and level. The sign of a good electrician is the neatness of his work.

ARTICLE 360

Flexible Metallic Tubing Type FMT

360.2. FMT is a raceway that is circular in cross section, flexible, metallic, and liquidtight WITHOUT a nonmetallic jacket.

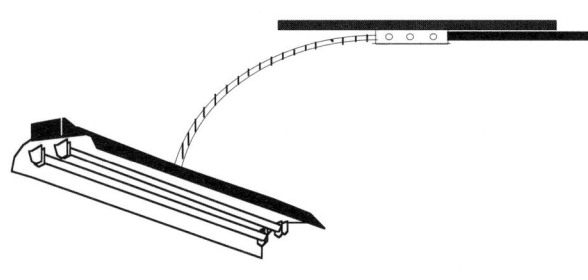

Flexible metal tubing is used often for *fixture whips*. Fixture whips are 4 to 6 feet in length and are used to connect light fixtures to a junction box such as in a suspended ceiling. This is done often in commercial buildings. The above ceiling wiring is installed with EMT or another wiring method to a junction box. The fixture whip is installed from the junction box to the light fixture.

II. Installations

360.10. FMT is limited to branch circuits only installed in dry locations either concealed or accessible.

360.20. FMT smaller than 1/2" is permitted:

Exception 1: 3/8" can be installed in accordance with 300.22(B) and (C).

Only MI cable, MC cable, EMT, **flexible metal tubing**, Flexible metal conduit not over 4', IMC, or rigid metal conduit without nonmetallic covering shall be installed in ducts or plenums specifically fabricated to transport environmental air.

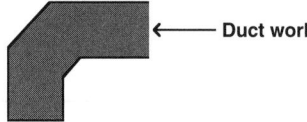

Exception 2: If part of a listed assembly 3/8" shall be permitted in lengths not in excess of 6' for light fixture whips.

ARTICLE 362

Electrical Nonmetallic Tubing Type ENT

362.2. A plastic raceway which is a pliable corrugated raceway. It is made of material that is resistant to moisture and chemical atmospheres and is flame retardant. ENT can be bent by hand. Called "smurf tube" by an electrician.

II. Installation

362.10. The first floor of a building shall be that floor that has 50% or more of the exterior wall surface area level with or above finished grade. One additional level that is the first level and not designed for human habitation and used only for vehicle parking, storage, or similar use shall be permitted.

The use of ENT shall be permitted:

(1) In any building not exceeding three floors above grade as follows:
  a. For exposed work, where not prohibited by 362.12
  b. Concealed within walls, floors, and ceilings

(2) In any building exceeding three floors above grade, ENT shall be concealed within walls, floors, and ceilings where they provide a thermal barrier of material that has at least a 15 minute finish rating.

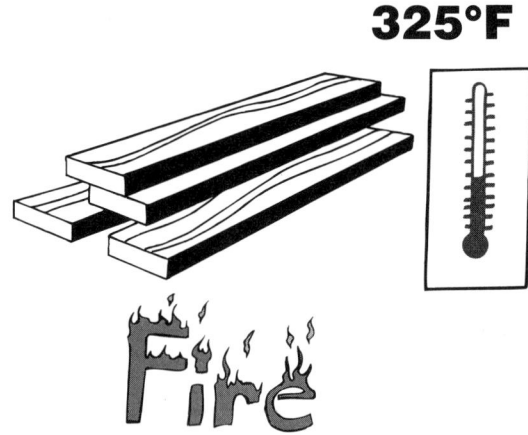

FPN: A finish rating is established for assemblies containing combustible (wood) supports. The finish rating is defined as the time at which the wood stud or wood joist reaches an average temperature rise of 250°F or an individual temperature of 325°F as measured on the plane of the wood nearest the fire. A finish rating is not intended to represent a rating for a membrane ceiling.

362.24. Bends shall be permitted to be made manually without auxiliary equipment, and the radius of the curve to the centerline of such bends shall not be less than shown in Table 2, Chapter 9 using the column "Other Bends".

Table 2 Radius of Conduit and Tubing Bends

Conduit or Tubing Size	One Shot and Full Shoe Benders	Other Bends
Trade Size	Inch	Inch
1/2"	4"	4"
3/4"	4 1/2"	5"
1"	5 3/4"	6"
1 1/4"	7 1/4"	8"
1 1/2"	8 1/4"	10"
2"	9 1/2"	12"
2 1/2"	10 1/2"	15"
3"	13"	18"
3 1/2"	15"	21"
4"	16"	24"
5"	24"	30"
6"	30"	36"

III. Construction Specifications

362.100. ENT shall be made of material that does not exceed the ignitibility, flammability, smoke generation, and toxicity characteristics of rigid (nonplasticized) polyvinyl chloride.

ENT, as a prewired manufactured assembly, shall be provided in continuous lengths capable of being shipped in a coil, reel, or carton without damage.

Articles 342 - 362 Quiz #1 - Open Book

QUIZ #1

1. The smallest rigid metallic conduit permitted to be used is _____ inch.

(a) 1/4   (b) 1/2   (c) 3/4   (d) 5/8

2. The largest rigid non-metallic conduit permitted to be used is _____ inches.

(a) 3   (b) 4   (c) 5   (d) 6

3. What is the **MAXIMUM** allowable voltage that conductors within electrical nonmetallic tubing may carry?

(a) 150v   (b) 300v   (c) 600v   (d) 1000v

4. Where liquidtight flexible metal conduit is installed as a fixed raceway, it shall be secured at intervals not exceeding 4 1/2' and within ____ on each side of every outlet box or fitting.

(a) 6"   (b) 8"   (c) 10"   (d) 12"

5. According to the National Electrical Code, disregarding any exceptions, rigid nonmetallic conduit shall not be used ____.

(a) in cinder fill
(b) for underground work
(c) for the support of fixtures
(d) in walls, floors and ceilings

6. Factory assembled nonmetallic underground conduit with conductors is not permitted ___.

(a) in cinder fill
(b) in exposed indoor locations
(c) encased or imbedded in concrete
(d) in underground locations subject to severe corrosive influences

7. 100 feet of rigid nonmetallic conduit is run between two cabinets. If its thermal expansion is less than _____ inches, an expansion joint is not required.

(a) .25   (b) .28   (c) .30   (d) .35

Articles 342 - 362 Quiz #1 - Open Book

QUIZ #1

8. Electrical nonmetallic tubing is permitted ____.

I. concealed in walls, floors and ceilings with a 15 minute fire rating
II. embedded in concrete provided with approved fitting
III. directly buried
IV. above a suspended ceiling with a 15 minute fire rating

(a) I only   (b) I, II and IV   (c) I, II and III   (d) all of the above

9. You are to install a 1/2" flexible metallic tubing in an area so that after installation its use will be infrequent flexing, the radius of bends shall not be less than ____ inches.

(a) 3 1/2   (b) 4   (c) 12 1/2   (d) 17 1/2

10. You are installing a 75 foot run of 4" rigid metal conduit, using threaded couplings. The Code requires you to support this conduit within 3 feet of termination, and then a maximum of ____ feet apart.

(a) 12   (b) 14   (c) 16   (d) 20

11. ____ of conductors in rigid nonmetallic conduit shall be made only in junction, outlet boxes or conduit bodies.

(a) Splices   (b) Splices and taps   (c) Connections   (d) none of these

12. Where conduit is threaded in the field, it is assumed that a standard cutting die should provide ____ taper per foot.

(a) 1/4"   (b) 1/2"   (c) 3/4"   (d) 1'

13. The largest conductor permitted in 3/8" flexible conduit is ____.

(a) #12   (b) #16   (c) #14   (d) #10

14. EMT shall not be used ____.

(a) for exposed work   (b) where protected from corrosion solely by enamel
(c) for concealed work   (d) none of these

Articles 342 - 362 Quiz #2 - Open Book

QUIZ #2

1. Flexible metal conduit shall be secured at which of the following?

(a) at intervals not exceeding 4 1/2 feet
(b) within 12 inches on each side of a box where fished
(c) where fished
(d) lengths not exceeding 3' at motor terminals

2. Rigid metal conduit shall be _____ every 10 feet as required by section 110.21.

(a) stamped   (b) clearly and durably identified
(c) marked   (d) none of these

3. Where practicable, dissimilar metals in contact anywhere in the system shall be avoided to eliminate the possibility of _____.

(a) hysteresis   (b) galvanic action   (c) specific gravity   (d) resistance

4. The smallest electrical nonmetallic tubing permitted is _____.

(a) 3/8"   (b) 1/2"   (c) 3/4"   (d) 1"

5. How many #12 XHHW conductors can you install in a 3/8" flexible metal conduit with the use of inside fittings?

(a) 1   (b) 2   (c) 3   (d) 0

6. Rigid metal conduit shall be permitted to be installed in concrete, in direct contact with the earth, or in areas subject to severe influences where protected by _____ and judged suitable for the condition.

(a) ceramic   (b) corrosion protection   (c) PVC   (d) orangeburg

7. Liquidtight flexible metal conduit is shipped in what sizes minimum and maximum?

(a) 1/2" to 4"   (b) 1/2" to 6"   (c) 3/4" to 5"   (d) 1/2" to 2"

8. The voltage limitation for electrical nonmetallic tubing is _____ volts.

(a) 600   (b) 500   (c) 450   (d) 300

TH
215

QUIZ #2

Articles 342 - 362 Quiz #2 - Open Book

9. Liquidtight flexible metal conduit may be used in which of the following locations?

(a) in areas that are both exposed or concealed
(b) in areas where the ambient temperature is to be greater than 194 degrees C
(c) in areas that are subject to physical damage
(d) in connection areas for gasoline dispensing pumps

10. All cut ends of rigid conduit shall be ____.

(a) threaded   (b) electrically continuous   (c) reamed   (d) cut square

11. Which of the following is **not** true regarding rigid PVC conduit?

(a) extreme cold may cause some nonmetallic conduits to become brittle and therefore more susceptible to damage from physical contact
(b) can be used to support fixtures
(c) all cut ends shall be trimmed inside and outside to remove rough edges
(d) expansion joints shall be provided to compensate for thermal expansion and contraction

12. Electrical nonmetallic tubing is permitted to be used in sizes up to ____.

(a) 1"   (b) 2"   (c) 3"   (d) 4"

13. Rigid PVC conduit of the 3" trade size, the maximum spacing between supports is ____.

(a) 12'   (b) 10'   (c) 8'   (d) 6'

14. Aluminum fittings and enclosures shall be permitted to be used with ___.

(a) both ferrous and nonferrous conduits
(c) electrical nonmetallic tubing
(b) PVC schedule 80 conduit
(d) steel electrical metallic tubing

QUIZ #3

Articles 342 - 362 Quiz #3 - Open Book

1. In a straight run of rigid PVC conduit between securely mounted boxes, expansion joints are required where the computed length change due to thermal expansion or contraction is at least ___ inch or more.

(a) 1/8   (b) 1/4   (c) 3/8   (d) 1/2

2. The maximum number of quarter bends in one run of EMT is ___.

(a) two   (b) four   (c) five   (d) none of these

3. A pliable raceway is a raceway which can be bent ___ with a reasonable force, but without other assistance.

(a) with heat   (b) without heat   (c) by hand   (d) easily

4. When installing rigid PVC conduit ___.

I.   all joints shall be made by an approved method
II. there shall be support within 2 feet of each box, cabinet
III. all cut ends shall be trimmed inside and outside to remove rough edges

(a) I, II and III   (b) I and III   (c) I and II   (d) II and III

5. Rigid PVC conduit may be used ___.

(a) above ground in direct sunlight
(b) as a support for lighting fixtures
(c) as a grounding conductor
(d) all of these

6. 2" rigid metal conduit shall be supported every ___ feet.

(a) 10   (b) 12   (c) 14   (d) 16

7. Electrical nonmetallic tubing shall be clearly and durably marked at least every ___ feet.

(a) 3   (b) 6   (c) 8   (d) 10

Articles 342 - 362 Quiz #3 - Open Book

QUIZ #3

8. EMT installed in a wet location, shall have its coupling and connectors ____.

(a) protected against corrosion   **(b) corrosion resistant**
(c) listed for wet locations   **(d) none of these**

9. The minimum radius of the inside of a bend for a 3/4" flexible metallic tubing used for flexing is ____ inches.

(a) 17 1/2   **(b) 12 1/2**   **(c) 10**   **(d) 5**

10. Liquidtight flexible metal conduit shall not be permitted ____.

(a) in hazardous locations
(b) in high temperature areas
(c) in exposed and concealed work
(d) where installations requires flexibility or protection from liquids, vapors or solids

11. Straight runs of 1 1/4" rigid metal conduit may be secured at not more than ____ intervals.

(a) 5'   **(b) 10'**   **(c) 12'**   **(d) 14'**

12. Minimum and maximum sizes of EMT are ____ except for special installations.

(a) 5/16" to 3"   **(b) 3/8" to 4"**   **(c) 1/2" to 3"**   **(d) 1/2" to 4"**

13. A 3/8" flexible fixture "whip" with external connectors may contain one bare #12 grounding conductor plus ____ #12 THHN circuit conductors.

(a) 2   **(b) 3**   **(c) 4**   **(d) 6**

14. Rigid metal conduit shall be fastened in place within ____ feet of each box, outlet, cabinet or fitting and may be increased to ____ feet where structural members interfere.

(a) 1;2   **(b) 2;4**   **(c) 3;5**   **(d) 4;6**

ARTICLE 366

Auxiliary Gutters

366.2. Auxiliary gutters can be sheet-metal or nonmetallic troughs in which conductors are installed after the gutter has been installed. They can have either removable or hinged covers.

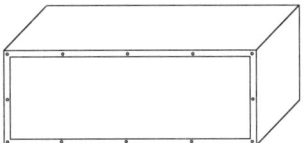

An auxiliary gutter serves the same function as a long junction box would. Sometimes it is necessary to run large conductors for a short distance but to make several *taps* to the conductors, in the case of multiple services.

II. Installation

366.10. The Code permits gutters to supplement wiring spaces at meter centers, distribution centers, etc.

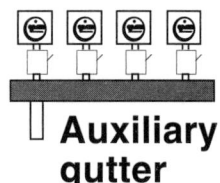

Auxiliary gutter

The auxiliary gutter may enclose conductors or busbars.

366.12. A gutter shall NOT extend more than 30 feet beyond the equipment it supplements. The gutter shall *NOT* be used to enclose switches, overcurrent devices, appliances, or other similar equipment.

366.22(A). The sum of the cross-sectional areas of all contained conductors at any cross section shall not exceed 20% of the interior cross-sectional area.

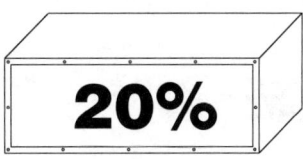

366.23(A). The current carried continuously in bare copper bars in the gutter shall not exceed 1000 amps per square inch.

copper busbar

The current carried continuously in aluminum bars in the gutter shall not exceed 700 amps per square inch.

aluminum busbar

366.30. Gutters shall be supported throughout their entire length at intervals not exceeding 5 feet.

Not exceeding 5 feet

366.56(A). Splices or taps within gutters is permitted where they are accessible by means of removable covers or doors. The conductors, including splices and taps, shall not fill the gutter to more than 75% of its area.

366.56(D). Tap connections from conductors in gutters shall be provided with overcurrent protection.

III. Construction Specifications

366.100(E). Bare conductors shall be securely and rigidly supported so that the minimum clearance between bare current-carrying metal parts of different potential mounted on the same surface will not be less than 2", nor less than 1" for parts that are held in free air. A clearance not less than 1" shall be secured between bare current-carrying metal parts and any metal surface.

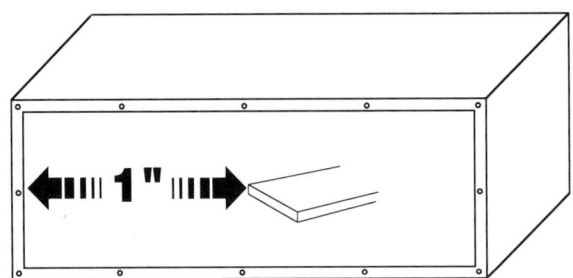

ARTICLE 368

Busways

368.2. A busway is a grounded metal enclosure containing factory-mounted, bare or insulated conductors, which are usually copper or aluminum bars, rods, or tubes.

BUSWAY

A busway is a prefabricated electrical distribution system that consists of busbars installed in a protective enclosure. This type of system is used in commercial and industrial buildings. Busway wiring provides a convenient method of supplying power to machinery. In industrial plants the layout of machines is often changed to meet manufacturing conditions. With busway wiring the machinery is moved to the new location and the wiring is tapped to the existing bus.

II. Installation

368.10(A). Busways shall be installed only where located in the open and are visible.

368.10(B). Totally enclosed, nonventilating-type busways, installed so that the joints between sections and at fittings are accessible for maintenance purposes, shall be permitted to be installed behind panels where means of access are provided, and:

(1) The space behind the access panels is not used for air-handling purposes; or;
(2) The space behind the access panels is used for environmental air, other than ducts and plenums, in which case there shall be no provisions for plug-in connections, and the conductors shall be insulated.

368.10(C). It shall be permissible to extend unbroken lengths of busway through dry walls. It shall be permissible to extend busways vertically through dry floors if totally enclosed (unventilated) where passing through and for a minimum distance of 6' above the floor to provide adequate protection from physical damage. In other than industrial establishments where a vertical riser penetrates two or more dry floors, a minimum 4" high curb is required.

368.12. Busways shall NOT be installed where subject to severe physical damage or corrosive vapors; in hoistways; in any hazardous location, unless specifically approved for such use; or outdoors or in wet or damp locations unless identified for such use.

Lighting busway and trolley busway shall not be installed less than 8' above the floor or working platform unless provided with a cover identified for the purpose.

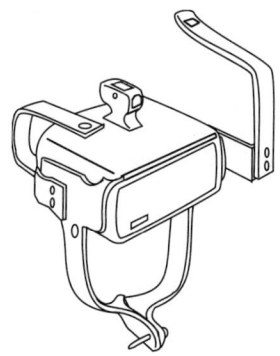

368.17(B). Overcurrent protection shall be required where busways are reduced in ampacity.

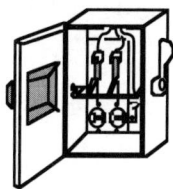

Exception: For industrial establishments only, omission of overcurrent protection shall be permitted at points where busways are reduced in ampacity, provided that the length of the busway having the smaller ampacity does not exceed 50' and has an ampacity at least equal to 1/3 the rating or setting of the overcurrent device next back on the line, and provided that such busway is free from contact with combustible material.

368.30. Busways shall be securely supported at intervals not exceeding 5' unless otherwise designed and marked.

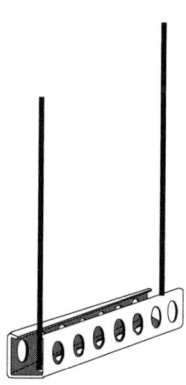

368.56(B). Suitable cord and cable assemblies approved for extra-hard usage or hard usage, and listed bus drop cable shall be permitted as branches from busways provided:

(1) The cord or cable shall be attached to the building by an approved means.

(2) The length of the cord or cable shall not exceed 6'.

(3) The cord or cable shall be installed as a vertical riser from the tension take-up support device to the equipment served.

(4) Strain relief grips shall be provided for the cord or cable at the busway plug-in device and equipment terminations.

Exception to (B2): In industrial establishments where maintenance and supervision ensure that only qualified persons service the installation the 6' maximum length can be increased to 8'.

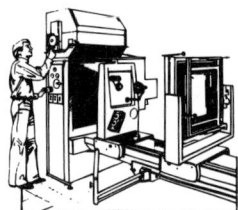

IV. Requirements for Over 600 Volts

368.234(B). Electrical installations in hollow spaces, vertical shafts, and ventilation or air-handling ducts shall be made so the possible spread of fire or products of combustion will not be substantially increased. Openings around electrical penetrations through fire-resistance-rated walls, partitions, floors, or ceilings shall be fire-stopped by using approved methods to maintain the fire-resistance rating.

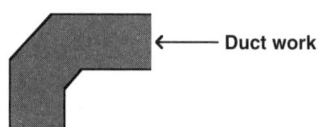

ARTICLE 370

Cablebus

370.2. Cablebus is an assembly of spaced insulated conductors in a completely enclosed ventilated metal structure including fittings and conductor terminations. Ordinarily cablebus is assembled at the point of installation. The cablebus system is highly desirable in industrial applications for large feeders or branch circuits.

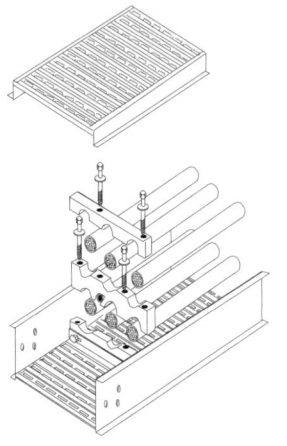

370.3. Cablebus shall be installed for exposed work only. It may be installed outdoors or in corrosive, wet, or damp locations if identified for such use.

Cablebus shall NOT be installed in hoistways or hazardous locations unless specifically approved for such use.

The cablebus framework is an all-welded construction for maximum strength. High-pressure splice joints between framework sections provide an excellent path or ground, and serves as a grounding conductor.

370.4(A). The insulation rating shall be 75°C or higher.

370.4(B). Since cablebus is a ventilated enclosure and conductors are separated by insulating blocks, conductor ampacities may be determined by Table 310.17 for single conductors in free air.

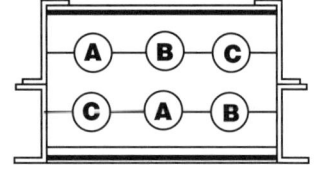

370.4(C). Conductors shall be #1/0 or larger.

ARTICLE 372

Cellular Concrete Floor Raceways

372.2. The floor is constructed of precast reinforced-concrete member. These precast members have hollow voids which form smooth, round cells. The cells form raceways for the wires. Connection to the cells is made by metal header ducts that run horizontally across the precast slab. Connection from these metal headers to the cells is made through handhole metal junction boxes. An outlet can be located at any point along a cell. A hole is drilled through the concrete slab into the cell. The hole is then fitted with the proper outlet fitting, and the wires fished from a handhole junction box to the outlet.

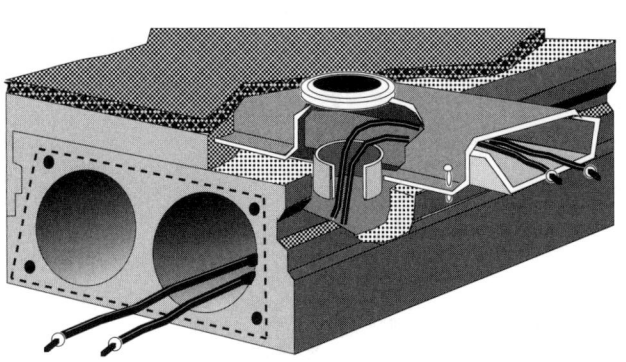
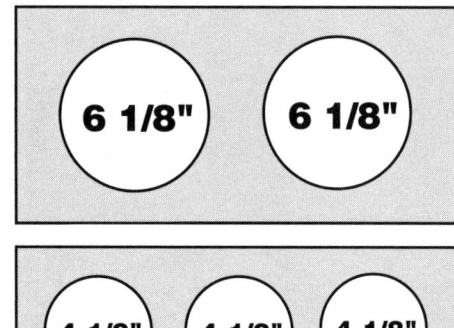

372.4. Conductors shall NOT be installed in precast-cellular-concrete-floor raceways where subject to corrosive vapor; in hazardous locations except where permitted; in commercial garages except for supplying ceiling outlets or extensions to the area below the floor but not above. No electrical conductors shall be installed in any cell or header which contains a pipe for water, air, gas, drainage, steam, or any service other than electrical.

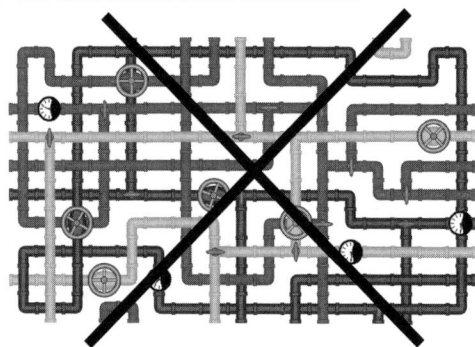

372.5. The headers shall be installed in a straight line, at right angles to the cells. It shall be mechanically secured to the top of the precast cellular-concrete floor. The end joints shall be closed by metallic closure fittings and sealed against penetration of concrete.

372.10. No conductor larger than #1/0 shall be installed, except by special permission.

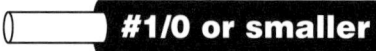

ARTICLE 374

Cellular Metal Floor Raceways

374.2.  Cellular metal floor raceway is a type of floor construction designed for use in steel frame buildings in which the members supporting the floor between the beams consist of sheet steel rolled into shapes to form cells.

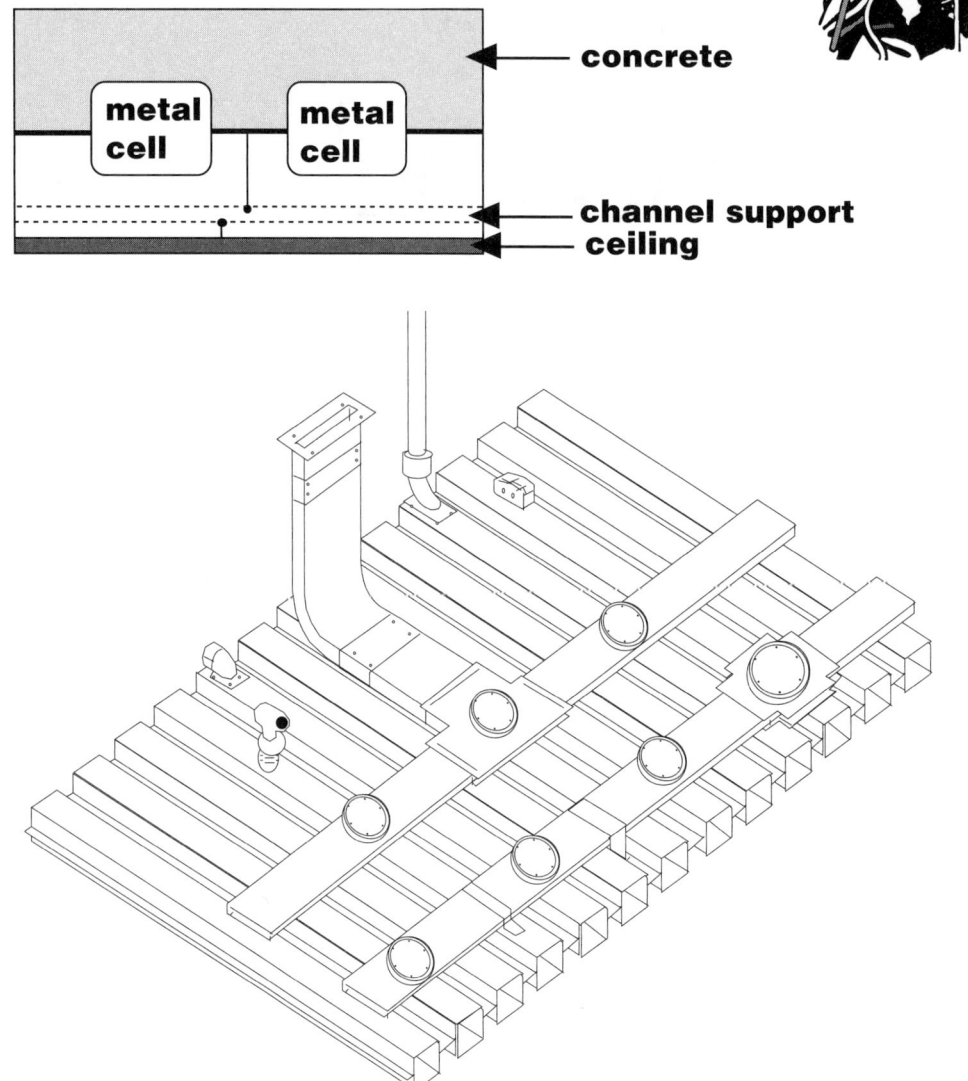

Cellular metal raceway systems are a special type of corrugated sheet steel flooring material which, when installed, forms the cells which are used for the electrical conductors. After the metal flooring is in place, concrete is poured for the floor leaving the cells open for the installation of the conductors.

Cellular metal floor raceways follow mostly the same code rules for cellular concrete floor raceways as for use not permitted, cell, header, size of conductors, splices, etc.

ARTICLE 376

Metal Wireways

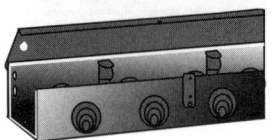

376.2. A wireway is a sheet metal trough used instead of conduit to run large wires a considerable distance to several locations. The cover may be hinged or removable. Conductors are laid in place after the wireway has been installed as a complete system.

Holes are punched in three sides of the wireway by the manufacturer have either eccentric or concentric rings.

ECCENTRIC RINGS   CONCENTRIC RINGS

The rings are a combination of different size hole knockouts to accommodate several sizes of conduit. The electrician removes only those knockout rings which provide the size of hole needed for the conduit being installed.

Wireway is available in standard lengths from one foot to 10 feet, 2" to 12" square, so runs can be made without cutting the duct.

II. Installations

376.10. Wireways may be installed only for exposed work, except as extensions to pass transversely through walls. They are NOT permitted where subjected to severe physical damage or to corrosive vapors or in any hazardous location except as permitted.

376.22. The purpose of a wireway is to provide the industry a flexible system of wiring in which the circuits can be changed to meet changing conditions. Wireways are also used to carry control wires. Wireways may contain up to 30 current-carrying conductors at any cross section. The total cross-sectional area of the group of conductors must not be greater than 20% of the interior cross-sectional area of the wireway.

ARTICLE 378
Nometallic Wireways

378.2. Nonmetallic wireways are flame retardant, nonmetallic troughs with removable covers for housing and protecting wires.

Most of the rules for a nonmetallic wireway are the same as the metal wireway. Support requirements are slightly different as 378.30(A) requires support at 3' intervals for the nonmetallic wireway, whereas the metal raceway support is required every 5'.

ARTICLE 380

Multioutlet Assembly

380.2. Multioutlet assemblies (Plugmold) consist of a wiring channel that the conductors are installed into and the receptacles are installed into the cover strip. Multioutlet assemblies are used where many outlets are needed in one location such as a workbench.

These assemblies are intended for surface mounting except that the metal type may be surrounded by the building finish or recessed so long as the front is not covered.

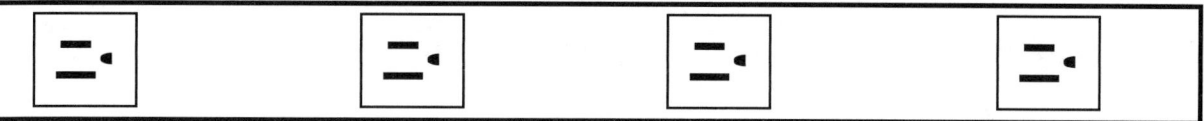

ARTICLE 382

Nonmetallic Extensions

382.2. A nonmetallic extension is an assembly of two insulated conductors with a nonmetallic jacket or an extruded thermoplastic covering. They can be mounted directly on the surface of walls or ceilings. Nonmetallic extensions are permitted only if the extension is from an existing oulet on a 15 or 20 amp branch circuit and the extension is run exposed in a dry location. Nometallic surface extensions are limited to residential or office buildings. Where identified for the use, concealable nonmetallic extensions shall be permitted more than 3 floors abovegrade.

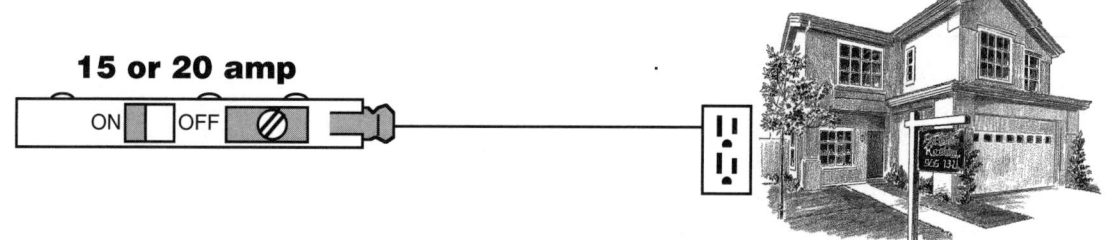

Articles 366 - 382 Quiz #1 - Open Book

QUIZ #1

1. An auxiliary gutter shall not extend a greater distance than ____ feet beyond the equipment which it supplements.

(a) 10   (b) 20   (c) 30   (d) 40

2. Nonmetallic extensions shall be supported every ____ inches with an allowable 12" to the first fastening where the connection to the supplying outlet is by means of an attachment plug.

(a) 6   (b) 8   (c) 10   (d) 16

3. A copper bus bar is 4" wide by 1/2" thick. What is the ampacity?

(a) 500 amps   (b) 1000 amps   (c) 1500 amps   (d) 2000 amps

4. A transverse metal raceway for electrical conductors, furnishing access to predetermined cells of a precast cellular concrete floor, which permits installation of conductors from a distribution center to the floor cells is called ____.

(a) an underfloor raceway   (b) a header
(c) a cellular raceway   (d) a mandrel

5. Multi-outlet assembly may be used ____.

(a) where concealed   (b) in hoistways
(c) in dry locations   (d) in storage battery rooms

6. Splices and taps shall be permitted within a wireway provided they are accessible. The conductor including splices and taps shall not fill the wireway to more than ____ percent of its area at that point.

(a) 25   (b) 80   (c) 125   (d) 75

7. In auxiliary gutters, the minimum clearance between bare current-carrying metal parts of different potential mounted on the same surface will not be less than ____ for parts that are held free in the air.

(a) 3/4"   (b) 1"   (c) 1 1/2"   (d) 2"

Articles 366 - 382 Quiz #1 - Open Book

QUIZ #1

8. Expansion fittings for nonmetallic wireway shall be provided to compensate for thermal expansion and contraction where the length change is expected to be ____ or greater in a straight run.

(a) .025 in.   (b) .050 in.   (c) .75 in   (d) 1/4"

9. Omission of overcurrent protection shall be permitted at points where busways are reduced in size, provided that the smaller busway doesn't extend more than ____ feet.

(a) 10   (b) 20   (c) 50   (d) 70

10. In cellular metal floor raceways all of the following are true **except** ____.

(a) splices and taps can be made in junction boxes
(b) disconnected outlets are removed
(c) entry boxes are installed flush to the floor
(d) the combined cross sectional fill cannot exceed 45%

11. A cellular concrete floor raceway's grounding conductor shall connect the insert receptacles to a positive ground connection provided on the ____.

(a) junction box   (b) cell   (c) fitting   (d) header

12. Sheet metal auxiliary gutters shall be supported throughout their entire length not exceeding ____ feet.

(a) 5   (b) 6   (c) 8   (d) 10

13. Horizontal installations of nonmetallic wireways shall be supported at distances not exceeding ____ unless listed for other support intervals.

(a) 2'   (b) 3'   (c) 4'   (d) 5'

14. Except where fire stops are required, it shall be permissible to extend cablebus vertically through dry floors and platforms, provided the cablebus is totally enclosed at the point where it passes through the floor or platform and for a distance of ____ feet above the floor or platform.

(a) 6   (b) 8   (c) 10   (d) 4

Articles 366 - 382 Quiz #2 - Open Book

QUIZ #2

1. At what angle does a header attach to the cells?

(a) parallel   (b) straight   (c) right angle   (d) none of these

2. In general, busways shall be supported at intervals of ____ feet.

(a) 3   (b) 5   (c) 6   (d) 10

3. Auxiliary gutters shall be permitted to supplement wiring spaces at meter centers, distribution centers, switchboards, and similar points of wiring systems and may enclose ___.

I. switches   II. overcurrent devices   III. conductors   IV. busbars

(a) I & II only   (b) I & III only   (c) I & III only   (d) III & IV only

4. For over 600v busways having sections located both inside and outside of buildings shall have a ___ at the building wall.

(a) vapor seal   (b) fire barrier   (c) condulet   (d) ventilated enclosure

5. Connections from headers to cabinets and other enclosures in cellular concrete floor raceways, shall be made by means of ____ raceways and approved fittings.

(a) rigid nonmetallic   (b) metal   (c) non-metallic   (d) all of these

6. Cablebus shall be securely supported at intervals not exceeding ____ feet.

(a) 6   (b) 8   (c) 10   (d) 12

7. A transverse metal raceway for electrical conductors, furnishing access to predetermined cells of a precast cellular concrete floor, which permits installation of conductors from a distribution center to the floor cells is called ____.

(a) an underfloor raceway   (b) a header duct
(c) a cellular raceway   (d) a mandrel

QUIZ #2

Articles 366 - 382 Quiz #2 - Open Book

8. Cablebus shall be installed only for ____ work.

(a) exposed   (b) commercial   (c) concealed   (d) hazardous

9. Except by special permission, no conductor larger than ____ shall be installed in cellular metal floor raceways.

(a) #1/0   (b) #2/0   (c) #250 kcmil   (d) #500 kcmil

10. The current carried continuously in bare copper bars in auxiliary gutters shall not exceed ____ amperes per square inch.

(a) 560   (b) 700   (c) 800   (d) 1000

11. Cablebus framework, where ____, shall be permitted as the equipment grounding conductor for branch circuits and feeders.

(a) bonded as required by Article 250
(b) welded
(c) protected
(d) galvanized

12. For industrial establishments only, omission of overcurrent protection shall be permitted at points where busways are reduced in size, provided that the smaller busway does not extend more than ____ feet and has a current rating at least equal to ____ the rating or setting of the overcurrent device next back on the line.

(a) 30' ... 80%   (b) 50' ... 1/3   (c) 20' ... 1/2   (d) 40' ... 75%

13. In no case shall the distance between supports of nonmetallic wireway exceed ____ feet.

(a) 3   (b) 5   (c) 8   (d) 10

14. A 300 foot run of 800 amp busway is installed in a commercial warehouse building. The last 20' of the busway run is reduced to a bus rating of 200 amps. Which of the following best describes requirements for installation of the smaller bus?

(a) This installation meets Code requirements.
(b) It must be protected by an overcurrent device.
(c) Busway is not permitted in commercial buildings.
(d) It must be at least 1/3 the ampere rating of the larger bus.

TH

QUIZ #3

Articles 366 - 382 Quiz #3 - Open Book

1. Which of the following is the maximum number of current-carrying conductors that can be used at any cross-section of a wireway?

(a) 100   (b) 30   (c) 50   (d) 40

2. For the use of nonmetallic surface extensions the building _____.

I.   cannot exceed three floors
II. is occupied for office purposes
III. is occupied for residential purposes

(a) I only   (b) II only   (c) II and III   (d) I, II and III

3. An auxiliary gutter shall not extend a greater distance than ____ feet.

(a) 10   (b) 30   (c) 50   (d) 75

4. Multioutlet assembly may be used ____.

(a) where concealed   (b) in storage battery rooms
(c) in dry locations   (d) in hoistways

5. Where devices containing a disconnecting means are mounted out of reach, suitable means shall be provided to operate the disconnecting means from the floor on a busway. Which of the following is permitted?

(a) devices cannot be mounted out of reach
(b) ladders
(c) sticks
(d) no method is permitted

6. Nonmetallic surface extensions with one or more extensions shall be permitted to be run in any direction from an existing outlet, but not on the floor or within ____ inches from the floor.

(a) 6   (b) 4   (c) 3   (d) 2

7. Vertical and horizontal spacing between supported cablebus conductors shall not be less than ____ at the points of support.

(a) 1"   (b) 1 1/2"   (c) 2"   (d) one conductor diameter

TH

Articles 366 - 382 Quiz #3 - Open Book

QUIZ #3

8. Metal-enclosed busways over 600v shall be installed so that ____ from induced circulating currents in any adjacent metallic parts will not be hazardous to personnel or constitute a fire hazard.

(a) stray currents   (b) magnetic flux   (c) the impedance   (d) temperature rise

9. Surface metal raceways when extended through walls or floors must be in ____ lengths.

(a) 8 foot   (b) 3 foot   (c) 5 foot   (d) none of these

10. In which of the following locations would nonmetallic wireway not be permitted unless marked for the use?

(a) Where subject to corrosive vapors.   (b) In wet locations.
(c) Where exposed to sunlight.   (d) In exposed locations.

11. A flexible cord connection is made directly to the load end terminals of a busway plug-in device. The maximum length of this cord to a tension take-up device is ____ feet.

(a) 3'   (b) 4'   (c) 5'   (d) 6'

12. The individual conductors in a cablebus shall be supported not greater than ____ for vertical runs.

(a) 18"   (b) 3'   (c) 6'   (d) 12'

13. Splices or taps shall be permitted within gutters when they are accessible. The conductors, including splices and taps, shall not fill the gutter to more than ____ of its area.

(a) 20%   (b) 40%   (c) 75%   (d) 80%

14. Listed nonmetallic raceways are permitted for all of the following uses **EXCEPT** ____.

(a) where subject to physical damage   (b) in exposed work
(c) where subject to corrosive vapors   (d) in wet locations

ARTICLE 384

Strut-Type Channel Raceway

384.2. Channel raceways are metallic and permitted for a variety of applications, for power poles to feed receptacles, electrified partitions, undercarpet or underfloor applications, etc.

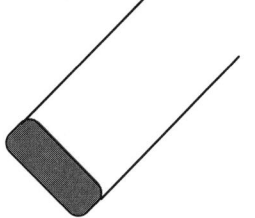

II. Installation

384.10. Strut-type channel raceways are permitted where exposed, in dry locations, and must be protected from corrosion.

384.12. Strut type channel raceways shall NOT be concealed or permitted subject to severe corrosion when solely protected by enamel.

384. 22. The number of conductors permitted shall not exceed the percentage fill from Table 384.22.

384.30. A surface mount strut-type channel raceway shall be secured with retention straps external to the channel at intervals not exceeding 10' and within 3' of each box.

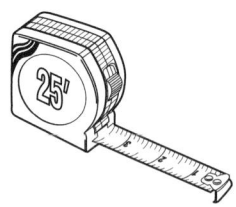

384.60. Where a snap-fit metal cover is used to achieve electrical continuity, this cover shall NOT be permitted as the means for providing electrical continuity for a receptacle mounted in the cover.

ARTICLE 386

Surface Metal Raceways

386.2. A metallic raceway that is intended to be mounted to the surface of a structure. Surface raceway has become popular for new works as well as for modernization.

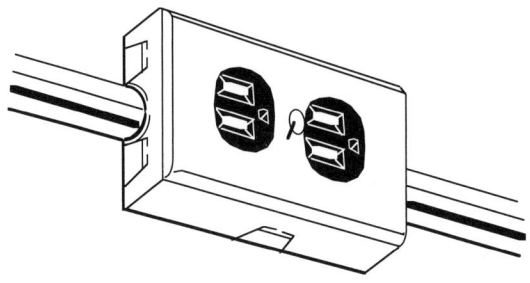

II. Installation

386.21. No conductor larger than that for which the raceway is designed shall be installed.

386.22. Ampacity derating factors shall NOT apply where:

(1) The csa exceeds 4 square inches
(2) The current-carrying conductors does not exceed 30
(3) The sum of the csa of all conductors does not exceed 20% of the interior csa

386.56. Splices and taps shall be permitted in surface metal raceways having a removable cover.

386.60. Surface metal raceway enclosures providing a transition from other wiring methods shall have a means for connecting an equipment grounding conductor.

ARTICLE 388

Surface Nonmetallic Raceways

388.2. Basically surface nonmetallic raceways follow the same rules as the metal raceways. The nonmetallic raceway is to have the necessary moisture and corrosion resistance, mechanical strength, flame retardance and low-smoke-producing characteristics

Look for the "LS" (low-smoke producing) marking on the raceway.

ARTICLE 390

Underfloor Raceways

390.2. An underfloor raceway system consists of ducts laid below the surface of the floor and interconnected by means of special cast-iron floor junction boxes.

Underfloor raceway systems (sometime called Walker duct) are used in office buildings where a large number of receptacles and phone outlets must be installed into the floor at desk or cubicle locations. This system consists of ducts which are installed below the finished surface of the floor. The outlet fittings are installed into inserts that are spaced at regular intervals along the duct.

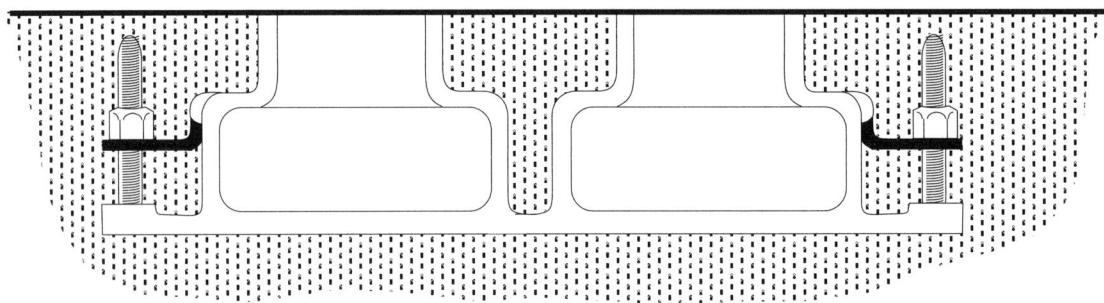

Underfloor raceway shall be permitted beneath the surface of concrete or other flooring material or in office occupancies where laid flush with the concrete floor and covered with linoleum or equivalent floor covering.

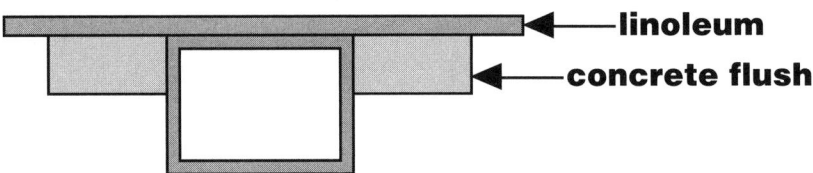

390.3(A). Half-round and flat-top raceways not over 4" wide shall have at least 3/4" concrete or wood above the raceway.

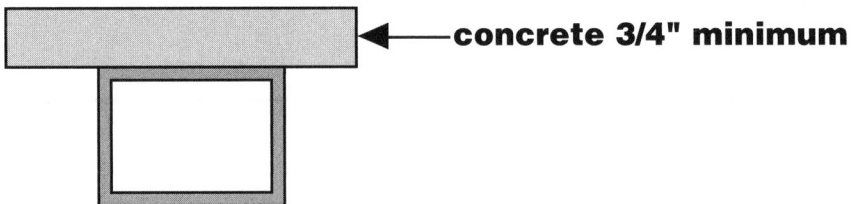

390.3(B). Flat-top raceways over 4" wide but not over 8" wide with a minimum 1" spacing between raceways shall be covered with at least 1" of concrete. Raceways spaced less than 1" apart shall be covered with at least 1 1/2" of concrete.

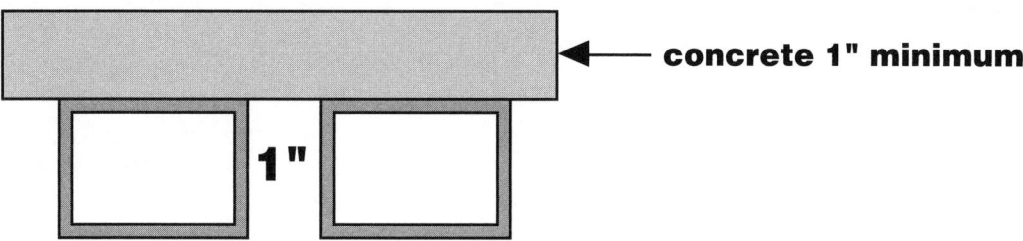

390.5. The csa of all conductors or cables shall not exceed 40% of the interior csa of the raceway.

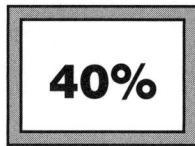

390.6. Splices and taps shall be made only in junction boxes.

Loop wiring shall NOT be considered a splice or tap.

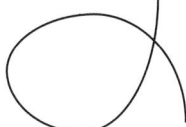

390.7. When an outlet is abandoned, discontinued, or removed, the sections of circuit conductors supplying the outlet shall be removed from the raceway.

ARTICLE 392

Cable Trays

392.2. Cable tray is not a wiring method, but is used as a mechanical support system for conduit. Multiconductor cables designed for use in cable trays, and single conductors of size #1/0 or larger with insulation that is approved for cable tray wiring may be installed in cable tray. Cable tray is manufactured in steel, aluminum, and fiberglass.

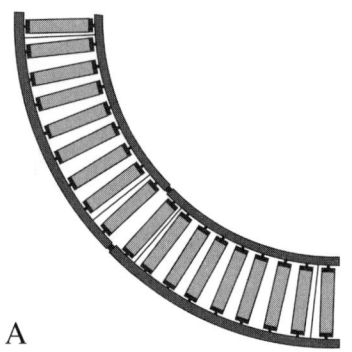

Cable tray is assembled in sections using the proper fittings and when completed, forms a continuous tray system. A variety of fittings are manufactured for use in installing cable tray, such as elbows, tees, reducers, dividers, and offsets for changes in elevation. Cable tray is often used in industrial buildings where many control, signal, and power cables are required.

•Note: A raceway must be an *enclosed* channel for conductors. A cable tray is not an enclosed channel, therefore cable tray is not a raceway, it is a *support* system.

392.3. Cable tray shall be permitted to be used to support service conductors, feeders, branch circuits, communications circuits, control circuits, and signaling circuits. Cable tray installations are not limited to industrial establishments. Insulated conductors and cables where exposed to the sun shall be sunlight resistant.

392.3(B). The wiring methods in Table 392.3(A) shall be permitted to be used in industrial establishments under the conditions in their articles. Where qualified persons sevice the cable tray system, any of the cables in 392.3(B1) and (B2) shall be permitted to be installed in ladder, ventilated trough, solid bottom, or ventilated channel cable trays.

(1) Single-conductor cables shall be permitted:

(a) Single-conductor cable shall be #1/0 or larger and listed for use in cable trays.

(b) Welding cables shall comply with Article 630, Part IV.

(c) Single conductors used as equipment grounding conductors shall be insulated, covered, or bare, and #4 or larger.

392.3(B2)

392.3(B2). The most common conductors used in cable trays are Type MC metal-clad cable and Type TC tray cables.

392.4. Cable tray systems shall NOT be used in hoistways or where subject to severe physical damage. Cable tray may be used in air-handling ceiling space but only to support the wiring methods permitted in such space by section 300.22(C). This recognizes cable trays simply as supports for raceways or cables permitted in hung ceilings used for air conditioning.

392.6. Cable trays shall be installed as a complete system. Field bends or modifications shall be so made that the electrical continuity of the system is maintained.

392.6(F). Cables rated over 600 volts and those rated 600 volts or less installed in the same cable tray shall comply with either of the following:

(1) The cables rated over 600 volts are Type MC.

(2) The cables rated over 600 volts are separated from the cables rated 600 volts or less by a solid fixed barrier compatible material of the cable tray.

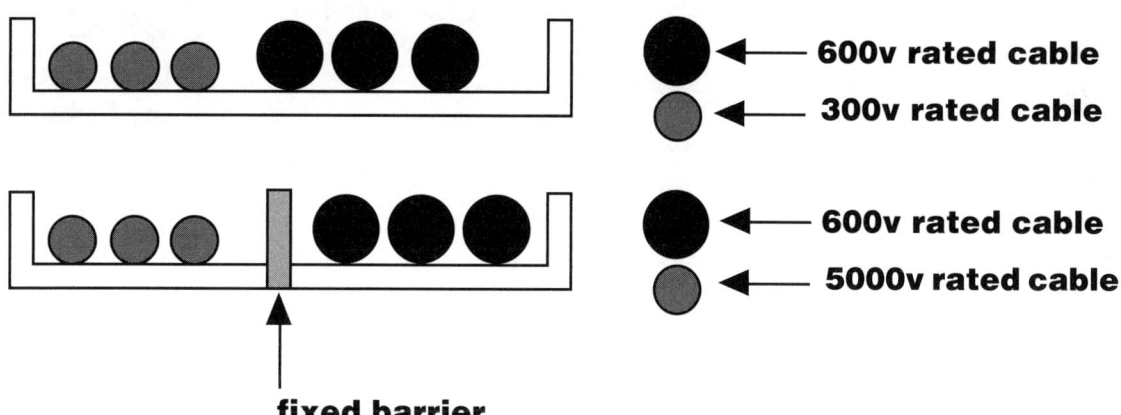

392.6(H). Cable trays shall be exposed and accessible.

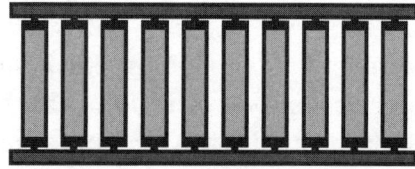

392.7(B). Steel or aluminum cable tray systems shall be permitted to be used as equipment grounding conductors provided: (2) The minimum csa of cable trays shall conform to Table 392.7(B).

392.8(A). Cables splices made an insulated by approved methods are permitted in a cable tray, provided they are accessible and do not project above side rails. Splices shall be permitted to project above the side rails where not subject to physical damage.

392.8(D). Where single conductor cables comprising of each phase and a neutral are connected in parallel they shall be installed in groups consisting of not more than one conductor per phase to prevent current imbalance in the parallel conductors due to inductive reactance.

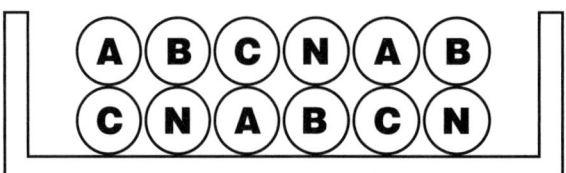

392.9. The number of multiconductor cables, rated 2000 volts or less, permitted in a single cable tray shall NOT exceed the requirements of this section. The conductor sizes apply to both copper and aluminum conductors.

2000 volts or less

392.9(A). Any mixture of cables shall:

(1) Where all of the cables are **#4/0 or larger**, the sum of the diameters of all the cables must not exceed the cable tray width, all the cables shall be installed in a single layer.

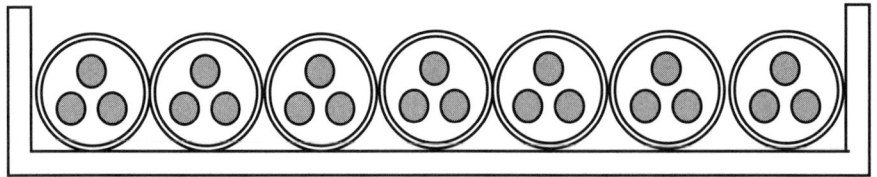

**Cable width must be at least the sum of all the cable diameters
and the sum of the required spacing widths between the cables.
All cables must lie flat, side by side in one layer.
Ladder or ventilated trough cable tray.
All of the cables are #4/0 or larger.**

392.9(A2)

392.9(A2). Where all the multiconductor cables in the tray are made up of conductors **smaller than #4/0**, the sum of the csa of all the cables must not exceed the maximum cable fill area in column 1 of Table 392.9 for the particular width of cable tray being used.

392.9(A3). Where a tray contains one or more multiconductor cables **#4/0 or larger** along with one or more multiconductor cables **smaller than #4/0**, the sum of the outside csa of all the cables **smaller than #4/0** must not be greater than the maximum permitted fill area resulting from the computation in column 2 of Table 392.9 for the particular tray width. The multiconductor cables that are #4/0 or larger must be installed in a single layer, and no other cables may be placed on top of them. The available tray csa which can properly accommodate cables smaller than #4/0 installed in a tray with #4/0 or larger cables is, in effect, equal to the allowable fill area from column 1 for each tray width minus 1.2 times the sum of the outside diameters of the #4/0 or larger cables.

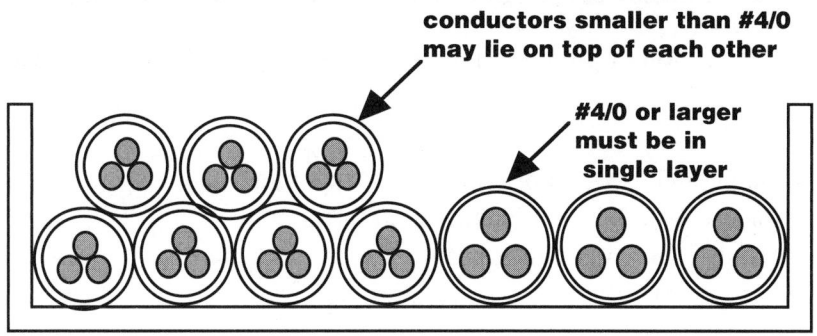

392.11. When cable assemblies of more than one conductor are installed as required by 392.9, each conductor in any of those cables will have an ampacity as given in Table 310.16 or 310.18.

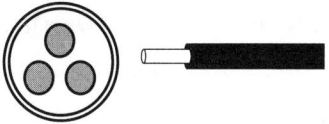

392.12. This section applies to high-voltage circuits in a cable tray. Type MV cable is a high-voltage cable.

Type MV and Type MC high-voltage cables must conform as shown in sketch below.

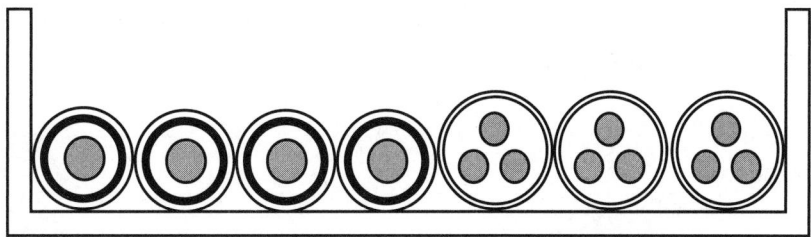

Cable tray must be wide enough for all high-voltage cables in a single layer

ARTICLE 394
Concealed Knob-and-Tube Wiring

394.2. Concealed knob-and-tube wiring is restricted to use for extensions of existing installations and is NOT Code accepted today for new electrical work. In the old days of plaster and lath walls you'll still find this wiring as it was used extensively at one time. It has been bypassed today in favor of the NM cable (romex).

ARTICLE 396
Messenger Supported Wiring

396.2. The basic construction of this wiring method has been used for many years as service-drop cable.

396.30. The messenger shall be supported at dead ends and at intermediate locations so as to eliminate tension on the conductors. The conductors shall not be permitted to come in contact with the messenger supports or any structural members, walls, or pipes.

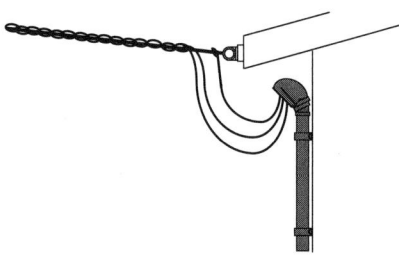

ARTICLE 398
Open Wiring on Insulators

398.2. An exposed wiring method using cleats, knobs, tubes, and flexible tubing for protection and support of single insulated conductors run in or on buildings.

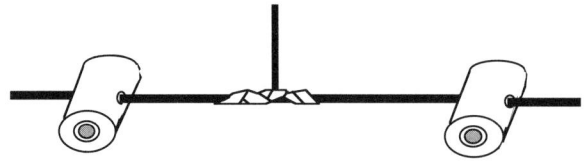

398.10. Open wiring on insulators shall be permitted only for industrial or agricultural establishments on 600v or less systems as follows:

(1) Indoors or outdoors
(2) In wet or dry locations
(3) Where subject to corrosive vapors
(4) For services

Articles 384 - 398 Quiz #1 - Open Book

QUIZ #1

1. The general rule is half-round and flat-top raceways not over ____ in width shall have not less than 3/4" of concrete or wood above the raceway.

(a) 2"   (b) 3"   (c) 4"   (d) 6"

2. Cable tray systems shall not be used in ____ or where subject to severe physical damage.

(a) tunnels   (b) hoistways   (c) hazardous locations   (d) 600 volt systems

3. Which of the following is/are correct about open wire systems on insulators?

I.   surface-type snap switches do not need boxes
II. conductor supports shall be within 6" of a tap
III. surface-type snap switches shall be mounted on insulating material

(a) I only   (b) II only   (c) I and III only   (d) I, II and III

4. In general, the voltage limitation between conductors in a surface metal raceway is ____ volts.

(a) 300   (b) 600   (c) 900   (d) 1000

5. When an outlet from an underfloor raceway is discontinued, the circuit conductors supplying the outlet ____.

(a) may be spliced
(b) may be reinsulated
(c) may be handled like abandoned outlets on loop wiring
(d) shall be removed from the raceway

6. Cable trays include fittings or other suitable means for ____.

I.   temperature
II. electric continuity
III. changes in direction and elevation of runs

(a) I only   (b) I and II only   (c) III only   (d) I and III only

7. Loop wiring for underfloor raceways, shall not be considered ____.

I. a splice   II. a tap

(a) I only   (b) II only   (c) both I and II   (d) neither I or II

TH
255

Articles 384 - 398 Quiz #1 - Open Book

QUIZ #1

8. Single conductors in a cable tray shall be securely bound in circuit groups to prevent ____ due to fault-current magnetic forces unless single conductors are cabled together, such as triplexed assemblies.

(a) current unbalance (b) inductive reactance
(c) excessive movement (d) voltage surges

9. Knob and tube wiring splices shall be ____ unless approved devices are used.

(a) taped   (b) bolted   (c) clamped   (d) soldered

10. Field bends or modifications shall be so made that the ____ of the cable tray system and support for the cables shall be maintained.

(a) temperature   (b) electrical continuity   (c) strength   (d) rigidity

11. Unbroken lengths of surface nonmetallic raceways may pass through which of the following?

(a) Dry walls   (b) Damp walls   (c) Damp floors   (d) Wet locations

12. Steel cable trays shall not be used as equipment grounding conductors for circuits protected above ____ amperes.

(a) 200   (b) 60   (c) 600   (d) 1200

Articles 384 - 398 Quiz #2 - Open Book

QUIZ #2

1. When derating the ampacity of multiconductor cables to be installed in cable tray, the ampacity deration shall be based on ___.

I. the total number of current carrying conductors in the cable tray
II. the total number of current carrying conductors in the cable

(a) I only   (b) II only   (c) either I or II   (d) both I and II

2. Where space is too limited to provide minimum clearances, such as at meters, panelboards, outlets, and switch points, concealed knob and tube wiring shall be enclosed in ___ which shall be continuous in length between the last support and the enclosure or terminal point.

(a) rigid metal conduit   (b) EMT   (c) IMC   (d) flexible nonmetallic tubing

3. Underfloor raceways not more than 100 millimeters wide shall have no less than ___ concrete or wood above them.

(a) 1/2 inch   (b) 3/4 inch   (c) 2 inches   (d) 4 inches

4. Which of the following locations is **not** permitted for the use of surface metal raceways?

(a) dry location   (b) hoistways   (c) under raised floors   (d) hazardous

5. Where single conductors #1/0 through #4/0 are installed in a ladder or ventilated trough cable tray they shall be installed in no more than ___.

I. a depth of 4"   II. a depth of 6"   III. a single layer

(a) I only   (b) II only   (c) III only   (d) I or II only

6. When installing open wiring on insulators in a dry location, conductors shall be permitted to be separately enclosed in flexible nonmetallic tubing. The tubing shall be in continuous length not exceeding ___ feet and secured to the surface by straps at intervals not exceeding 4 1/2 feet.

(a) 6   (b) 10   (c) 15   (d) 50

7. Where single conductor cables in sizes #1/0 through #500 kcmil are installed, continuously covered for more than 6 feet with unventilated covers, the ampacities shall not exceed ___ percent of the allowable ampacities in Tables 310.17 and 310.19.

(a) 50   (b) 60   (c) 65   (d) 80

Articles 384 - 398 Quiz #2 - Open Book

QUIZ #2

8. It shall be permissible to extend ____ of surface metal raceways through dry walls, dry partitions, and dry floors.

(a) 2 feet (b) 3 feet (c) 6 feet (d) unbroken lengths

9. Where single conductors are installed in a triangular or square configuration in uncovered cable trays, with a maintained free air space of not less than ____ times one conductor diameter of the largest conductor contained within the configuration and adjacent conductor configurations, the ampacity of #1/0 AWG and larger cables shall not exceed the allowable ampacities of two or three single insulated conductors rated 0 through 2000 volts supported on a messenger.

(a) 3 (b) 2 (c) 2.15 (d) 2.75

10. Splices and taps in surface nonmetallic raceways shall not fill the raceway at the point of the splice or tap to more than ____.

(a) 20% (b) 50% (c) 75% (d) 80%

11. Concealed knob-and-tube wiring shall not be used in the hollow spaces of walls, ceilings and attics where such spaces ____.

(a) exceed 30 degrees C
(b) are insulated by loose or rolled insulation material
(c) are not fire rated for 3 hours
(d) are not ventilated

12. A unit or assembly of units or sections, and associated fittings, forming a rigid structural system used to securely fasten or support cables and raceways is a ____.

(a) flat cable assembly (b) wireway (c) multioutlet assembly (d) cable tray system

Articles 384 - 398 Quiz #3 - Open Book

QUIZ #3

1. Cables rated over 600v may be installed in the same cable tray with cables rated 600v or less ____.

(a) Where cables over 600v are Type MC
(b) where separated by a solid fixed barrier of a material compatible with the cable tray
(c) both (a) and (b)
(d) neither (a) nor (b)

2. Open conductors shall be separated from metal conduits, piping or other conducting materials by no less than ____.

(a) 8"   (b) 6"   (c) 4"   (d) 2"

3. Cable trays shall ____.

I.   have side rails or equivalent structural members
II. not present sharp edges or burrs
III. have suitable strength and rigidity

(a) I only   (b) I and II only   (c) III only   (d) I, II and III

4. Loop wiring for underfloor raceways, shall not be considered ____.

(a) a splice   (b) a tap   (c) both (a) and (b)   (d) neither (a) nor (b)

5. Concealed knob-and-tube wiring shall be permitted to be used only for extensions of existing installations and elsewhere only by special permission under the following conditions ____.

I.   in unfinished attic and roof spaces when such spaces are insulated by loose or rolled insulating material
II. in the hollow spaces of walls and ceilings
III. in unfinished attic and roof spaces as provided in section 394.23

(a) I only   (b) I and II only   (c) II and III only   (d) I, II and III

6. Single conductor cables shall be ____ or larger and shall be of a type listed for use in cable trays.

(a) #1   (b) #1/0   (c) #4/0   (d) #250 kcmil

7. ____ or larger conductors supported on solid knobs shall be securely tied thereto by tie wires having an insulation equivalent to that of the conductor.

(a) #12   (b) #10   (c) #8   (d) #6

TH

Articles 384 - 398 Quiz #3 - Open Book

QUIZ #3

8. Cable splices made and insulated by approved methods shall be permitted within a cable tray provided they are accessible and ____.

(a) have a hinged cover
(b) are crimped properly
(c) are not over 600 volt
(d) do not project above the side rails

9. Underfloor raceways may be occupied up to ____ percent of the area.

(a) 55   (b) 30   (c) 40   (d) 38

10. Messenger supported wiring shall not be used ____.

I. where subject to severe physical damage
II. in hoistways

(a) I only   (b) II only   (c) both I and II   (d) neither I nor II

11. In industrial establishments, when single conductor cable, #1/0 or larger, is installed in ladder cable tray the maximum allowable rung spacing shall be ____.

(a) 4"   (b) 6"   (c) 9"   (d) 12"

12. A surface metal raceway enclosure providing a transition from other wiring methods shall have a means for connecting ____.

(a) a metal box to the raceway
(b) a nonmetallic box to the raceway
(c) an ungrounded conductor to the raceway
(d) an equipment grounding conductor

Articles 384 - 398 Quiz #4 - Open Book

1. Which of the following wiring methods is not permitted to be installed as a "Messenger supported wiring" system?

(a) Multiconductor service entrance cable
(b) Metal-clad cable
(c) Power and control tray cable
(d) Nonmetallic sheathed cable

2. Where cable trays are continuously covered for more than six feet with solid unventilated covers, not over ____% of the allowable ampacities of Table 310.16 and Table 310.18 shall be permitted for multiconductor cables.

(a) 70   (b) 75   (c) 80   (d) 95

3. Strut-type channel raceway shall be secured at intervals not exceeding ___ feet and within 3 feet of each outlet box.

(a) 3   (b) 4 1/2   (c) 10   (d) 12

4. The sum of the diameters of all single conductors shall not exceed ___ when installed in a ventilated channel cable tray 4 inches inside width.

(a) 2 inches   (b) 3 inches   (c) 4 inches   (d) none of these

5. In general, the voltage limitation between conductors in surface metal raceways is ____ volts.

(a) 300   (b) 500   (c) 600   (d) 1000

6. Where nails are used to mount knobs, they shall not be smaller than ____ penny.

(a) 6   (b) 8   (c) 10   (d) 16

7. Aluminum cable trays shall not be used as equipment grounding conductors for circuits with ground-fault protection above ____ amperes.

(a) 600   (b) 800   (c) 1200   (d) 2000

Articles 384 - 398 Quiz #4 - Open Book

QUIZ #4

8. Disregarding any exceptions, surface metal raceways shall be permitted ____.

(a) in dry locations
(b) in any hazardous location
(c) where subject to corrosive vapors
(d) where the voltage is 300 volts or more between conductors

9. Underfloor flat-top raceways over 4 inches but not over 8 inches wide with a minimum of 1 inch spacing between raceways shall be covered with concrete to a depth of not less than ___.

(a) 3/4" (b) 1" (c) 1 1/2" (d) 2"

10. Of the following, ____ is not permitted for installation in cable trays.

(a) nonmetallic sheathed cable
(b) multiconductor service entrance cable
(c) single conductor smaller than #1/0
(d) multiconductor underground feeder and branch circuit cable

11. Where screws are used to mount knobs, or where nails or screws are used to mount cleats, they shall be of a length sufficient to penetrate the wood to a depth to at least ____ the height of the knob and the full thickness of the cleat.

(a) twice (b) one-half (c) one-quarter (d) 3 times

12. The conductors, including splices and taps in metal surface raceway shall not fill the raceway to more than ____ percent of its area at that point.

(a) 75 (b) 40 (c) 38 (d) 53

FINAL EXAM

Final Exam

FINAL EXAM   50 Questions   -   Open Book

1. Which of the following requires a moisture seal at all points of termination?

(a) underplaster extensions
(b) bare conductor feeders
(c) liquidtight flexible metal conduit
(d) mineral-insulated cable

2. If made up with threadless couplings, a 1" rigid metal conduit shall be supported at least every ____ feet.

(a) 6   (b) 8   (c) 10   (d) 12

3. Where NM cable is used, the cable assembly, including the sheath, shall extend into the box no less than ____.

(a) 1/2"   (b) 3/4"   (c) 1/4"   (d) 1"

4. ____ of the following is a true statement.

I.   Wiring above a nonfire rated ceiling shall not be supported by the ceiling support wires.
II. Wiring above a fire rated ceiling shall not be supported by the ceiling support wires.
III. Cables and raceways shall not be permitted to be supported by ceiling grids.
IV. The ceiling support wires shall be permitted to support branch circuit wiring if in accordance with the ceiling manufacturer's instructions.

(a) I & II only   (b) II & III only   (c) IV only   (d) I, II, III & IV

5. Electrical ducts shall include any of the electrical conduits recognized in Chapter 3 as suitable for use ____.

(a) over 600v   (b) as bus bars   (c) underground   (d) exposed

6. In cellular metal floor raceways all of the following are true **except** ____.

(a) splices and taps can be made in junction boxes
(b) disconnected outlets are removed
(c) entry boxes are installed flush to the floor
(d) the combined cross sectional fill cannot exceed 45%

7. Steel cable trays shall not be used as equipment grounding conductors for circuits protected above ____ amperes.

(a) 200   (b) 60   (c) 600   (d) 1200

Final Exam

8. Cabinets and cutout boxes that contain devices or apparatus connected within the cabinet or box to more than ___ conductors, including those of branch circuits, meter loops, feeder circuits, power circuits, and similar circuits, but not including the supply circuit or continuation thereof, shall have back wiring spaces or one or more side wiring spaces, side gutters, or wiring compartments.

(a) 8   (b) 10   (c) 21   (d) 30

9. A protective layer which is installed between the floor and type FCC flat conductor cable to protect the cable from physical damage and may or may not be incorporated as an integral part of the cable is the ___.

(a) transition assembly   (b) outer sheath   (c) bottom shield   (d) header

10. The number of #12 conductors permitted in a 3" x 2" x 1 1/2" deep device box is ___.

(a) 6   (b) 5   (c) 4   (d) 3

11. Except where fire stops are required, it shall be permissible to extend cablebus vertically through dry floors and platforms, provided the cablebus is totally enclosed at the point where it passes through the floor or platform and for a distance of ___ feet above the floor or platform.

(a) 6   (b) 8   (c) 10   (d) 4

12. All but which of the following shall be continuous between cabinets, boxes, fittings or other enclosures or outlets?

(a) short sections of raceways used to provide support or protection of cable assemblies
(b) metallic or non-metallic raceways
(c) cable armors
(d) cable sheaths

13. Factory assembled PVC underground conduit with conductors is not permitted ___.

(a) in cinder fill
(b) in exposed indoor locations
(c) encased or embedded in concrete
(d) in underground locations subject to severe corrosive influences

14. Which of the following statements about MI cable is correct?

(a) it may be used in any hazardous location
(b) it may be mounted flush on a wall in a wet location
(c) it shall be supported every 10 feet
(d) a single run of cable shall not contain more than four quarter bends

15. Where space is too limited to provide minimum clearances, such as at meters, panelboards, outlets, and switch points, concealed knob and tube wiring shall be enclosed in ____ which shall be continuous in length between the last support and the enclosure or terminal point.

(a) rigid metal conduit   (b) EMT   (c) IMC   (d) flexible nonmetallic tubing

16. What is the ampacity of four #6 THW copper current-carrying conductors enclosed in schedule 80 PVC conduit, 8 feet in length entering a trench?

(a) 65 amps   (b) 52 amps   (c) 44 amps   (d) 40 amps

17. Flat cable assemblies may be installed ____.

I. for small power loads outdoors, not subject to physical damage
II. as tap devices for lighting and small appliances
III. for small power loads in hoistways

(a) I only   (b) II only   (c) I and III only   (d) I, II, and III

18. Surge arresters over 1kV shall be permitted to be located ____ and shall be made inaccessible to unqualified persons unless listed for installation in accessible location.

I. outdoors   II. indoors

(a) I only   (b) II only   (c) either I or II   (d) neither I nor II

19. The internal depth of outlet boxes intended to enclose flush devices shall be at least ____.

(a) 1/2"   (b) 7/8"   (c) 15/16"   (d) 1 1/2"

20. Where a single AC conductor carrying current passes through metal with magnetic properties, the inductive effect shall be minimized by ____.

I. cutting slots in the metal between the individual holes through which individual conductors pass
II. passing all the conductors in the circuit through an insulating wall sufficiently large for all the conductors of the circuit

(a) I only   (b) II only   (c) both I and II   (d) neither I nor II

21. Which of the following is **true** concerning type NM cable?

(a) it may be installed where exposed to corrosive fumes
(b) it may be fished in air voids in masonry block or tile walls
(c) it may be embedded in masonry, concrete, or plaster
(d) it may be covered with plaster, adobe, or similar finish

TH

22. The temperature rating of a conductor is the maximum temperature, at any location along its length, that the conductor can withstand over a prolonged time period without ____.

(a) tripping the breaker
(b) serious degradation
(c) short circuiting
(d) a ground fault

23. Auxiliary gutters shall be permitted to supplement wiring spaces at meter centers, distribution centers, switchboards, and similar points of wiring systems and may enclose ____.

I. switches   II. overcurrent devices   III. conductors   IV. busbars

(a) I & II only   (b) I & III only   (c) I & III only   (d) III & IV only

24. Type ____ cable is a factory assembly of one or more conductors, each individually insulated and enclosed in a metallic sheath of interlocking tape, or a smooth or corrugated tube.

(a) MI   (b) AC   (c) MC   (d) MV

25. 100 feet of rigid PVC conduit is run between two cabinets. If its thermal expansion is less than ____ inches, an expansion joint is not required.

(a) .25   (b) .28   (c) .30   (d) .35

26. A means shall be provided in each metal box over 100 cubic inches for the connection of an equipment grounding conductor. The means shall be permitted to be ____.

I. a tapped hole   II. the cover screw   III. a screw used to mount the box

(a) I only   (b) II only   (c) I and II only   (d) I, II, or III

27. There shall be an air space of at least ____ between walls, back, gutter partition, if of metal, or door of any cabinet, or cut out box and nearest exposed current-carrying parts of devices mounted within the cabinet where the voltage exceeds **251** volts.

(a) 1/4"   (b) 1/2"   (c) 1"   (d) 1 1/2"

28. Which of the following methods is **not** approved for conductor supports?

(a) deflecting of cables in junction boxes
(b) insertion of boxes
(c) clamping devices
(d) loop connectors

29. Nonmetallic sheath cable: If the attic is **not** accessible by stairs or permanent ladder, the cable needs to be protected only within ____ feet of a scuttle hole.

(a) 2   (b) 3   (c) 6   (d) 10

30. Cable trays include fittings or other suitable means for ____.

I. temperature
II. electric continuity
III. changes in direction and elevation of runs

(a) I only   (b) I and II only   (c) III only   (d) I and III only

31. Where single conductors or multiconductor cables are stacked or bundled longer than ____ without maintaining spacing and are not installed in raceways, the ampacity of each conductor shall be reduced.

(a) 12"   (b) 18"   (c) 20"   (d) 2'

32. Which of the following is a false statement?

(a) direct buried conductors are required to be spliced in a splice box.
(b) direct buried conductors are permitted to be soldered.
(c) where wire connectors are used for splicing direct buried conductors, the connectors must be listed for such use.
(d) where necessary to prevent physical damage, direct buried conductors shall be protected by raceways, boards sleeves, or other approved means.

33. The largest conductor permitted in 3/8" flexible conduit is ____.

(a) #12   (b) #16   (c) #14   (d) #10

34. When installing open wiring on insulators in a dry location, conductors shall be permitted to be separately enclosed in flexible nonmetallic tubing. The tubing shall be in continuous length not exceeding ___ feet and secured to the surface by straps at intervals not exceeding 4 1/2 feet.

(a) 6   (b) 10   (c) 15   (d) 50

35. Where nonmetallic sheathed cable is used with boxes no larger than ___ mounted in walls or ceilings and where the cable is fastened within 8 inches of the box, securing the cable to the box shall not be required.

(a) 2 1/4" x 4"   (b) 2/12" x 4"   (c) 2" x 4"   (d) 1 1/4" x 4"

36. ____ of insulating material shall be permitted to be used without boxes in exposed cable wiring.

I. Switch devices   II. Outlet devices   III. Tap devices

(a) I only   (b) II only   (c) III only   (d) I, II and III

37. A copper bus bar is 4" wide by 1/2" thick. What is the ampacity?

(a) 500 amps   (b) 1000 amps   (c) 1500 amps   (d) 2000 amps

38. If a nipple 18" long contains 24 conductors, the ampacity for each conductor must be reduced to ____ of Table 310.16 and Table 310.18.

(a) 80%   (b) 70%   (c) 60%   (d) 0%

39. Which answer best completes the following sentence describing the Code requirements for the use of short radius capped elbow type conduit bodies containing conductors smaller than #6? Capped elbow type conduit bodies ____.

(a) are not permitted by the Code   (b) may be used to enable the installation of the raceway
(c) may contain devices   (d) may contain splices and taps

40. Messenger supported wiring shall not be used ____.

I. where subject to severe physical damage
II. in hoistways

(a) I only   (b) II only   (c) both I and II   (d) neither I nor II

41. The following letter suffixes shall indicate the following:

____ for two insulated conductors laid parallel within an outer nonmetallic covering.

(a) D   (b) M   (c) R   (d) N

42. Liquidtight flexible metal conduit shall not be permitted ____.

(a) in hazardous locations
(b) in high temperature areas
(c) in exposed and concealed work
(d) where installations requires flexibility or protection from liquids, vapors or solids

43. Enclosures that are not over 100 cubic inches in size and which have two conduits supported within three feet on either side of the enclosure and the enclosure does not contain devices or support fixtures shall not be required to have the enclosure supported if the conduits are ____.

(a) rigid nonmetallic conduits
(b) threaded into hubs identified for the purpose
(c) installed with locknuts inside and outside enclosure
(d) shoulders of fittings outside and locknuts inside the box

44. Nonmetallic surface extensions with one or more extensions shall be permitted to be run in any direction from an existing outlet, but not on the floor or within ____ inches from the floor.

(a) 6   (b) 4   (c) 3   (d) 2

45. The ampacity of a #250 kcmil IGS cable is ____ amperes.

(a) 119   (b) 168   (c) 215   (d) 255

46. Where two different ampacities apply to adjacent portions of a circuit, the higher ampacity shall be permitted to be used beyond the point of transition, a distance equal to 10 feet or ____ percent of the circuit length figured at the higher ampacity, whichever is less.

(a) 10%   (b) 15%   (c) 20%   (d) 25%

47. Electrical nonmetallic tubing is permitted ____.

I.   concealed in walls, floors and ceilings with a 15 minute fire rating
II. embedded in concrete provided with approved fitting
III. directly buried
IV. above a suspended ceiling with a 15 minute fire rating

(a) I only   (b) I, II and IV   (c) I, II and III   (d) all of the above

48. Type SE service-entrance cables shall be permitted in interior wiring systems where all of the circuit conductors of the cable are of the ____ type.

I. rubber-covered   II. thermoplastic   III. metal

(a) I and II only   (b) II only   (c) II and III only   (d) I, II and III

49. Determine the allowable ampacity of 13 - #12 THHN conductors in a raceway, when passing through an area where the ambient temperature is 40° C.

(a) 13.65 amps   (b) 15.0 amps   (c) 26.4 amps   (d) 30.0 amps

50. What size octagon box is required for 4 - #12 and 3 - #14 conductors?

(a) 1 1/4"   (b) 1 1/2"   (c) 2"   (d) 2 1/8"

ANSWERS

ANSWERS

Article 280 Quiz #1

1. (a) #14 — 285.26
2. (d) I,II,III, IV — 285.23(B)
3. (c) either I or II — 285.11
4. (c) I or III — 285.3(3)
5. (b) #6 copper — 280.23
6. (d) I,II, III — 285.3 FPN

Article 300 Quiz #1

1. (b) I and II — 300.22(C2)
2. (d) I, II, III, IV — 300.11(1,2) ex.
3. (b) 1/4" — 300.6(D)
4. (b) hysteresis — 300.20(B) FPN
5. (b) 8' — 300.5(D)
6. (a) 1 1/4" — 300.4(A1)
7. (b) #4 — 300.4(F)
8. (b) 6" — 300.14
9. (a) increased — 300.21
10. (d) 18" — 300.5(D)(3)
11. (c) pigtail — 300.13(B)
12. (a) less 600v — 300.3(C1)

Article 300 Quiz #2

1. (a) short sections — 300.12 ex.
2. (c) I, III, IV — 300.22(B)
3. (a) MI cable — 300.37
4. (b) 8 times — 300.34
5. (d) loop — 300.19(C1,2,3)
6. (c) I and II — 300.15(A)
7. (c) I and II — 300.20(B)
8. (d) inductive — 300.20(A)
9. (a) 1" — 300.39
10. (a) filled — 300.7
11. (a) metal — 300.22(C1)
12. (d) I, II or III — 300.50(A2)

Article 300 Quiz #3

1. (a) EMT — 300.22(B)
2. (d) inductive — 300.20(A)
3. (a) 1/16" — 300.4(A1)
4. (a) maximum — 300.3(C1)
5. (b) hystersis — 300.20 FPN
6. (a) spliced — 300.5(E)
7. (a) energized — 300.31
8. (d) raceway — 300.5(C)
9. (a) sealed — 300.7(A)
10. (d) none of these — 300.22(A)
11. (d) flexible — 300.4(A2) ex.
12. (d) 5 supports — T. 300.19(A)
13. (d) 12 times — 300.34
14. (d) enamel — 300.6(A)
15. (a) rigid — 300.4(A2) ex.
16. (c) any conductor — 300.3(C1)

Article 310 Quiz #1

1. (c) #8 — 310.3
2. (a) ozone — 310.6
3. (a) 65a — 310.15(B2a) ex.4
4. (d) 35% — 310.15(B2a)
5. (a) D — 310.11(C)
6. (d) lowest — 310.15(B3)
7. (d) all of these — 310.11(A1,2,3)
8. (d) enclosed — 310.4(B)
9. (d) 24" — 310.11(B1)
10. (c) underground — 310.60(A)
11. (d) maintained — 310.15(B2b)
12. (a) MTW — 310.8(C2)
13. (b) 50a — 310.15(B2) ex.3
14. (c) I, II, IV — T. 310.13

ANSWERS

Article 310 Quiz #2

1. (c) shielded   310.6
2. (c) 90°C   T. 310.13
3. (c) 90°C   T. 310.16
4. (d) 0%   310.15(B2) ex.3
5. (c) 45%   T. 310.15(B2a)
6. (d) I,II,III,IV   310.10 FPN
7. (d) degradation   310.10 FPN
8. (a) lowest   310.15(A2)
9. (a) 65a   310.15(B2) ex.3
10. (c) #1   310.4
11. (c) 86°F   T. 310.16
12. (d) 2'   310.15(B2a)
13. (c) #2/0   T. 310.15(B6)
14. (c) insulation   310.10

Article 310 Quiz #3

1. (d) I, II, III   310.4
2. (d) voltage drop   310.15(A1) FPN1
3. (c) ambient   310.10(4)
4. (a) 70%   310.15(B2a)
5. (c) 40°F   T.310.15(B2c)
6. (d) 90°C   T. 310.13
7. (c) #4/0   T. 310.15(B6)
8. (a) RHH   T. 310.13
9. (c) #10   310.3
10. (c) 110a   T. 310.17
11. (b) 6   310.15(B4a) & (B5)
12. (a) 10%   310.60 ex.

Article 310 Quiz #4

1. (c) 24a   310.15(B4a)
2. (d) 16a   T. 310.15(B2a)
3. (c) 28a   T. 310.15(B2a)
4. (c) 160a   T. 310.15(B2a)
5. (d) no derating   T. 310.15(B2a) ex.3
6. (a) 65a   T. 310.15(B2a) ex.4
7. (d) 176a   T. 310.16
8. (d) 41.6a   T. 310.13 = 40a x 1.04
9. (c) 20.5a   T. 310.16
10. (a) 13.65a   T. 310.15(B2a)•T.310.16
11. (a) 150.9a   T. 310.15(B2a)•T.310.16
12. (d) not required   T. 310.15(B2a) ex.3
13. (a) 30a   *see 240.4(D)
14. (b) 41a   T. 310.16
15. (c) 44a   T. 310.15(B2a) & (B4c)

Article 312 Quiz #1

1. (a) 1/4"   312.3
2. (c) 30a   312.11(B)
3. (a) 0.053"   312.10(B)
4. (b) #4   312.6(C)
5. (b) corrosion   312.10(A)
6. (a) 8 conductors   312.11(C)
7. (b) weatherproof   312.2
8. (a) offset   312.6(B2) FPN
9. (a) without   312.2 ex.
10. (c) 1"   312.11(A3)

ANSWERS

Article 314   Quiz #1

1. (c) 8 times   314.28(A1)
2. (b) separate box   314.28(D)
3. (b) 1/8"   314.21
4. (a) .0625"   314.40(B)
5. (c) 36 times   314.71(B1)
6. (b) #4   314.28(A)
7. (a) round   314.2
8. (c) 1/4"   314.17(C)
9. (b) twice   314.16(C)
10. (d) I,II,III,IV   314.23(D1)
11. (a) 1/4"   314.20
12. (b) 50 pounds   314.27(B)
13. (d) 3 conductors   T. 314.16(A)
14. (a) one conductor   314.16(B1)
15. (d) 12"   314.23(H2)

Article 314   Quiz #2

1. (c) 10 cu.in.   T. 314.16(A)
2. (a) 2 1/4" x 4"   314.17(C) ex.
3. (c) box listed   314.27(C)
4. (a) I only   314.40(D)
5. (c) 8 times   314.28(A1)
6. (b) enable   314.5
7. (b) 3"x2"x2 1/4"   T. 314.16(A)
8. (b) 1/4"   314.20
9. (a) 1/32"   314.41
10. (c) 15/16"   314.24(B)
11. (d) rendered   314.29
12. (a) 1/2"   314.24(A)
13. (d) removable   314.71(C)
14. (c) largest   314.16(B3,4)
15. (d) 18"   314.23(F)

Article 314   Quiz #3

1. (c) 1" x 2"   314.23(B2)
2. (c) assembled   314.16(A)
3. (d) 48 times   314.71(A)
4. (a) 8"   314.17(C) ex.
5. (b) weight   314.27(B)
6. (c) I and II   314.25 • 314.28(B)
7. (d) Danger   314.72(E)
8. (b) threaded   314.23(E)
9. (d) flush   314.20
10. (d) 100 pounds   314.30(D)
11. (d) 6 pounds   314.27(A) ex.
12. (b) 1.75 cu.in.   T. 314.16(B)

Article 314   Quiz #4

1. (b) 1 1/2"   T. 314.16(B)•T. 314.16(A)
2. (b) 15.75 cu.in.   T. 314.16(B1)•T. 314.16(B)
3. (d) 10 cu.in.   T. 314.16(B)
4. (b) 12"   X = 6 x 2" = 12"
5. (a) 21.5 cu.in.   314.16(B)
6. (c) 27 cu.in.   314.16(B1) & (B2)
7. (b) 6.75 cu.in.   314.16(B5)(B1) T.314.16(B)
8. (c) 22" x 22"   6 x 3"=18"+ 2 1/2"+ 1 1/2"

Article 314   Quiz #5

1. (d) 17 cu.in.   314.16(B)• T. 314.16(B)
2. (d) 18 cu.in.   314.16(B1)(B2) T.314.16(B)
3. (d) 2 conductors   T. 314.16(A)
4. (d) 20.25 cu.in.   T. 314.16(B)
5. (c) 3 conductors   T. 314.16(A)
6. (c) 22.5 cu.in.   T. 314.16(B)
7. (b) one conductor   T. 314.16(A1)
8. X = 21"   6 x 3" = 18" + 2" + 1" = 21"
   Y = 18"   6 x 3" = 18"
   Z = 18"   6 x 3" = 18"

ANSWERS

Articles 320 - 330   Quiz #1

1. (b) adhesive — 324.41
2. (b) 194°F — 320.80(A)
3. (d) MV — 328.2
4. (a) transition — 324.40(D)
5. (b) 15a — 322.56(B)
6. (b) 2' — 320.30(D2)
7. (c) shield — 324.2
8. (a) #18 — 330.104
9. (d) I, II, III — 324.40(A)
10. (b) II only — 322.10(1)
11. (b) 2 crossings — 324.18
12. (c) 86°F — 324.10(F)
13. (d) 2001 volts — 328.2
14. (d) 20 pounds — 326.112
15. (a) white — 322.120(B)

Articles 332 - 340   Quiz #1

1. (b) 12" — 334.30
2. (a) hazardous — 332.10(7)
3. (d) 60°C — 340.80
4. (d) all of these — 340.12(2,4,5)
5. (c) NMC — 334.116(B)
6. (d) all of these — 332.104 & .108 & .116
7. (d) I, II, III — 340.10(3)
8. (a) 60°C — 334.80
9. (a) 5 times — 332.24(1)
10. (b) air voids — 334.10(A2)
11. (a) I and II — 338.10(B1)
12. (a) 6" — 334.15(B)

Articles 320 - 330   Quiz #2

1. (a) 24" — 320.30(D2)
2. (b) FC — 322.2
3. (d) I and II — 320.10(1)
4. (b) 300 volts — 324.10(B1)
5. (c) MC — 330.2
6. (a) AC cable — 320.10(4)
7. (d) I, II, III — 324.120
8. (a) 119a — T. 326.80
9. (c) carpet squares — 324.1
10. (c) 6' — 334.23 & 320.23(A)
11. (d) I, II, III — 324.40(A)
12. (b) 194°F — 320.80(A)
13. (c) I and II — 328.12
14. (d) FCC — 324.2
15. (a) 8' — 322.10(3)

Articles 332 - 340   Quiz #2

1. (b) appliances — 338.10(B3)
2. (c) burial — 340.10(1)
3. (c) I and II — 334.15(B) & 334.23
4. (b) 4 1/2' — 334.30
5. (a) #4/0 — 340.104
6. (b) corrosive — 332.12
7. (d) 5 times — 334.24
8. (b) service — 334.12(A3)
9. (b) twelve — 336.24
10. (b) USE — 338.2
11. (d) buried — 340.10(1)
12. (c) wet locations — 340.10(3)

TH

ANSWERS

Articles 332 - 340 Quiz #3

1. (b) II only — 336.10(2)
2. (c) 90°C — 334.112
3. (d) I, II, III — 340.116
4. (a) bare copper — 338.100
5. (a) hazardous — 332.10(7)
6. (d) V — 334.116(B)
7. (d) I, II, III — 334.40(B)
8. (d) uninsulated — 338.100
9. (d) I, II, III — 332.10(1,3,5)
10. (c) insulating — 332.80
11. (c) #14 - #2 — 334.104
12. (d) interior — 340.10(3)

Articles 342 - 362 Quiz #1

1. (b) 1/2" — 344.20(A)
2. (d) 6" — 352.20(B)
3. (c) 600v — 362.12(6)
4. (d) 12" — 350.30(A)
5. (c) support — 352.12(B)
6. (b) exposed — 354.12(1)
7. (a) .25" — 352.44
8. (b) I, II, IV — 362.10
9. (c) 12 1/2" — T. 360.24(A)
10. (d) 20' — T. 344.30(B2)
11. (b) splices & taps — 352.56
12. (c) 3/4" — 344.28
13. (d) #10 — T. 348.22
14. (b) enamel — 358.12(2)

Articles 342 - 362 Quiz #2

1. (a) 4 1/2' — 348.30(A)
2. (b) identified — 344.120
3. (b) galvanic — 344.14
4. (b) 1/2" — 362.20(A)
5. (a) 1 — T. 348.22
6. (b) corrosion — 344.10(B)
7. (a) 1/2" to 4" — 350.20(A,B)
8. (a) 600 volts — 362.12(6)
9. (a) both — 350.10
10. (c) reamed — 344.28
11. (b) support — 352.12(B)
12. (b) 2" — 362.20(B)
13. (d) 6' — T. 352.30(B)
14. (d) EMT — 358.12 ex.

Articles 342 - 362 Quiz #3

1. (b) 1/4" — 352.44
2. (b) four — 358.26
3. (c) by hand — 362.2
4. (b) I and III — 352.28 & 352.48
5. (a) sunlight — 352.100
6. (d) 16' — T. 344.30(B2)
7. (d) 10' — 362.120
8. (c) listed — 358.42
9. (a) 17 1/2" — T. 360.24(A)
10. (b) temperature — 350.12(2)
11. (d) 14' — T. 344.30(B2)
12. (d) 1/2" to 4" — 358.20(A&B)
13. (b) 3 — T. 348.22 *note
14. (c) 3;5 — 344.30(A)

ANSWERS

Articles 366 - 382 Quiz #1

1. (c) 30' 366.12(2)
2. (b) 8" 382.30
3. (d) 2000a 366.23(A)
4. (b) header 372.5
5. (c) dry 380.2
6. (d) 75% 376.56
7. (b) 1" 366.100(E)
8. (d) 1/4" 378.44
9. (c) 50' 368.17(B) ex.
10. (d) 45% 374.5
11. (d) header 372.9
12. (a) 5' 366.30
13. (b) 3' 378.30(A)
14. (a) 6' 370.6(C)

Articles 366 - 382 Quiz #2

1. (c) right angle 372.5
2. (b) 5' 368.30
3. (d) III & IV 366.10
4. (a) seal 368.234(A)
5. (b) metal 372.6
6. (d) 12' 370.6(A)
7. (b) header duct 374.2
8. (a) exposed 370.3
9. (a) #1/0 374.4
10. (d) 1000a 366.23(A)
11. (a) bonded 370.3
12. (b) 50'...1/3 368.17(B) ex.
13. (d) 10' 378.30(A)
14. (b) protected 368.17 ex.

Articles 366 - 382 Quiz #3

1. (b) 30 376.22(B)
2. (d) I, II, III 382.10(C)
3. (b) 30' 366.12(2)
4. (c) dry 380.2
5. (c) sticks 368.17(C)
6. (d) 2" 382.15
7. (d) one conductor 370.4(D)
8. (d) temperature 368.214
9. (d) none of these 376.10(4)
10. (c) sunlight 378.12(3)
11. (d) 6' 368.56(B2)
12. (a) 18" 370.4(D)
13. (c) 75% 366.56(A)
14. (a) damage 378.12(1)

Articles 384 - 398 Quiz #1

1. (c) 4" 390.3(A)
2. (b) hoistways 392.4
3. (d) I, II, III 398.30(A1)•.42• 404.10(A)
4. (a) 300 volts 386.12(2)
5. (d) removed 390.7
6. (c) III only 392.5(E)
7. (c) I and II 390.6
8. (c) movement 392.8(D)
9. (d) soldered 394.56
10. (b) continuity 392.6(A)
11. (a) dry walls 388.10(2)
12. (c) 600a T. 392.7(B) **note b

ANSWERS

Articles 384 - 398   Quiz #2

1. (b) II only — 392.11(A1)
2. (d) flexible — 394.19(B)
3. (b) 3/4" — 390.3(A)
4. (b) hoistways — 386.12(4)
5. (c) III only — 392.8(E)
6. (c) 15' — 398.30(B)
7. (b) 60% — 392.11(B2)
8. (d) unbroken — 386.10(4)
9. (c) 2.15 — 392.11(B4)
10. (c) 75% — 388.56
11. (b) insulated — 394.12(5)
12. (d) cable tray — 392.2

Articles 384 - 398   Quiz #4

1. (d) NM — T. 396.10(A)
2. (d) 95% — 392.11(A2)
3. (c) 10' — 384.30
4. (c) 4" — 392.10(B)
5. (a) 300 volts — 388.12(3)
6. (c) 10 penny — 398.30(D)
7. (d) 2000a — T. 392.7(B) note b
8. (a) dry — 386.10(1)
9. (b) 1" — 390.3(B)
10. (c) single — 392.3(B1a)
11. (b) one-half — 398.30(D)
12. (a) 75% — 386.56

Articles 384 - 398   Quiz #3

1. (c) both — 392.6(F1,2)
2. (d) 2" — 398.19
3. (d) I, II, III — 392.5(A,B,D)
4. (c) both — 390.6
5. (c) II and III — 394.10
6. (b) #1/0 — 392.3(B1a)
7. (c) #8 — 398.30(E)
8. (d) side rails — 392.8(A)
9. (c) 40% — 390.5
10. (c) I and II — 396.12
11. (c) 9" — 392.3(B1a)
12. (d) equip. grd. — 386.60

ANSWERS

FINAL EXAM

1. (d) MI cable	332.40(B)	26. (a) I only	314.40(D)
2. (c) 10'	344.30(B1)	27. (c) 1"	312.11(A3)
3. (c) 1/4"	314.17(C)	28. (d) loop	300.19(C1,2,3)
4. (d) I, II, III, IV	300.11(1,2) ex.	29. (c) 6'	334.23 & 320.23(A)
5. (c) underground	310.60(A)	30. (c) III only	392.5(E)
6. (d) 45%	374.5	31. (d) 2'	310.15(B2a)
7. (c) 600a	T. 392.7(B) **note b	32. (a) buried	300.5(E)
8. (a) 8 conductors	312.11(C)	33. (d) #10	T. 348.22
9. (c) bottom shield	324.2	34. (c) 15'	398.30(B)
10. (d) 3	T. 314.16(A)	35. (a) 2 14" x 4"	314.17(C) ex.
11. (a) 6'	370.6(C)	36. (d) I, II, III	334.40(B)
12. (a) short sections	300.12 ex.	37. (d) 2000a	366.23(A)
13. (b) exposes	354.12(1)	38. (d) 0%	T. 310.15(B2) ex.3
14. (a) hazardous	332.10(7)	39. (b) enable	314.5
15. (d) flexible	394.19(B)	40. (c) I and II	396.12
16. (a) 65a	310.15(B2a) ex.4	41. (a) D	310.11(C)
17. (b) II only	322.10(1)	42. (b) temperature	350.12(2)
18. (c) I or II	280.11	43. (b) threaded	314.23(E)
19. (c) 15/16"	314.24(B)	44. (d) 2"	382.15
20. (c) I and II	300.20(B)	45. (a) 119a	T. 326.80
21. (b) air voids	334.10(A2)	46. (a) 10%	310.60 ex.
22. (b) degradation	310.10 FPN	47. (b) I, II, IV	362.10
23. (d) III & IV	366.2	48. (a) I and II	338.10(B1)
24. (c) MC	330.2	49. (a) 13.65a	T. 310.15(B2a) T. 310.16
25. (a) .25"	352.44	50. (b) 1 1/2"	T. 314.16(B) T. 314.16(A)

THE ELECTRICIANS BOOKSTORE

VIDEO's DVD's

THE BLOCKBUSTER
By Tom Henry

THE LIBRARY
SAVE $230
MASTER COMBO #4

BEST VALUE!

30 of *Tom Henry's* electrical books for **$16.63** per book when purchased as a library! The TOP seller!!!

ITEM #513 - JOURNEYMAN SERIES includes tapes or DVD's #501 through #509. A total of 9 videos/DVD's for $299.00

ITEM #514 - MASTER SERIES includes all 12 videos or DVD's for $399.00

*VIDEOS or DVD's CAN BE ORDERED SEPARATELY USE ITEM # BELOW $39.95 each

EACH VHS TAPE/DVD IS 75-90 MINUTES

THE EXAM **OHMS LAW - THEORY** **VOLTAGE DROP & RESISTANCE** **AMPACITY CORRECTION FACTORS**
Item #501   Item #502   Item #503   Item #504

MOTORS **COOKING EQUIPMENT DEMAND FACTORS** **DWELLING-RESIDENTIAL SERVICE SIZING**
Item #505   Item #506   Item #507

BOX and CONDUIT SIZING **SINGLE-PHASE TRANSFORMERS** **THREE-PHASE TRANSFORMERS**
Item #508   Item #509   Item #510

COMMERCIAL-MULTI-FAMILY SERVICE SIZING **MOTOR CONTROL - SWITCH CONNECTIONS**
Item #511   Item #512

ITEM #224 - Master Combo #4 - **Start your own library!** 30 of Tom Henry's study-aid books and instructor guides. Every school program and electrical contractor should have this combo. The complete study guide. Why take the exam more than once? Properly prepare yourself with this combo. Save $230 total price is **$499.00**

☎ **CALL TODAY!** ☎
1-800-642-2633
E-Mail: tomhenry@code-electrical.com
http://www.code-electrical.com